'WE SEEK THE HIGHEST'
RAF COLLEGE, CRANWELL
A CENTENARY CELEBRATION

ROGER ANNETT

Pen & Sword
AVIATION

First published in Great Britain in 2019 by
PEN AND SWORD AVIATION
an imprint of
Pen & Sword Books Limited
Yorkshire – Philadelphia

ISBN 978 1 52671 218 9

Printed and bound in England by TJ International,
Padstow, Cornwall, PL28 8RW

Typeset in Times New Roman 11/13.5 by
Aura Technology and Software Services, India

Pen & Sword Books Ltd incorporates the imprints of Pen & Sword
Archaeology, Atlas, Aviation, Battleground, Discovery,
Family History, History, Maritime, Military, Naval, Politics, Railways,
Select, Social History, Transport, True Crime, Claymore Press,
Frontline Books, Leo Cooper, Praetorian Press, Remember When,
Seaforth Publishing and Wharncliffe.

For a complete list of Pen and Sword titles please contact
PEN & SWORD BOOKS LTD
47 Church Street, Barnsley, South Yorkshire, S70 2AS, England
E-mail: enquiries@pen-and-sword.co.uk
Website: www.pen-and-sword.co.uk

Or

PEN & SWORD BOOKS
1950 Lawrence Rd, Havertown, PA 19083, USA
E-mail: Uspen-and-sword@casematepublishers.com
Website: www.penandswordbooks.com

Contents

Foreword

Air Chief Marshal Sir Sandy Wilson, KCB, AFC, FRAeS

The year 2020 marks the centenary of the founding of the Royal Air Force College, Cranwell, one of Marshal of the Royal Air Force Lord Trenchard's 'Three Pillars' for the future of the new Royal Air Force of 1918. The two others were the Apprentice School at Halton and the Staff College at Andover. Whilst a number of books have been published about Cranwell, *We Seek the Highest* captures life at the College as seen through the eyes of the officer cadets themselves.

The author traces how the College has developed over the past 100 years, during which time it has aimed to provide future officers prepared to face the realities of operations. Policing of colonies and mandated territories from the air was a major feature of RAF life between the two World Wars, followed by action across the globe during the Second World War. Then came the uneasy peace of the Cold War and the withdrawal from Empire. Today, we have conflicts in the Middle East and the threat of terror attacks.

The book's core narrative is the story of No. 81 Entry, who entered the College in September 1959 and graduated as Pilot Officers in July 1962. At the time, a new academic syllabus for Cranwell's Flight Cadets was being devised, one which was more closely aligned to those of the fast-expanding universities. Co-incidentally, the RAF was making greater use of jet aircraft and to cater for this, the Jet Provost was introduced right from the basic stage of flying training. No. 81 was the first entry expected to take on both those challenges and this they did with a will, the result being a hard-won success on the flying side and sufficiency on the academic front, with half-a-dozen attaining external degree-level results.

Sadly, within a few years it became obvious that such an academic task alongside exacting pilot and navigator training was too demanding to be maintained by all but a small minority of cadets. The College was

FOREWORD

also failing to woo the stars away from university and into the depths of Lincolnshire. By the 1970s, the aim became the recruitment of graduates only, most of whom had been members of University Air Squadrons, where they had learnt the basics of flying.

By the 1980s, the focus had switched again. The College became an Initial Officer Training establishment, with a carefully selected intake from schools and colleges and, for the first time, the NCO ranks. After a six-month concentrated Officer Training course at Cranwell, those who made the grade moved on for their professional training elsewhere. Today, the RAF College has become the sole point-of-entry for RAF officers of all trades.

I can vouch for the authenticity of this book's narrative, which in itself makes an important contribution to the social history of the Royal Air Force. For those readers who served as cadets, or on the College staff it will, I am sure, bring back all manner of memories. For others I trust it will provide an interesting insight into the life of Cranwell's officer cadets over the first ten decades of the Royal Air Force.

I was a proud member of No. 81 Entry and the memories, friendships and respect generated during those three years at Cranwell will never be forgotten. I am pleased to commend this book to you.

October 2019

Prelude

It's the last weekend of the sunny August of 1959, and grand weather for hiking in the Western Highlands of Scotland.

At the country's most remote Youth Hostel, Craig, sitting on the rocky and roadless point at the head of Upper Loch Torridon, four young men and four young Irish nurses splash about in the sparkling, cool waters of the nearby mountain beck. Two of the men are undergrads from Leicester, the girls are from Cork and the other two blokes are grammar school boys from Kingston upon Thames – just finished with the sixth form and not believing their luck.

One of the grammar-grubs, Mark, has a promising relationship going on in Kingston but that's not on his mind just now. What's concerning him is that it's his turn to pop down to Inveralligan Post Office and pick up a few groceries, together with any mail that might be at the *poste restante*. That's three miles down the track and it's early-closing day. He ought to have left an hour ago.

Panting, sweaty and midge-bitten, he makes it – just as well as he finds there are two letters for him, posted a week before from the Thames Valley. One of them is from his mother and the other from his girlfriend. Without hesitation, he opens Sally's first.

Among other things, the letter tells him she's learned from his mother that he's been offered a place at the RAF College Cranwell, in Lincolnshire. She lets him know that she's not best pleased – this Easter she went on the 'Ban the Bomb' march from Aldermaston.

He quickly tears open the envelope from his mother, who writes:

> I suppose you will seize on Sally's letter and open it before your poor old mother's, so I shall not really have given you the news. Never mind.
>
> You have to be at Cranwell on September 8th, so that doesn't give you much time. The Air Ministry has sent a railway warrant and all particulars about what to bring.

1

'WE SEEK THE HIGHEST'

> Among other things, such as suit, jacket and flannels and
> tooth brush, you have to take – One Hat!

Mark's mum also breaks the news that his A-level results have just arrived – passes in French, Spanish and English Literature. They have won him a County Major Scholarship and Bristol and Durham Universities want to talk, the latter about going up to read Economics, this coming term. It's clearly decision time.

Trudging back up to Craig, he considers his options. For the past half-dozen years, he's been an enthusiastic member of the school Combined Cadet Force RAF Section and with a spell as an RAF pilot in mind, in 1956, aged just sixteen, he took and passed the Aircrew Aptitude tests at RAF Hornchurch. As a result, he'd won an RAF Flying Scholarship, giving him thirty thrilling hours in Tiger Moth biplanes out of Fairoaks airfield near Woking – chasing motorbikes out of Guildford and along the Hog's Back road to Farnham and gaining a Private Pilot's Licence (PPL) into the bargain.

On Summer Camps, his Cadet Officer had made sure that a couple of visits to RAF Officers' Messes gave him a taste for the organised Service Officer life. But Cranwell – that had never been what he'd had in mind. All a bit heavy, that. But somehow or other the Cadet Officer must have got him to sign the application form.

He'd then spent three days with the RAF Officer Selection Board at Daedalus House, on the west side of RAF Cranwell camp, taking all those potentially embarrassing tests – crossing deep chasms with too-short planks and that sort of thing. But he must have done something right because now they want him.

He's not sure where Durham is and what Economics are all about. The whole idea of university life's a big mystery for him, whereas from CCF camps he's got a good feel for what the RAF world would have in store. Anyhow, if it came to it and everything went pear-shaped at Cranwell, they'd be keeping the place at Durham open for a year, at least.

He makes his decision and announces to a passing seagull, 'Let's give Cranwell a try.'

***

In the evening, Mark gets some help from his pals. First problem – how to get from the back of nowhere down to the Thames Valley in the shortest time possible. He came up as a passenger in his schoolmate's parents' Humber Hawk, and they are somewhere across the mountains – fly fishing, and won't be back for a fortnight.

PRELUDE

Against all the odds, one of the Leicester blokes comes to the rescue – he has a return rail ticket to London which he's willing to swap for a lift in the Hawk. What luck! That'll do it.

At the crack of a misty Highland dawn, with very mixed feelings, Mark takes his leave of the nurses and students and hoofs the miles to the nearest bus. After some hours, of which he has precious few, this gets him to the West Highland Line, Glasgow and the South.

Feet up in the carriage, with moors and mountains passing leisurely by, he has a chance to review this extraordinary chain of events. Between the Flying Scholarship and the final medical for an intended eight-year Short-Service Commission, he'd grown some inches and was declared by the medics to be above the six-foot-three height limit for a pilot. His dream of flying shattered, university beckoned and a third A-level course was hastily arranged.

Then fate picked him out for a spot of good fortune. The Air Ministry had decided to buy a brand-new, shiny fleet of jet-powered trainers, Jet Provosts, destined to be the sole aircraft for pilot training in the RAF, including Cranwell. Crucially for him, it had a bigger cockpit than the current Vampire. Hasty visits were arranged to the aeromedical people at Farnborough, where careful measurements were taken, and to Hunting Aircraft at Luton, where he was able to show he could sit comfortably in the Jet Provost itself, safe in the knowledge that in the event of an ejection he wouldn't lose his knees and everything below them. The dream of a flying career was up there again, in full Technicolour.

Behind the scenes, his headmaster and the CCF chief had got to work. They'd been keen to get a boy into Cranwell for some time so when they found out that an old boy of the school, Air Commodore Denis Spotswood, was to be the new Commandant, they saw their chance. The new Commandant co-operated and Mark's fate was sealed.

Swept along with the tide, here he sits, speeding south to London's Euston Station – a sunburned beatnik with just four days to get himself cleaned up and his affairs in order. Then, he'll be setting off up north again, be-hatted and flannelled, from London's King's Cross.

He's lucky to have the chance. He'll make it in time.

School CCF group.

De Havilland Tiger Moth.

OFFICER CADETS

	Weekly Rates of Pay		
	£	s.	d.
On becoming an Officer Cadet at the R.A.F. College, Cranwell or the R.A.F. Technical College, Henlow.	4	4	0
On completing 1 years service.	5	5	0

The Cranwell pay packet. (*Air Ministry 1958*)

The RAF College for officers was established as the world's first Air Academy, at Cranwell, at the end of 1919. An institution modelled on the Royal Military Academy, Sandhurst and the Britannia Royal Naval Academy, Dartmouth, it was the brainchild of the Great War Royal Flying Corps pilot and commander Major-General Hugh Trenchard, as well as that of Winston Churchill – at the time of its opening, Secretary of State for War and Air.

Entry No. 1 arrived in February 1920, less than two years after the birth of the RAF on 1st April 1918. Save for the years of the Second World War, when it was regrouped into a busy Advanced Flying Training School (AFTS), the College has been grooming Royal Air Force officers ever since.

The newcomers are entering a unique world. It's isolated from home, family, girlfriends and civilisation but it's one in which they aim to fulfil their dream – that of becoming aircrew officers in the world-famous Royal Air Force.

With hard work and good luck, Cranwell will be home to them for three eventful years.

The escorting sergeant announces, 'That grand building and its lime trees, respectively built and planted in 1933, is the home of the Senior Mess Flight Cadets. It's not the destination for you gentlemen, yet.' The driver turns south towards the airfield and past a cluster of military buildings. The most imposing of those is flying the RAF Ensign and the Union Flag. 'The College Headquarters,' remarks the sergeant. 'You'd do well to remember that, Gentlemen.'

The new arrivals debus near a brick archway behind what turns out to be the Junior Mess. They are welcomed by three smartly turned-out Drill Sergeants. One unsuspecting fellow is roundly harangued for sporting a non-regulation flat cap. Another, a grammar school lad who 'thought they were joking about the hat' and whose suit is deemed by the sergeants to be 'more New York than Savile Row', is dispatched forthwith to Messrs Gieves, the tailors, handily situated nearby, to put that right.

He's firmly instructed to watch out on the way back for passing officers, to whom it is imperative to raise the hat in the approved manner. Now no one's in doubt as to why they're juggling all those titfers.

Flight Cadet Entry arrival. (*RAF College Journal*)

Junior Mess and Parade Ground. (*JGL*)

Messrs Gieves. (*RAF College Journal*)

In the spartan surroundings of the Junior Mess Orderly Room, the lads are informed that they'll be forming Flight Cadet Entry No. 81. They'll be fifty-six in number. There are five other entries in residence – No. 76, the senior, down to No. 80. All of the new arrivals are training to become General Duties officers, with just three being aspiring navigators, GD(N), the rest looking to be trained as pilots, GD(P). They're all allocated to the Junior Flights of the three Cadet Squadrons, 'A', 'B' and 'C'. Mark's down for 'C'.

Each of the Flights has a Flight Commander – Flight Lieutenants responsible for the lads' welfare and instruction in matters military, while monitoring, and regularly reporting on, their charges' progress. They are also to be the arbiters on disciplinary issues. First-line discipline as well as the all-important drill are the responsibility of the sergeants.

Still struggling with luggage, the lads are marshalled along a concrete-block pathway to a line of pre-war redbrick huts, the so-called South Brick Lines – their quarters. Each hut houses four or five of the lads, allocated alphabetically by squadron. Mark and his three room-mates, two English and one Scots, take stock of their surroundings. The entrance door leads straight into the ablutions area, beyond which is the living-space with its highly-polished lino floor, central coke-fired stove and old-fashioned cast-metal casement windows.

A chap in smart RAF battledress rises from his chair to say hallo. He introduces himself as the resident Flight Cadet mentor, from 80 Entry, there to keep order and to show the newcomers the ropes. To the right, he points out a cubbyhole. 'That's for the batman. He'll not have a lot to do for you in your first term, except look after your uniforms and shoes. If you treat him right, he might bring you a cup of tea in the mornings.'

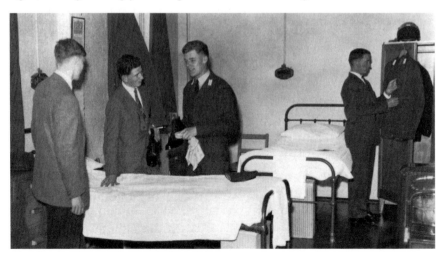

A mentor explains. (*RAF College*)

The living-space seems generous enough, with wardrobe, shelving, chair and bed for each of four cadets. A door to the rear leads to a further room, with utility armchairs, work tables, and a second coke-fired stove. 'This is the domestic area,' announces the mentor. 'It's for relaxation – not much of that – and work, lots of it.'

Having emptied the contents of their bulging suitcases, it's straight into the Junior Mess block for a drastic haircut, regardless of whether or not they've had a smart trim before leaving home.

Scissors fly. 'There – that's a bit tidier, isn't it, Sir?' grins the demon barber. A long-serving civilian from Cranwell Village, Mr Riley has doubtless wrecked all manner of trendy hairstyles over the decades. Mark's carefully-chosen trilby no longer fits – it slips down onto his ears and some paper padding is urgently required.

There's a welcome early supper in the Junior Mess dining-room and Flight Commanders note that some newcomers need work on knife and fork drills. Then, there's a chance to try out the offerings of the Junior Mess bar and the separate NAAFI shop. From the latter, cadets can buy the small necessities of life – toothpaste, boot polish, cigarettes and a cup of tea. From the former, at certain times of the day, they can purchase alcoholic beverages, at well below pub prices. The mentor tells them to call it the Junior 'FGS', short for Fancy Goods Store – which it has been since the 1920s.

With refreshment in hand, the lads now have a chance to learn something about their new, multi-cultural colleagues.

***

To Mark, most of these blokes look like they could already be officers – dapper, well-spoken and able to carry off brutal haircuts with a semblance of dignity. A fellow member of 'C' Squadron, Robert, is no exception:

> I come from a military background – my father was an army officer and my grandfather served in the Indian Army.
>
> At the Salesian College in Farnborough I joined the cadets. My first flight was with a friend's RAF father – Commandant of the Empire Test Pilots' School. The College was under the Farnborough flight path so there was plenty of aviation on view.
>
> After Hornchurch and Daedalus House, they gave me an RAF Scholarship. So I had financial support in the sixth form and a place at Cranwell, subject to passing two A-levels and a final medical. I managed that and here I am, ready to go.

'B' Squadron's Mac has a ready Irish wit:

> At Dulwich College, I got a taste of flying and air force life from the CCF and applied for Cranwell. All went well, until the final panel interview at Daedalus, where I fell foul of a prickly Wing Commander.
>
> He asks me, 'Which newspaper do you read?' I say, 'The Times', which causes him to scowl and ask, 'Why?' I say, 'Because the paper's offered to students at half-price.'
>
> Still scowling, the Wingco asks me what books I read. I say, 'Anything by Damon Runyan.' Now the Chairman, a Group Captain, sits up. There follows a lively two-way discussion on the writer's merits – and I'm in.

Mac's 'B' Squadron colleague, John, educated at Ampleforth, and another CCF stalwart and RAF Scholar, says he was always a cert to give the RAF a go:

> My late father was an RAF pilot in the Second World War and two of my uncles, together with an aunt, were all aircrew, the latter with the ATA. And my stepfather's a Captain in the Royal Navy. I was born to serve the Queen, so to speak.
>
> After I'd completed my Flying Scholarship, Aunt Marion massively widened my biplane experience by letting me fly her Hornet Moth. On top of that, there were the Farnborough Air Shows. New aircraft every year, all trying to impress and excite – and succeeding with me, for sure.

Chris is a third 'B' Squadron man, another RAF Scholar, from Cheltenham College. He too has strong RAF connections:

> My father was a pilot in the RFC and then the RAF – he retired as an Air Vice-Marshal. My much older brother was a graduate of 46 Entry – the first cadets to arrive at Cranwell after the Second World War.
>
> I did three one-week CCF camps at RAF Cranwell and managed to fly half-a-dozen hours on the Piston Provost. So I'm fairly well-acquainted with the College.

That's four public-school boys in a row, notes Mark. Michael, also of 'B' Squadron, is yet another, from St Edward's Oxford:

> It was inevitable that I'd have a shot at the RAF. I'll be the next in a line of RFC and RAF pilots – grandfather, three uncles, and my father, who's an Air Commodore. I've had an RAF Scholarship too, to keep me tied in – no chance of escape for me.
>
> But I'm not complaining. I'm looking forward to joining all my folks in the ranks of the boys in blue.

Andy, an 'A' Squadron man, confides:

> I've taken much the same route to Cranwell as the rest of you. I was studying at Tonbridge to become a doctor but, with National Service in prospect, I decided to apply for an RAF Flying Scholarship so that I might be able to fly on a Short Service Commission. Tigers at Fairoaks had hooked me on flying.
>
> Then, earlier this year I was one of those representing the CCF at the tenth Anniversary celebrations of Indian Independence – an amazing adventure.
>
> All this persuaded me to apply for an RAF Scholarship to Cranwell. I passed all the tests and my parents were very happy to accept the financial help.
>
> And here I am, hoping one day to become a fighter pilot.

Mark can see that Andy might well do that – he has a lucky face. He's the sixth from public school so far but it's good to meet someone who's also enjoyed Fairoaks airfield and the Tiger Moth.

He notes that all these lads have a lot to thank the CCF and their schools for and wonders again how many doors his CCF Officer had to open for him to get a place at the College.

He goes in search of others, maybe another grammar school lad. He finds Dave, a friendly-looking bloke, and soon learns that he was born in Dorset:

> My father had been a skilled boilermaker at Swan Hunter in Newcastle but in the 1930s Great Depression he moved to the South Coast for ship repair work in Portland Harbour.

After the war, living in Southampton, we children were free to roam in the woods and fields, and on the foreshore. Life was an adventure.

When we were twelve, a chum and I persuaded the Chief Instructor of Air Service Training at Hamble to take us up in an Airspeed Oxford. I was hooked.

From the background of the Air Training Corps and as a pupil at Taunton's Grammar in Southampton, I made two attempts at satisfying Hornchurch. At the first, my outdoor life stood me in good stead on the Daedalus tests.

But they said, 'You're obviously keen – come back in a year.' In that year, I learnt to fly gliders and passed an additional O-level – Applied Aeronautics.

That did the trick. I won a Flying Scholarship, and an RAF Scholarship. Throughout my time in the sixth form, that paid a helpful two pounds a week to my mum.

A place was reserved for me at Cranwell, I got my A-levels, and here I am.

Nigel comes up to shake Dave's hand, telling Mark that they were both on the same Flying Scholarship course together earlier this year.

Is Nigel also an RAF Scholarship man?

I certainly am.

I've some military background in the family. Grandad was a private soldier in the Great War – survived the Somme. Father was the same in the Second World War. On demob he joined the police – finished up as Chief Inspector.

As a war-baby, I was well aware of the RAF from an early age. Then, at Peter Symonds Grammar in Winchester, the CCF summer camps opened up the Air Force world. And of course there were the Farnborough Air Shows.

It was my CCF master who set me off on the Hornchurch and Daedalus route. Daedalus was a real test – aged just fifteen and being grilled by officers who'd seen war service.

But it turned out all right. I'm here.

A compact fellow with a broad smile and a Yorkshire accent joins the chat. Mike has been a pupil at Leeds Modern, which he says is 'a grammar school in all but name'. He'd been the Hornchurch and Daedalus route too, and he's yet another awarded an RAF Scholarship. But he's quick to explain:

> I took up the RAF pilot option late in the game. The scholarship was awarded to me with only three months to go before the end of what turned out to be my last year at school – it was essentially a nominal award. At the end of May I got the letter saying I was accepted for Cranwell, subject to my passing two of Physics, Chemistry and Maths A-levels – which I did.
>
> This summer I've been too busy mountaineering to have time for a Flying Scholarship and here I am, a seventeen-and-a-half-year-old flying virgin.

It seems to Mark that almost everyone except him has had the benefit of an RAF Scholarship. What about this chap over here – slightly built, and sporting glasses. He's got a small audience in thrall:

> So then I wander into the Orderly Room to find out what I should be doing next – and Sergeant Ross gives me a rocket for not standing to attention before ordering me to have a haircut.
>
> 'But Sergeant,' says I, 'I've had one already – just this morning.'
>
> 'Then have another, Sir,' says he. So I do.
>
> Back in the Orderly Room, Sergeant Ross has been replaced by Sergeant McDill, so I ask him what I should be doing next. Without looking up from his paperwork, he says, 'Go for a haircut.'
>
> To save any further bother, I do. Three haircuts in a single day! Surreal.

Mark asks this fellow, whose name is Bill, about the route he's taken to Cranwell:

> I have a brother who's ten years older than me. In 1946, he became a sixteen-year-old boy-entrant Electrician Apprentice at the Radio School here, before going on to OCTU and getting commissioned as a pilot. He was my inspiration for trying for the College. The CCF at my school, Worksop College, also helped, with summer camps at Church Fenton and Linton-on-Ouse.

Then, at Daedalus, it turned out that one of the Assessors knew my brother and what he'd achieved, and that helped a lot. I got an RAF Scholarship and a Flying Scholarship – Tigers at Marshalls of Cambridge. Great fun.

And the glasses? They're for long-sightedness. At the time I went to Hornchurch I didn't need them – by the time I had the check medical, I did. They said it didn't matter and I didn't argue.

They are joined by Robin, another RAF Scholar:

Without it, I couldn't have got through the sixth form. My father had seen me – his new-born only son – just briefly before sailing off, as a bombardier in the RA, on a troopship to the Far East. Turned out to be a one-way trip to a Jap camp. Two stepfathers and one half-brother later, my mum needed the scholarship money to keep me at Bournemouth Grammar.

I'm very lucky and I'm very pleased to be here – ready for whatever's in store.

Standing on the edge of the group are the two Colonials from the bus. They turn out to be ex- Apprentices. One, a tall muscular chap from Rhodesia called Phil, introduces the other, a craggy New Zealander, who says he's known as 'Kiwi'. Under the Commonwealth Air Forces Scholarship scheme they've just had three years at the No. 1 School of Technical Training, at RAF Halton in Buckinghamshire. Having come out top of their entry, they've been rewarded with three more at Cranwell. Kiwi's brother turns out to have won the top prize here, the Sword of Honour, four years ago.

The two Halton men point out three other ex-Apprentices, one more from Halton and two from the No. 1 Radio School of Apprentice Training at RAF Locking, near Weston-super-Mare. They're chatting to the pair of exotic Middle-Easterners, both from the Royal Jordanian Air Force. Mark's about to say hallo when he hears the Mess Stewards politely informing the young gentlemen that it's time to return to the huts. The boys wind their way back to their allocated quarters.

Mark falls in alongside room-mate Sid. He seems a down-to-earth chap – must be a grammar-grub like him. Yes, brought up in a Leicestershire village, Sid was a boarder at Loughborough College School:

ARRIVAL

I don't have a military family background – it was the aeroplanes at Farnborough that turned me on, plus the summer camps with the ATC. I went the Aircrew Officer Selection route and won an RAF Scholarship.

'That,' says Mark to himself, 'was inevitable.'

***

Back in the South Brick Lines, with ablutions tested (basic but spotlessly clean) civvy kit stowed and cherished photographs in position, at eleven o'clock it's time for lights-out.

For bed-time stories, the first of many, the mentors share their know-how, such as:

> You'll find out soon enough that you're going to be known by every one of the other cadets as 'Junior Entry Crows'. Airmen recruits are 'Rookies' – Cranwell new boys are 'Crows'. You must stand to attention when Flight Cadets from more senior entries come into the room and address them all as 'Sir'.
>
> There's a Crow Song that you'd better learn quick – save you a great deal of bother with the bully-boys. And start thinking about some entertainment that might distract them when it comes to your turn. Also, although you're unlikely to meet them much, be sure you get the names and decorations of the Commandant and Assistant Commandant off pat.

And:

> You'll be drawing your kit tomorrow afternoon. You'll have to stow it and make a regulation bedroll of your blankets and sheets. Then you'll have to mark every single piece of kit, from heavy cloth flying-helmet to shoe brushes, with the service number they give you.
>
> Then there's your boots. You'll be issued with two pairs – the ceremonial ones have to be polished to a mirror finish – it's called bulling. You'll learn how to get a shine on the stove and lino as well as your buttons.
>
> Mind you, I'll only be telling you what to do – I won't be doing it for you. I'd be in trouble if I did – as I'd also be if any

of you end up on Restrictions parade, which we call 'Strikers'. If you fall foul of the rules, then the deal here is that I carry some of the can too – understood?

Together with:

> It's said that the first boss of the RAF, the famous Lord Trenchard, chose Cranwell as a location for the Cadet College because it's remote in rural Lincs, far from the sinful temptations of London. It's certainly that, all right.
>
> But don't think too badly of the South Brick Lines. It was worse for Entry Number One, pretty well forty years ago – they were billeted in old wooden naval huts.
>
> Those early guys' parents had to pay for their sons to be here – you're being paid. On the other hand, they were only here for two years – you're here for three. But you'll only be in the South Brick Lines for one term.
>
> Sleep tight!

***

Mark lies in his wire-strung bed, his head full of the mentor's remarks:

> Apart from the haircut, the hat, and an officer-type Mess, it's already much like cadet camp – fierce sergeants and living in huts.
>
> It's going to be a real sweat, that's for sure, but what did I expect? And anyhow – it's not much more than a dozen weeks till Christmas.

None of the new boys yet knows that their entry, No. 81, have been chosen as guinea-pigs for radical change. That, for many, will be the greatest challenge.

At the same time, they'll unwittingly be helping to sow the seeds of a revolution that will lead to the demise of the current Flight Cadet system – just nine years after the successful among them graduate.

Chapter 2

The Deep End

Week 1: Wed 9th-Sun 14th Sep 1959

The first full day as Junior Crows is a whirlwind of activity, directed mostly by ever-watchful NCOs.

Reveille is at 0630 hours and breakfast at 0730. At 0800, Tannoy loudspeakers throughout the station squawk, before announcing: 'Standby for Crash Alarm Test!' followed by the wail of the siren. That's to be a daily reminder that Cranwell is an active flying station.

The first gathering of the day is at 0830 in the Junior Mess, where Flight Commanders supervise the paperwork, including the all-important Attestation Form 60, which outlines the Contract of Enlistment (for five years) and requires the recruits to fill in personal details – date and place of birth, religious denomination and so forth. The form also contains the words of the Oath of Allegiance that all, save for the ex-Apprentices and the Jordanians, are going to be required to take today. It reads:

> I swear by Almighty God that I will be faithful and bear true allegiance to Her Majesty Queen Elizabeth the Second, Her Heirs and Successors, and that I will, as in duty bound, honestly and faithfully defend Her Majesty, Her Heirs and Successors, in Person, Crown and Dignity against all enemies, and will observe and obey all orders of Her Majesty, her Heirs and Successors, and of the Air Officers and Officers set over me. So help me God.

This is going to be a big commitment, and the enormity of it strikes Mark for the first time. But he realises that it's a requirement for an officer serving in Her Majesty's Royal Air Force.

One of the lads gets puzzled by the box headed 'Religious Denomination' and in a stage whisper asks for guidance from one of the sergeants. 'I don't know what to put down – I don't really have a religion.' 'In that case, Sir,' is the snappy response, 'put down C of E.'

On riffling through the completed forms, the 'C' Squadron Flight Commander, Flight Lieutenant Gilliatt (a navigator by trade) is brought up short. In the 'Marital Status' box, one of his charges, the third man from Halton, has written 'Married'. That disqualifies him from being a Flight Cadet at the RAF College. There's a muffled conversation and both Flight Commander and Apprentice hastily leave the room. The chap isn't seen in the South Brick Lines again.

The entry is one down already. Fortunately, the remaining fifty-five lads are bachelors and their written responses are declared all in order.

The stately College building. (*RAF College*)

Still in civvies, the new boys are bussed up to the stately College building they glimpsed beyond the gilded gates. Following the Flight Commander, they troop through a side door and along corridors made splendid with stone-tiled floors, high ceilings and polished woodwork. Portraits of the College's great and good of the previous four decades loom as they approach the Rotunda, a two-storey atrium, complete with circular gallery, right in the centre of the building, beneath the tower.

At the end of the corridor, just off the carpeted Rotunda, lies the colonnaded Founders' Gallery. The aspiring Flight Cadets form up in an orderly queue. Mark finds himself standing in front of another tall chap who, in reverential whispers, in deference to the setting and occasion, introduces himself as Pete. Mark is sure that Pete was not around the previous evening and so it turns out.

Despite years of experience in train travel with the ATC, Pete had misread the timetables, arrived at Grantham late and had to have a special bus come to collect him, all on his own. Not too much missed though – just supper and the haircut. For Mark, Pete's story is a moment of bathos in what is an event of some solemnity.

Oath of Allegiance. (*RAF College*)

Face-to-face with his Flight Commander, alongside a portrait of the Monarch, and clutching a Bible, each new recruit solemnly takes the oath of allegiance. Invited to sign the Form 60, for regular service as Aircraftman II, with the rate of pay and legal status of that grade, Mark, with pen in hand, has a momentary wobble. He's about to commit to this status for the entire three years to planned graduation and commissioning.

'Well,' he reckons, 'given I do all right and graduate, it'll mean a commission, and pilot's Wings. If I don't and I get chopped, as long as it's not for a court-martial offence, I'll be free to go up to Durham.'

He signs.

Like all the others who have enlisted with him, he's now a Cranwell Flight Cadet and has his own six-digit personal service number, beginning with the distinctive Cranwell-specific 'six-zero'. He's told this number will be with him for the whole of his service career.

***

At lunch in the Junior Mess at 1230, Mark meets up again with Jock, of 'A' Squadron – they were on Tiger Moths together at Fairoaks that summer of '57.

Jock had a globe-trotting early upbringing. Born in Tanganyika, he moved with his doctor father to Kenya and Uganda but the most formative years of his education were as a boarder at Surrey's Epsom College, destined for medicine and financed by a Medical Foundation Scholarship. But the Fairoaks experience, together with CCF trips and the inspiration of a wartime Spitfire-ace art master, persuaded him away from a medical to a flying career.

'It was those thirty hours on Tigers that were the clincher. That and a CCF trip to Malta.'

Three more join the conversation. Tony, also from 'A' Squadron, was at Hampton Grammar in Middlesex, while Terry, a 'C' Squadron man with a fine sense of humour, graced the halls of the 'Bec' Grammar, in Tooting. Both have been supported by an RAF Scholarship.

'C' Squadron's Danny is a fit-looking chap with determined jaw and ready laugh. He reveals, 'I'm another from the Thames Valley – Sutton Grammar.'

'Blow me down,' says Mark, 'that's just down the road from my school, Kingston Grammar. Might we have met before? I've been to Sutton a few times with the cricket team.'

'I don't play cricket. I'm a soccer man and your lot only play hockey in the winter. I enjoyed my time at Sutton – the CCF did me proud. I won a Flying Scholarship – thirty hours on Tiger Moths at Fairoaks.'

That seals it. Not only are they all Surrey grammar-grubs but Danny's yet another who's learnt the arcane arts of the three-point landing from Wing Commander Arthur. They're mates.

Five boys from CCF schools in the heart of the Home Counties. Obviously a well-stocked pool for the RAF to trawl for trainee Pilot Officers.

Having agreed on the high quality of W. E. Johns' *Biggles* books, and their important influence on their choice of career, the talk moves to the small matter of the oaths they've just taken. Danny reckons, 'That's all right and proper. Allegiance to the Queen is our defence against any potentially sinister government.'

Mark hadn't thought of that – it's a strong point.

Jock concurs with Danny's view. 'I accepted it as something that had to be done early on – it's one of the rules of the Cranwell game.'

***

The new, junior members of Her Majesty's Royal Air Force are transported along Cranwell Avenue to the Station Stores, where awaiting them are piles of kit ready for their selection. Included in the issue are blue serge airman's battledress, beret, shoes, boots, and greatcoat, plus officer-style raincoat. There's a tailor on hand to assist with matching uniforms to the lads' measurements.

Mark is pleased to see there's flying kit. Although they're all well aware that flying training's not till Term 4, the mentor's told them it'll be needed right up-front, for navigation sorties in the College's twin-engine Valettas and Varsities.

Everything is carried away in a personal kitbag. The lads are told they'll have to stencil on their service number in indelible ink. Robert's somewhat curious that he's been issued with a bag bearing the number of its previous user, crossed out. The storeman tells him that it had belonged to a Senior Flight Cadet killed in a mid-air collision in January just this year.

Anthony, mentor to Robert in 'C' Squadron, has more detail:

> I had a grandstand view of what happened – saw it all from the rugby pitch. It was horrifying. Two Vampires collided in the circuit over the South Airfield – fell out of the sky.
>
> It seems the pilot of one of them, the kitbag owner, a senior cadet on a solo sortie in an FB9, had failed to call up before letting down into the circuit. The other crew, instructor and pupil minding their own business in a T11, obviously didn't get any warning.
>
> None of them had a chance.

It's a sobering reminder that in this profession, danger is always just around the corner.

Cranwell Vampires. (*RAF College Journal*)

A further indication that they are entering a fighting service is a trip to the Station Armoury to be issued with a .303 rifle – for drill and the firing range. When not in use it has to be secured under each cadet's bed-frame, with D-ring and padlock, while the bolt's to be locked in a bedside drawer. The mentor says that's to foil the IRA and others with evil intent. 'Guard it with your life,' is the message.

***

After tea at 1630, it's down to 'domestic' work in the South Brick Lines. They make a start on marking all items before stowing them away in regulation manner. This is a highly time-consuming process, involving the writing of service number onto strips of white tape with Indian ink, before painstakingly sewing them onto every garment. For shoe brushes, however, the service number has to be scored into the wood. In addition, they are required to sew onto the collars of the uniform blouse the white tab gorgets of Flight Cadets, each with a coloured vertical cord – red for 'A' Squadron, yellow for 'B', and blue for 'C'.

There's discussion about the anomaly that, despite all the domestic work required of the lads, they'll be enjoying the services of locally-recruited civilian batmen, one per two or three huts. The mentor has told them:

> They'll brush, sponge and press your uniforms, clean and polish your shoes – but not, repeat not, your boots. Also, they'll

26

scrub up the loos and showers. Mostly from Cranwell Village, these men are highly-respected servants – some have been at the College since the time of Number One Entry. For batting, the College bears the majority of the cost while we cadets give them a pound a month as a top-up.

You'll also get a laundry service – a free one on the station which shrinks everything or the better civilian one in Sleaford which must be paid for. Clothes for the wash are collected every Friday and delivered back, ironed and aired, by Monday.

All the new cadets are soon speaking highly of the batmen, including those in Mark's hut, where 'Mickey' greets them in the morning, come rain, shine or wall-to-wall fog with, 'Turned out nice again, Gentlemen.'

Robert is the only one with a problem. 'Our batman has polished my brown suede shoes!'

Second day official photograph of 81 Entry 'C' Squadron. Just ten were to make it to the entry's 1962 Graduation. (*RAF College*)

The marking-up extends into day two, before on the morning of day three, in their new uniforms, they are ready to pose for squadron and individual photographs. Squadron shots are to be pinned up in the Orderly Room as an aid for the staff in matching names and faces. The individual images are for mounting on identification cards, in due course.

Then, again by squadron flights, gingerly in unbroken boots, the tyros take their first steps on the drill square. For the ex-Apprentices, this is a breeze and most of the other lads are familiar with basic drill from their time with the CCF and ATC but some, obviously, are not. It's soon clear which of the lads have arms uncoordinated with legs, and difficulty in distinguishing left from right.

Mishaps and collisions, and the fact that it's all three squads on the same square, give the Drill Sergeants the opportunity for much verbal interplay. The protesting Scottish brogue of 'A' Squadron's McDill competes with the ironic South London whine of 'C' Squadron's Cliff Ross. 'B' Squadron's Flight Sergeant Harvey is notably less confrontational. His most frequent, and highly appropriate advice is, 'Remember, Gentlemen, forewarned is forearmed.' In a discussion on matters nutritional, McDill's assertion that 'baked beans, Gentlemen, are not an officer's vegetable', goes down in the record books.

The uniforms of the new Flight Cadets are ready targets for attention. Bill has sewn on his Coronation ribbon. This he's done with Sergeant Ross's permission but nevertheless it's a chance not to be missed. 'Remind me what the medal ribbon's for, Mr Wood.'

'Coronation Medal – Sergeant.'

'And tell us what you did for Her Majesty, Mr Wood.'

'I sang in the choir, Sergeant,' adding, in a boyish treble, 'Vivat Regina – Sergeant.'

Bill gets away with that – the occasional flash of humour's obviously tolerated.

The process of bulling gets under way. The ceremonial pair of boots needs much elbow-grease with Kiwi Parade Black while belt and gaiters require treatment with blue Blanco on the webbing parts and Brasso on the shiny bits – and 'never the twain shall meet'.

The lads are now issued with their brand-new laminated-plastic Forms 1250. Showing name, rank and number as well as photo, they are, so they are firmly told, the most important document they'll ever own. 'Lose at your absolute peril,' is the message.

Albeit at the very bottom, the new boys are part of the hierarchy now.

***

The days proceed, with lectures from Squadron and Flight Commanders on rules of the game, expectations and requirements of cadets through to table manners and etiquette.

They are measured by Messrs Bates and Co for their officer-pattern service hats with RAF badge (and the distinctive white band of a Flight Cadet around the rim), by Messrs Poulson Skone for one pair of officer-pattern black shoes and by Gieves for a pair of unlined brown-leather gloves.

Bates & Co. (*RAF College Journal*)

Poulsen, Skone & Co. (*RAF College Journal*)

The Medical Officer arrives, to talk (embarrassingly and scarily) about personal hygiene, following which, there's a series of vaccinations which leave the arm swollen and stiff for at least a couple of painful days.

This makes the Friday evening bulling of ceremonial boots even more of a trial, before Saturday morning brings some relief with a tour of the stately College building.

The pillared portico entrance is out of bounds to all cadets save for the Senior Entries – so the visitors from the Junior Mess are required to use a side entrance, to be escorted by a guide. A mentor has told them that that's one of the extra duties taken on by the Senior Entry, as part of their personal skills training.

This guide's certainly done his homework:

> The foundation stone of the College building was laid in 1929 by Lady Hoare, the wife of the then Secretary of State for Air. It was a hurried affair, with no band, flags or ceremony. A change of government was expected and Air Marshal Trenchard and his supporters feared that the new one might yet reverse the whole RAF enterprise.
>
> The building is constructed in what is called 'rustic and moulded' brickwork, with the more important features picked out in Portland stone. There are three wings of two storeys, housing 150 Flight Cadets, but building work's under way to add a fourth wing for a further squadron.
>
> Between the 800-feet-wide building and an oblate spheroid of manicured lawn, called the 'Orange', extends 600 feet of Parade Ground.

Following their leader, the junior lads make their way along the lofty corridors, lined with classical scenes as well as portraits of Commandants from the year dot, and are shown the spacious anterooms. Three of those, furnished with leather armchairs, low tables and wall-hung pictures of heroic scenes, are allocated one each to the three squadrons of Senior Mess Flight Cadets. A fourth is given over to a billiards room, with three full-size tables and all the fixings. Yet another houses a grand piano.

They briefly take in the Senior Mess FGS. Here, says their guide, cadets can spend their relaxed hours enjoying beer and spirits, highly competitive darts, bar billiards and gramophone music. Arriving at the Rotunda, with its broad and deep-patterned carpet, the guide warns:

> Mind you don't step on the carpet. Only officers and the Senior Entry are allowed to do that. The route across the Founders'

Gallery is also out of bounds. All cadets, again other than the Senior Entry, must take the longer back-route round by the Dining Hall.

Here, we're directly underneath the 120-foot tower. That houses not only a clock face on each of its four facades but also a peal of bells, presented in 1952 by the Shell Group in memory of all College graduates who gave their lives in the Second World War. Those chime not only the hours and the quarters but also the Retreat at the evening Sunset Ceremony.

Just above your heads, is the spot where, one foggy wartime night, an off-course Whitley bomber crashed into the roof, killing not only the crew but also a sleeping student pilot.

Outside, on the gable-end above the entrance, is mounted the College Coat of Arms. The College of Arms granted this in December 1929, with a design based on that of a local feudal landowner, de Cranewell, but with a new motto, Superna Petimus – which can be translated as 'We Seek the Highest'.

The tourists can see that in the Founders' Gallery, where they pledged themselves to serve the Queen, hang full-length oil-paintings of Lord Trenchard, Air Vice-Marshal Sir Charles Longcroft, the first Commandant, and Sir Winston Churchill, in stern bulldog pose. Also featured is a portrait of Air Commodore Sir Frank Whittle, who while at the College in 1928, wrote his ground-breaking thesis on jet-propulsion.

They then take that route round the back to look in on the main lecture theatre, the 'Longcroft Room', impressive with three-score rows of seats and proscenium stage. The corridor walls en route the Dining Hall are lined with photos of entries, prize-winners and sports teams from the year it all began. The Hall itself has top table and three sprigs, all in weighty mahogany, arranged, they're told, for one of the regular, formal Guest Nights, when the whole of the Senior College, staff and guests will be seated. Behind the western-end top table stands a tall plinth with an impressive banner affixed at the slant, surmounted by a magnificent bronze eagle.

'That's the Queen's Colour,' the guide informs, 'the College Standard.' It's paraded on Graduation and other ceremonial parades.'

RAF College Coat of
Arms, as granted 1929.
(*RAF College*)

Queen's Colour for the Royal Air Force College.
(*RAF College*)

Bell Tower.
(*RAF College*)

Around the sidewalls hang portraits of mostly stern-looking, senior officers of the RAF while the eastern-end wall boasts a minstrels' gallery. 'That's where,' their guide reports, 'the College Band entertains the assembled diners with a selection of military marches as well as songs from the shows – the Post-Horn Gallop's the party piece.'

To finish the tour, they climb a broad carpeted staircase to the elegant and well-stocked College Library, housing an impressive array of books, magazines and newspapers as well as an in-depth archive and display of the history and traditions of the RAF and the College. It gives the new boys a glimpse of how the RAF College Cranwell came to be.

In just a little more than a decade after the Wright Brothers in December 1903 had made the world's first controlled powered flight at Kittyhawk, the air of Northern Europe was about to become a battlefield – in the Great War of 1914-18. It was in that war that the airbase alongside Cranwell village was founded.

In 1912, the British government had established the Royal Naval Air Service (RNAS) as the air arm of the Royal Navy, and the Royal Flying Corps (RFC), as that of the Army. By May 1916, difficulties in coordinating the control of two services led to the RNAS being entrusted with home and coastal defence and the RFC, under Trenchard, with operations in Europe.

In seeking to counter the German threat from both the sea and the air, the RNAS in 1915 established HMS Daedalus, on 3,000 commandeered acres of farmland outside the village of Cranwell. It was set up as a training base for crews of naval aircraft and balloons, to be based at a string of RN Air Stations planned for East Anglia.

It transpired that the RNAS was not equipped with the resources to deal with German Zeppelin airships and Botha bomber night marauders. The raids caused considerable fatalities and damage. Public opinion demanded a response from the newly-incorporated Air Board, which in turn called on General Jan Smuts, a respected former foe in the turn-of-the-century Boer War, to investigate.

In August 1917, Smuts recommended a complete shake up including, for the services involved, a contentious proposal that a new air service should be formed, equal in status to the Army and Navy. Created by merging the RNAS and the RFC, the new air service would receive direction from a new Air Ministry.

Army and Navy chiefs were utterly opposed to the concept of the RAF as a separate independent service and tried by every available means to divide up available air assets between themselves. However, with the support of, among others, Winston Churchill, Smuts's suggestion was taken up. On 1st April 1918, the Royal Air Force came into being, the world's first independent air force, with Brigadier General Hugh Trenchard in command.

On the formation of the RAF, HMS Daedalus *became RAF Cranwell. Within a year Trenchard, who had stated from the outset that a key requirement for the new RAF was the facility to train its own officers, had chosen the station as the home for his Air Academy. The first Cadet Entry arrived on 5th February 1920 and within the decade, Trenchard had secured the budget for a new College building. He foresaw an imposing edifice and in 1933, he got it. Giving the RAF College a measure of instant tradition and stature, the very presence of the building helped in successfully fending off further takeover bids from rival Services.*

The Senior College visit over, it's back to the Junior Mess for a hurried lunch before domestic business in the South Brick Lines. On Monday, there's to be a Flight Commander's Inspection so now's the time to polish rifles (the barrels made spotless with a pull-through lanyard and duster), together with bayonet (with Solvol-Autosol courtesy of the Halton chaps) and everything in the hut that doesn't move. It's all something of a chore and a bit more bull than many had anticipated but at least it's all done in what already has become home. And the work's shared – by blokes that they already count as pals.

Therefore it's a most unwelcome violation of their space and peace of mind when every hut is invaded by 80 Entry men, well-oiled from a Saturday evening in one of the local pubs. These raiders are looking for likely lads on whom to practise their ritual sadism.

Cocksure, secure in their seniority and sporting the best in officer-style twill and chukka-boots, they move through the living areas, pulling apart bedrolls with cries of, 'That's rubbish!' and emptying shelves with, 'Filthy!' and, 'Squalid!' taking pleasure in undoing hours of painstaking work.

Then, while the mentor sensibly takes shelter in his cubbyhole, the hut's occupants are herded into the domestic area at the rear. Slouching in the armchairs, and squatting on the tables, the marauders order the new boys, one by one, to perform. It can be a song, a witty poem, dirty story or a stunt. If they decide they don't reckon it cuts the mustard, then ferocious forfeits follow.

This process is known as 'crowing', a brutal welcome for newcomers to the stresses of service life.

Mark renders a version of *Who Killed Cock Robin?* with added hand gestures. They've not seen those before, and he gets away with it. Sid does a pretty professional card trick and survives. But one of the hut-mates, a Glaswegian with an accent to match, freezes in mid-performance – and loses his trousers.

For a climax, they are all required to sing the *Crow's Song*, to the tune of *All Creatures that on Earth do Dwell*. Prompted by their tormentors, the lads bellow as loud as they can:

> Three big black crows sat on a tree,
> They were as black as black could be.
> Said one black crow unto the other,
> Get off my foot, you big black bugger!

It takes a while, but at last, the crowing party is satisfied.

With the last of their sneers and jeers, they swagger off back to the Junior Mess and the FGS, there to drink to their triumphs.

The mentor emerges from his hiding-place:

> Well done! You've survived.
>
> What was that all about? Well, alongside the drill, bulling and discipline, it's meant to beat down cocky young sixth-formers such as you and develop resilience. Unless there's grievous bodily harm, the authorities let it go on.
>
> And remember, you're being spared the boxing torture – that's just been abolished. We, 80 Entry, were the last to endure that. At the end of Term One, after being given a couple of sessions in the rudiments of fisticuffs, we were paired off for a series of bouts down in the gym.
>
> It was always after a black-tie dinner up in the Senior Mess and down they came – Senior Entries, Commandant and all, cigars in hand – to watch the bouts. Three one-minute rounds to each, in gym kit and boxing gloves. We didn't hold back. Slogged each other to a standstill. Couldn't be seen to show any weakness.

After close-on forty years, there's not to be any more boxing. Cadets have been so badly beaten up – vision impaired, sinuses damaged – that they lost their medical category. No more flying. Expensive for the victims and for the College.

But there'll be plenty more crowing. Get used to it.

The public-school boys, as well as many of the grammar-grubs, have seen it all before. Danny says his hut has had it pretty mild. 'I quite enjoyed playing basketball without a ball.' Mike, the man from Leeds, reckons 'crowing's more banter and sending-up than bullying'. The news gets around on the field-telegraph that the crowers have met their match in two 'A' Squadron huts. One, a local man from Stamford, quite able to look after himself, has sent them on their way. 'It's nothing more than I've experienced at school – and there most boys are the sons of farmers, good with their fists.' This broad-faced and muscular chap, with his wicked smile, has quickly earned the nickname of 'Kraut'.

Another 'A' Squadron man has also given better than he got. Jim is one of the three navigator trainees in the entry, a tough Yorkie and ex-Apprentice from No. 1 Radio School. 'I blew my top – left them in no doubt that they should desist immediately, and go forth and multiply. There was none of this nonsense at Locking. Short of resorting to fisticuffs, there was nothing else they could do and they shortly left us in peace. We've been expecting dire retribution but none's come.'

Michael and his 'B' Squadron roommates decide to take action. 'We in our hut reckon it's just plain silly. We're not going to play along with it. We'll see what they think of that.'

Before long, 81 Entry have collectively decided, not to 'kowtow to the bastards. Stand up straight and look 'em in the eye, like Kraut and Jim. If you can, make 'em laugh. Don't, at all costs, start blubbing!'

***

Day five, their first Sunday in the College, sees the whole entry, in best civvies, marching up to the Senior College to watch the first Church Parade of term. According to the mentors, the Queen's Colour will be on view.

They find a fair crowd of onlookers there already, mostly staff and their families. It's quite a show. The RAF College Band are in best Sunday fig on the College steps and at 1030 prompt, three ranks of Flight Cadets, from 76 Entry down to 80 – save those few given permission to be absent for some authorised activity, or who find themselves in sick quarters – march onto the Parade Ground from the western end of the square. Without rifles but in best Number One uniforms, they halt, turn to face the Orange and

'Crows' in Sunday Best. (*WMNG*)

stand to attention while undergoing inspection by the College Warrant Officer, a figure of considerable authority.

'This,' the mentor has warned, 'is an inspection not to be treated lightly. Even though it's the day of rest and worship, you can still be put on a charge for any slovenliness.'

The inspection completed to the CWO's satisfaction, he hands command of the parade to a cadet Senior Under Officer, who gives the order, 'Roman Catholics, non-Conformists and Jews may fall out'. Whereupon those individuals turn smartly to their right, salute and march off behind the ranks to their own religious observances or to while away the time before re-joining the parade for the return march.

The Parade Commander now gives the command, 'Parade – Move to the Left in Threes' followed by, 'Parade – Quick March'.

It's a few hundred yards to the Church of England chapel of St Michael and All Angels, housed under the corrugated roof of a former hangar. It stands alongside the North Airfield, 'Reckoned,' says the mentor, 'to be the biggest area of unfenced grassland in England.' He adds that the church is known as the 'Tin Tabernacle' – a permanent building is targeted for two years' time.

But the parade's a proper military affair. On the return march, the Commandant mounts a podium to take the salute.

For Mark, it's been an impressive and inspirational introduction to College ceremonial. On top of that, the service at St Michael's has made a change from the events of the first week. A section of the College Band has done justice to the music and the choir has sung with gusto.

It's also been good to hear that, apparently, God is still on our side.

Junior Mess Dining Room. (*FM*)

The generous Sunday lunch in the Junior Mess is impressive – 80 Entry men give the College's kitchen, staffed by the best RAF chefs in the Catering Branch, excellent reviews. Over the meal, the new lads learn more from the mentor about the Queen's Colour:

> Presented in 1953, it remains a symbol, for cadets and staff alike, of the authority of their boss, the Monarch. For the special occasions when it's needed – Battle of Britain Parade, which will be next week, Passing Out ceremonies and such – it's carried by an Under Officer of the Sovereign's Squadron.
>
> Under Officer? Think of him as a school prefect and a Senior Under Officer as the Head Prefect and you won't go far wrong. They're responsible for keeping discipline in the squadrons.
>
> Sovereign's Squadron? That's the one given the privilege of carrying and escorting the Queen's Colour. The title is held

by the squadron gaining a majority of wins in three inter-squadron competitions, in drill, athletics and such, held every term. You'll soon learn all about them.

For the last couple of terms, the Sovereign's Squadron has been, and still is, 'C'.

Refreshed in body and mind, the newcomers retire to the South Brick Lines back rooms for more bulling of boots.

The ceremonial boots are needing close-on a whole tin of Kiwi Parade Black – some have used the back of a hot spoon to get it on, most rely on tried and trusted spit and polish. On this and many other domestic matters the entry is pleased to have the experience of the Halton and Locking fellows to help them out.

They learn all about the shining of floors with underfoot remnants of old blankets, the black-leading of the stove and how to fold blankets and sheets into a kind of cubic Swiss roll. They get the latest tips on how to make everything from the taps in the ablutions to the woodwork on the rifle shine like a cavalry officer's breastplate.

Dave hits on a great wheeze to ease the strain of kit inspection. As well as having prepared a pre-formed bed roll, to be brought out from under cover on the appropriate morning, he's extended the idea to other items. 'I have one set of toilet gear that I don't use and it stays out of sight and immaculate – no hairs in the hairbrush, no bristles in the razor. Works a treat.' The idea catches on. Mercifully, visitors are confined to the Senior Entry coming down to say hallo and the bull somehow goes more easily when it's Cliff Richard and his *Living Doll* on Sid's portable Roberts Radio.

Back room,
South Brick
Lines – with
Nav Bag. (*JGL*)

Bulling… (*JGL*)

…and more bulling. (*JGL*)

Chapter 3

Moving Goalposts

Term 1: 9th Sep-15th Dec 1959

Monday's Flight Commanders' room and kit inspection kicks off at 0815 hours. There's to be no such thing as an easy introduction. Non-regulation bedrolls and 'filthy' razors and tooth brushes are not for one minute to be tolerated. All have to be remade, cleaned up or polished under a Drill Sergeant's beady eye. No nook or cranny escapes notice and the slightest 'grot' has to be dealt with there and then.

No one is put on a charge, yet, but it's clear that this is a world of zero-tolerance.

***

The inspection is followed in the afternoon by further Flight Commanders' briefings before the day finishes off with an hour's drill.

On the Parade Square, the sergeants announce that the next morning at 0900, there's to be a briefing by the Assistant Commandant, together with the Director of Studies, in the Junior Mess. 'Muster at 0830, Gentlemen – and not a moment later.'

In a routine evening session, the majority of crows spoil the crowers' fun by having the words of the *Crow's Song* off by heart, and by refusing to play along with their game.

Relieved, the lads fall asleep wondering what the morning briefing will bring.

***

Crowded into the Junior Mess anteroom, the entire entry, complemented by uniformed Senior RAF Education Branch Tutors and Squadron Commanders, are addressed by the Assistant Commandant, a Group Captain. He welcomes the new boys to Cranwell and Mark understands from his following words that they should consider themselves lucky to be here and to watch their step.

41

The Director of Studies, the suited and gowned Mr Antony Constant, MA, however, has something of a surprise. He lets the lads know that they've been selected against high standards at Hornchurch and Daedalus House – many of them have achieved above average A-level results into the bargain. There are therefore high hopes that they will be able to join in a bid to raise the academic bar at the Royal Air Force College.

At the beginning of the next week they will, like every Cadet Entry before them, begin the general syllabus of academic studies. This, comprising a mixture of Science and Humanities, has been running almost unchanged, since the College re-opened following the Second World War. But for their second term, starting in January, they are going to be invited to join one of three new academic streams.

'A' Stream will pursue courses balanced between humanities and science subjects relevant to the needs of trainee General List aircrew officers – such as Applied Mathematics, English, Physics, Economics and Military Studies. There will be examinations throughout their time at the College. Its members will be embarking on a syllabus that demands a higher and broader standard than has been asked of their predecessors.

'B' Stream will major in Scientific Studies. These will follow a syllabus targeted at qualification for Associated Fellowship of the Royal Aeronautical Society, known as AFRAeS. Examinations, equivalent to degree-level, will be taken at Cranwell – for Part I in the autumn of next year and Part II in their ninth, and final term.

'C' Stream will be studying for the University of London's external Bachelor of Arts General Degree. Examinations, in War Studies together with two other subjects, chosen from Geography, History, Economics, English and French, will be in London in the early summer of 1962.

The authorities realise that for 81 Entry students, this will present a challenge. They will be undergoing enhanced academic training while completing the syllabus of officer, ground school and flying training the same as everyone else. This will require careful management of time and priorities.

The Director concludes:

> This is to be a bold experiment in raising the academic standards necessary for today's new generation of trainee officers and those to come. The modern world demands it. The RAF College, together with its sister colleges at Dartmouth and Sandhurst must keep up with the University world, which is every year widening its catchment areas.

42

Tomorrow you will be invited to meet your relevant Senior Tutors face-to-face in individual discussions as to where your place will be in this new adventure.

We in the Academics Wing wish you all the best for your time at the Royal Air Force College and in your careers beyond.

The Orderly Room posts the proposed division of the 81 Entry cadets into the three streams, together with the times of their interviews. They show that nineteen will be in 'B' Stream (AFRAeS), and eight in 'C' (BA London). The remainder will form the 'A' Stream, for General Studies (with selected O- and A-levels for some).

These developments give many a cadet considerable pause for thought. They knew that there would be academic studies alongside the officer and flying training – it said so in the info packs. But this so-called 'bold new experiment', with enhanced brainwork – that's more than they bargained for.

How could this have come about?

For some years before 1959, the RAF as well as the RAF College had been falling short, by as much as 50%, of its aircrew recruiting targets.

A study commissioned by the Air Board was undertaken by Mr G.A. Roberts, a Senior Scientific Adviser to the Air Ministry. By the time of his report, in 1958, he had found that the problem was not one of a lack of applicants. Many who had passed the Aptitude Tests were being rejected at the final panel and one-on-one interviews. The simple fact was that assessing officers were being overly subjective in their decision criteria, mostly accepting, as briefed, those who looked and spoke like officers, and those who went to 'good schools'.

This had led to a skewing of the odds in favour of public school boys at the expense of many bright individuals from the technical side of education – the ones that the Air Force desperately needed in the new age of missiles and high technology. As a result of Mr Roberts's work, the criteria for selection were extended to include a box headed 'Potential'. Numbers accepted for training improved, with a noticeable increase in boys from technical schools.

The RAF College shared this experience. For 78 Entry in January 1958 the percentage coming from Head Masters' Conference Schools was 63.8 – for 81 Entry in September 1959, it was 41.8. More bright boys from Grammar and Technical schools were making it through

---

to a Cranwell cadetship, able to accept greater challenges on the academic front.

At the same time, there was an increasing realisation among sixth-formers, as well as their masters, that a university degree was the thing to aim for if they wished to advance in a world where technologists were infiltrating the British Establishment. Feedback from headmasters told the top brass that further education at the average military college no longer cut the mustard. Therefore, at the request of the Air Council, in April 1957, the Ministry of Education subjected the College syllabus to a searching examination. Twelve months later, the report it delivered did not pull its punches, concluding:

> *Cranwell has become little more than a Flying Training School, with an inadequate school regime tacked on to it. This is not the object of the College's being.*

In 1958, a Working Party delivered to the Air Council what was known as the Melvin Report, which offered the opinion that for Cranwell to fulfil its long-term objectives, cadets must be given the equivalent of a university education, with science at its core. Hence the three-stream course to be undertaken by 81 Entry.

Still under development on their arrival, it would not be ready for delivery before January 1960. Additional tutors, sufficient in quality and in number, were still being identified – the majority, serving officers on five-year tours. For them, the revised aim of the College was to be the basis for their briefing:

> *To provide the Service with officers of character and ability, whose education and service training will enable them progressively to develop their powers and faculties to meet the demands of service in the highest ranks.*

In Senior Tutor interviews, the 81 Entry cadets find out more about their intended academic path. The selections appear to have been made on the basis of A-level results and Head and Schoolmasters' recommendations. Reaction is mixed.

Robert, Pete, Mac, Michael and Mark are among those chosen for the 'C' Stream. Privately, Mark, whose allocated subjects after War Studies are

Economics and French, is delighted. Learning to fly and getting a degree at the same time, with Economics into the bargain. The best of both worlds.

Robert, with Geography and History, is also pleased, seeing studying for a BA as 'a useful insurance against the dreaded flying chop'.

Pete is surprised:

> At grammar school in Bournemouth, it took me an extra go to get my A-levels – now, I've been put in for a degree. But History and English – why not my best subject, French? All right – these days the Air Force probably has to show it can get degree-level candidates into Cranwell, but why me? We'll see.

John has an interesting situation:

> I'm the 'C' Stream, recommended to opt for Maths and History, both of which I passed at A-level. So now I've got a problem with logistics.
>
> I'm going to have to hare between the Humanities Huts, four hundred yards west of the College building on West Site, and the Science site the same distance over on the east. How to do that, without a bike and forbidden to run?
>
> All the same, it may well be worth it. We'll see how it goes in January.

Dave's in the 'B' Stream and with those four scientific A-levels under his belt, has no qualms about that:

> This AFRAeS affair seems at first glance to be no more than a continuation of the studies I've done so far. But the real challenge is going to be when we're doing academics and flying together.
>
> Mind you, I'm relaxed. My school headmaster's lined up a place at Southampton University in reserve.

Tony, on the other hand, is dubious:

> The AFRAeS studies and exams are sure to take up huge amounts of time. Will there be enough hours in the day to fit much else in? Flying training, for a start.

I was considering going to university but applied to Cranwell as I was dead set on learning to fly and also because that was the route my father felt he could support – he was in the RAF during the war. Now I'm also being given the chance of a degree-level qualification.

We'll have to see how it goes.

Sid, whose A-level qualifications are in Mathematics and Physics, is also on the AFRAeS route. He's somewhat taken aback by the whole development and confides to Mark:

It seems the twelve of us in the 'B' Stream are going to be asked to study Aerodynamics, Structures and Strength of Materials, together with Electronics, Thermodynamics and Meteorology. Alongside, we'll be expected to submit to the full three years of military training as well as learning to become pilots qualified to Wings standard.

I'm here to fly. This new direction isn't what I'd bargained for when I applied for a cadetship. But all right – for now I'll bow to the inevitable with as much grace I can muster.

The new 'A' Stream course syllabus is to be much expanded compared with that of previous entries. Jim the Nav's name is down for it:

I'm pleased to see English, Applied Maths and Physics on the menu – highly relevant for a potential General Duties officer, as should be Military Studies. I can't say the same for Economics, but we'll see – I've had zero exposure to the 'dismal science' so far.

Andy's also to be an 'A' Stream man, with the chance to study for Maths and Economics to A-level. Mike is alongside him:

I'm not disappointed. I'm here to learn to fly, and to become an officer. With A-levels, Chemistry and Biology, already in the bag, the 'A' Stream is fine by me. If I'd wanted a degree, I'd have gone to Cambridge as previously planned to become a doctor!

Bill, despite A-level passes in Maths, Physics, and Chemistry, together with Robin (similarly qualified, save for Chemistry) are surprisingly joining the 'A' Stream. Bill comments, 'I'm not bothered – it'll give me a chance to retake Maths and perhaps get a better grade.' Robin adds, 'I'm proud of my two passes. At the time of the study and the exams, with mum away in Brum with my second stepfather, I was living in digs. But I'm not complaining – low profile, that's me.'

Jock, also destined for the 'A' Stream, is another who's nonplussed:

> At Epsom, I passed the Zoology and Chemistry A-levels required for the First MB but failed the Physics, which I hated. But also, I'd qualified for Cranwell through the Civil Service exam, with specialist subjects in French and Chemistry. And, I have O-level Latin – from scratch, at prep school.
>
> I'd have loved the chance to take a degree in the 'C' Stream – but I'm not going to protest. I'm a conformist – grateful to be here.

Is there any element of choice for the Flight Cadets?

Danny, selected for the AFRAeS route, tells Mark, 'I was certainly given the option by Wingco Duckett but I'm going with the course. It's a chance to do something different.'

'Our Humanities tutor, Wing Commander Watts,' responds Mark, 'was a gallant Guards Officer in the war. There was no arguing when he let us know that he sees this as a first-class opportunity for us all.'

***

In the meetings with Wing Commander Watts, five of the 'C' Stream students are faced with an extra surprise. To satisfy London University's matriculation requirements, five of them (including Mark, Pete and Mac) are required to acquire a pass in O-level Latin.

Another 'C' Stream man, Robert, has Latin but needs O-level English Literature and Sid, in the 'B' is going to be faced with retaking A-level Applied Maths. The exams for these extra 0- and A-levels, which can be held at Cranwell, are scheduled for autumn 1960. Studies, mostly in the evening, get under way almost immediately. For the Latin students it's Virgil and the *Aeneid* while for Robert it's Shakespeare and Dickens.

Mark is struck by the oddity of it all. For the first twelve months of their new RAF career in the forefront of technology and in the midst of nuclear weapon-driven world tension, he and his 'C' Stream pals find themselves back in the archaic world of long-dead English and Roman poets and playwrights, all in the interests of furthering the needs of a 'bold experiment' dreamt up by the Air Ministry.

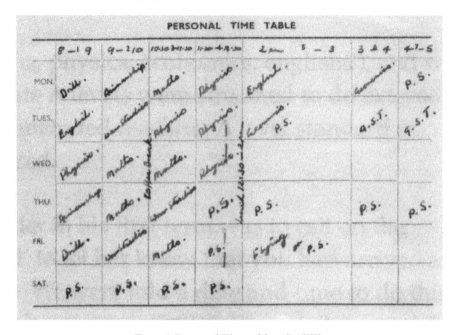

Term 1 Personal Timetable. (*RAFW*)

Meanwhile, Term 1 progresses.

It's back to drilling, bulling and PT until the Weekly Programme of College Instruction kicks off at the beginning of week three. The mix of subjects for the term consists of: Airmanship (including Navigation and Meteorology), English, Physics, Maths, Economics and War Studies. Squeezed in with those are two sessions of General Service Training (GST) – everything from Air Force Law to the basic Rules of Etiquette (introducing the gent to the lady and that sort of thing). Ground Defence Training (GDT), with the RAF Regiment contingent also has its place. In due course that will include (they're promised) range practice with .303 rifle, Smith-and-Wesson revolver and STEN sub-machine gun.

The Flight Commanders give their charges all the details of prizes that are there for the taking at the end of their nine terms. The Sword of Honour heads the list, awarded to the Flight Cadet 'who is recommended by the Commandant as having most distinguished himself in leadership and in general influence for the good of the College while in residence at Cranwell'. Next in line comes the Queen's Medal, awarded to the Flight Cadet who is placed first in the Order of Merit – this order depending on individual results in all aspects of training.

The Philip Sassoon Memorial Prize is another in the direct bequest of the Commandant –for the best all-round runner-up to the Sword winner. The Abdy Gerrard Fellowes Memorial Prize is for the man showing greatest proficiency in Maths, Aeronautical Science and Engineering and there's an Air Ministry Prize for Imperial and War Studies.

The flying awards consist of the R.M. Groves Memorial Prize and Kinkead Trophy for the first in the Order of Merit for flying – for the second in the Order, there's the Hicks Memorial Prize and for instrument flying, the Dickson Trophy.

There is also an Institute of Navigation Trophy and Air Ministry Prize for the man top of the Navigators' Order of Merit. The J.A. Chance Memorial Prize is for the chap who's outstanding in term work and examinations in all subjects from drill, PT, GST and flying. This latter depends heavily on the Squadron Commanders' assessments.

It's agreed that given that little lot, under-employment's not going to be a problem for 81 Entry.

***

There's a half-hour NAAFI break at 1000 (tea and buns), and one-and-a-half hours for lunch but a good slice of that is used up marching to and from the Junior Mess. The drill is that each squad or set, come rain or shine, musters twenty minutes before the first lesson is due to start. Under the close scrutiny of the sergeants, they form up in three ranks, with the handle of a sturdy blue navigation bag full of books, firmly grasped in the left fist.

The Duty Cadet calls the shots, bringing the lads to attention. Then it's, 'Righ-ert – Turn, Quick March', and off they set at a brisk pace, along tarmac tracks that become all too familiar after a couple of days. Should an officer appear, then it's a smart, 'Squad! Eye-ers – Right', or 'Left', from the Duty Cadet. At the destination, the squad is brought to a crisp halt and dismissed. Damp, rain-coated figures are swallowed up by the 'wrinkly-tin' Science Building to the east of the Senior College, or the wartime creosoted-wood huts of the Humanities Site to the west.

Talking in the ranks en route is strictly forbidden. The same rule applies when individual cadets, or small groups from a couple upwards, are hoofing it from place to place – always march in step, look smart and keep mouths shut.

***

A regular destination is the College swimming pool, down on the edge of the South Airfield. On an early visit, the 'C' Squadron Duty Cadet nervously garbles an order. 'By the Light…'

Quick as a flash, from Sergeant Ross it's, 'Of the silvery moon I suppose, Mr Coulson?' Straight, faces are not.

The pool, just twenty-five metres long, is a place of baptism for the new cadets into the business of the stiff upper-lip. Situated in a former hangar, it's cold as well as old. There's a five-metre high springboard and the drill is that all the lads, swimmers or not, are required to climb the steps and fearlessly dive or at least leap into the abyss below. The Physical Training Instructors (PTIs) fish out those who are struggling, while making note of any 'lack of moral fibre'.

A more popular visit is to the small workshop in the Science site where the budding officers hone their soldering skills in the assembly of small radio sets. More advanced mechanical work takes place in the Cadets' Instructional Workshops (CIW), where the lads are entrusted with basic tools with which to learn essential hand-crafting skills, such as wood-working, steel-filing, aluminium-turning on a lathe, as well as screw-tapping. The output there comprises small table lamps, in gleaming aluminium on a polished-wood base.

For those with thoughts of more exciting activities the CIW also houses a small museum, where stand a rare WWII Luftwaffe Messerschmitt ME 262 jet fighter, together with an even rarer 'Komet' ME 163 hydrogen-peroxide rocket-powered aircraft – the latter achieving 700mph in level flight in 1944. Alongside those sits a single-seat Vampire FB 5 – aspiring pilots can sit in its cockpit, to dream of a flying future.

***

The timetable allows for a couple of hours' drill a week – 0800 start on Monday and Tuesday. The mentor says, 'You're lucky blighters – we had it five days a week.' Navigation flying is to be on Monday afternoon. Wednesday afternoon is given over to sport and Saturday morning is designated, somewhat ingenuously it seems to Mark, Private Study time. 'Private bulling time more like,' he reckons.

From the beginning of this timetable, the sergeants' gloves are off. Punishments are dished out for the slightest transgression. These usually involve a routine: 'See me after, Mister Bloggs!' followed by, 'You're on a Charge!' before being marched by the sergeant into the Flight Commanders' Orderly Room. The sentence is a spell on Strikers from a day to a week, and sometimes more. Strikers entails all-day wearing of uniform ('and make sure it's immaculate'), no sports (on or off the station) and non-use of the FGS for the duration of the punishment. It also involves parading in full drill kit on the Junior Square for half an hour before breakfast and again at the 1630 sunset routine (1800 in the summer) both in front of the Duty Under Officer.

The lads are becoming increasingly aware of the cadet-administered system of discipline run in parallel by one Senior Under Officer (SUO) and at least two Under Officers (UOs) per squadron. It's said they all reside in some comfort in flats in the Senior Mess. However, on a weekly roster, one UO is banished to the Junior Mess, tasked with keeping order.

'It's a thankless task,' says the mentor. 'They're responsible for discipline in the entire Junior Mess – if there's any trouble in the South Brick Lines, they'll get it in the neck for letting it happen.'

Mark, who has early experience of Strikers (for 'creeping around like a half-closed penknife!') remarks to Sid:

> It's not so much the severity of the punishment – it's the shame of hearing your name followed by the dreaded, 'See me after!' It starts at your boots and climbs up to your neck. You've been tried in the balance and found very much wanting.

Andy says:

> Now we're in uniform, the pressure's on and the indoctrination's starting. It's all designed to strip us of our backgrounds and turn us into a homogenised group of Flight Cadets.
> It's a tough regime and, having spent five years climbing up the public-school ladder, it's not one I'm enjoying very much.

He very quickly gets a reputation for being something of a Houdini. One cold morning on the square Sergeant McDill takes Andy's bayonet out of its scabbard and complains, 'You've not rubbed the polish off your bayonet, have you, Sir?' Andy's response is lightning fast. 'Condensation, Sergeant.'

Apparently, if you can raise a laugh you've a chance of getting away with it. Welshman Frank, a lanky and engaging lad from Tredegar Grammar, is challenged by Sergeant McDill: 'How did you polish those buttons, Mister Hoare? Shaving cream?'

'I *hurred* on 'em, Sergeant.'

***

Early starts, square-bashing and crowing nights take it out of even the fittest of young men, and Newton's Laws of Motion are not guaranteed to hold the boys' complete attention. More than once, tutor and students manage to creep out of the hut and get halfway back to the Mess when pounding feet tell them the one they left behind has woken from his deep sleep.

The start of academics does not mean the cessation of bull. On 10th October, John writes home:

> Last Friday, we had a Squadron Commander's inspection. Mac, Michael and I cleaned the windows, doors and floor until the hut looked like a fairground Hall of Mirrors.
>
> We had everything at right angles to everything else and in exact symmetry, down to having opposite windows open the same exact amount. There was not a speck of dust anywhere.
>
> Our boots are coming along, thanks to much spit and polish. The spit goes onto one of those yellow dusters with red stitching before it's dug into the polish tin for a good gobbet of polish. Then, it's round and round and round until you get a shine, spitting on the boot so as to keep the duster damp.
>
> Much drudgery, but at the end of it, Squadron Leader Robinson said that he was pleased. If he had not been, well, then he would have had to lump it.

Despite the bull, bookwork and being shouted at from dawn to dusk, it's not all soul-destroying toil. There are uplifting moments. As the evenings draw in and mists begin to creep over from the fens to the east, Mark for one finds comfort in the march back from studies. Surrounded by ranks of fellow cadets, dressed in publicly-funded, warm kit, the day's work almost over and a mug of strong tea to come – well, that's all right, isn't it?

He comes back down to earth when the mentor barks in his ear, 'All right, lad. It's your turn to keep the stoves going overnight – tonight.' That's quite a task. Mark's hut may be closest to the Mess but it's the furthest from the coke bunker, which is right down the western end of the South Brick Lines, near the Sick Quarters. He sets his alarm for the four o'clock haul.

***

The crowing could be losing its edge – 80 Entry seem to have had their fill. The mentor comments:

> About time too.
>
> Groups from the Senior Cadet Mess usually come down to assert their traditional rights, as well as to take revenge for having endured this themselves a couple of years before. We've not seen any of that from them this term – just as well.
>
> Earlier this year, one young lad, starkers apart from a back-to-front flying-helmet on his head, was chased down the the walkways by a mob. He lost his footing and put his hand through a window. Seriously cut.
>
> Could be that the bosses have had enough and word's gone round.

But attacks on property, privacy and personnel are not restricted to crowing. In the close-confined quarters of the South Brick Lines there's occasional intense rivalry between huts. The most extreme example of what most in the entry reckon is just 'letting off steam', comes from 81 'A' Squadron. Mike has a grandstand view:

> One of our huts decides to launch an attack on the one next door. They climb onto the unsuspecting fellows' roof with a hosepipe and pour water down the chimney into the fire. This, of course, makes the wretched thing rattle and stink.
>
> The inmates counter-attack, storming in through the raiders' hut door with brimming fire buckets, bent on revenge. In the ensuing melée, beds get soaked and wrecked and there's much wrestling and fisticuffs.
>
> One chap, Martin, a dormitory fighter from Wellington College yells, 'I've lost my front teeth!' before resuming his

set-to with Sam, one of the wiry Jordanians. They'd have been at it all night if the Duty Under Officer hadn't arrived.

***

There's a frisson when brand-new Flying Log Books as well as navigation kit get issued on 21st September. It includes a Dalton Computer for calculating groundspeed and drift, a Douglas Protractor for measuring courses, headings and bearings, and a pencil box. They are soon brought into use as navigation instruction begins under the watchful eye of Flight Lieutenant 'Annie' Oakley, down in the South Airfield Flight buildings. Much of the instruction is reminiscent of school CCF Friday afternoon sessions but soon, they're to have the chance of practising the theory of triangulation for real – in the air.

The nav trips are operated by the Navigation Flight out of the satellite airfield of Barkston Heath, on Ermine Street, halfway to Grantham. They get off to a stuttering start. Scheduled for 28th September, half have to be postponed for lack of flying-helmets. The following Monday, a small selection of tyros, including the two trainee navigators, get to fly for over two hours in a Valetta – from Barkston to Cheltenham, Exeter, Shrewsbury and return. But not much navigation can be done, the ground being mostly invisible through cloud. On a repeat flight in November, Chris manages to plot a few fixes but finishes up complaining that someone's been sick over his parachute in its container.

But at least it's flying.

Into the Pig, and... (*RAF College*)

...in the Pig. (*JGL*)

After his first two days on Strikers, following a charge for 'having unsatisfactory greatcoat buttons', Chris comments:

> It seems that Strikers can be the start of a very slippery slope. With all the additional kit inspections, it's all too easy to be charged again and have extra days added. Then it can happen again – and again, escalating out of control.
>
> There's evidently just been an example of that with an 80 Entry man – lovely chap, son of an Air Chief Marshal. His Strikers' backlog has grown and grown, so much so that the poor fellow has just got the chop. Sobering thought.
>
> On the other hand, perhaps being at Cranwell was the wrong career path for him and it's a blessed relief for the bloke.

***

Sports sessions are under the control of Staff Officers. The mentor says they're allocated the job as a Secondary Duty but it's soon evident that most are more than reasonably proficient and the standards demanded and achieved are high. The more senior men that the lads meet on the sportsfield say that rivalry with Sandhurst and Dartmouth makes those annual fixtures keenly contested. That goes for inter-squadron matches as well as for fixtures against local clubs, universities and schools who all want to make their mark against the celebrated Air Academy.

As a result, a good few of 81 Entry new boys are summoned early to the colours. Mac finds himself straight away in the College 1st Rugby XV, and as early as the second Wednesday afternoon has been taken off-station to do battle in the Number 8 shirt with the well-muscled farmers of Brigg Rugby Club. Similarly, Chris, an athlete, and a pretty good hurdler, has walked into the athletics team, Jock's straight into the Shooting VIII and Danny's in the soccer squad. Lucky Mark, just four weeks into Term 1, has been selected to keep goal for the Hockey XI up at Sheffield University, where he and Vernon (a Solihull School full-back in 'B' Squadron) find there's student life to observe – and girls. 'A' Squadron's Brian, a mighty atom of a chap from the Channel Islands, is filling a vacancy in the Soccer XI and Bill is booked this first term to travel with the cross-country team to enjoy army and navy hospitality at Sandhurst and Dartmouth.

Hockey on the sports field… (*RAF College*)

… with rugby… (*RAF College*)

Right: …soccer… (*RAF College*)

Below: … running on the track, and... (*RAF College*)

…fencing in the gym. (*RAF College*)

Run with the beagles at Fulbeck… (*RAF College Journal*)

...or, follow the hunt! Belvoir at Cranwell, autumn 1961. (*RAF College Journal*)

These sports provide a much-needed alternative to the continuous round of studies, PT, drill – and bulling. On 18th October, John writes home:

> Life is fuller than ever here. We carry on with the old system but I still use all my private study for doing extra History, Maths or whatever. Something will have to give – either the senseless bull or our work. We cannot keep up the present pressure – we hardly get a moment to ourselves.
>
> So you can see why we're all looking forward to half-term.

***

With the continual activity, the weeks fly by, and on the evening of the last Thursday of October, just before the mid-term break starts at lunchtime on the Friday, there's what for most is a rite-of-passage experience – a full dress, full ceremonial Dining-in Night in the Junior Mess.

The new Flight Cadets get togged up in 'Hairy Mary' airman's blue-serge battledress, worn with white shirt, wing collar and black bow-tie – the tying of which gives some the stiffest test so far.

The meal itself offers high-class food (devils-on-horseback for a savoury) together with decades-old ceremonial for the newcomers to learn. The layout is top table and sprigs. At the centre of the top table sits the President, the Sovereign's Squadron Commander, while at the bottom end of the central sprig is 'Mister Vice'. This evening, the role is filled by the youngest cadet in 81 'C', Peter, still in his eighteenth year. He's in the Science stream so Mark's scarcely met him before now. He takes the chance to ask him how he's come to be at Cranwell:

> I was born in India, Uttar Pradesh, where my ex-military father was Chief Engineer on the railway during the Second World War. In the Great War, he'd commanded a mortar battery, before transferring to the RFC and winning the AFC.
>
> In 1945 we came home to the Thames Valley before finishing up in Bournemouth, where I followed my elder brother to Canford School as a day boy.
>
> I did Maths, Physics and Chemistry, joined the CCF, did gliding at Thruxton and took a Flying Scholarship.
>
> Only one way to go after that. Follow my brother, this time to Cranwell.

Peter's duties as Mister Vice are to stand and repeat the President's toasts in as loud a voice as he can nervously muster. 'Mister Vice, the Queen' – 'Gentlemen, the Queen'. Then, at the end of ceremonies, when the President departs for the anteroom, he walks halfway round the room to take the President's place at the top table – to sit there until the last diner has left.

An apparently vital ritual must be mastered – the passing of port decanters in the correct direction and approved manner (to the left, from hand to hand) at risk of instant forfeit.

The Dining-in Night also gives a chance for the new boys to get to know some of the members of 80 Entry (with whom, now the crowing's over, relations are good) as well as Flight and Squadron Commanders, in a more social atmosphere. But in conversation with the latter, it's wise for a cadet to watch what he says.

Etiquette lectures have made it clear that women, politics and religion are subjects definitely off the agenda, and talking shop is also frowned upon. There's still plenty to talk about – sport, activities from pot-holing to beagles, and aviation to the fore.

Nevertheless, anything said can be noted and written down in the continual round of Personal Reports, as Robert has already found out:

> I made a cock-up in sending my private kit to the service laundry and the batman had to help me sort it out. Nothing dramatic about that, I reckon. But Pete Gilliatt's asked the

batmen what they think of us and this has come out. Now, I'm marked down in my very first report as being 'confused'!

In post-port anteroom socialising, Mark gets into conversation with a further colleague from the entry. Guy is from 'the only boys' Catholic grammar within twenty miles of Birmingham':

> I'm in a hut with two ex-Apprentices, one Halton and one Locking, and a Bristolian grammar school lad. Our mentor's an Old Etonian – says he can't believe that none of us has tied a bow-tie before.
>
> No such background myself – father a Great War trooper and failed livestock trader and breeder who died seven years ago, leaving huge debts. I've aimed to steer well clear of livestock except riding horses – the stables here offer plenty of opportunity to keep that up.
>
> I came into aviation courtesy the ATC. Joined at thirteen – first flight on summer camp in a Sunderland. Landed at Gibraltar – captivated. Scrounged flights at weekends and holidays and won a Flying Scholarship, as well as a trip to Italy on the International Cadet Exchange.
>
> I was in the slot for 79 Entry but had conflicting advice on future career paths – aviation, university or RAF. Frittered away a whole year before accepting an RAF Cadetship.
>
> So here I am, and ready to make the most of it. My strategy for survival is to keep as low a profile as possible and graduate with a pilot's Wings.

One of Guy's 'B' Squadron hut-mates, Frank, the ex-Locking Apprentice, agrees. 'Yes, let's get on with the flying – that's what we're here for.'

***

The couple of nights of mid-term break bring relief from the strictures of the South Brick Lines, but, as with many servicemen he's read about, Mark finds it difficult to make the transition back to civvy life in so short a time.

He visits Sally at her lodgings in the Finchley Road. She's now at Drama School and, together with her friends, is already a world away in cultural terms from this gangling bloke with the disastrous haircut who's training for a possible role in World War III.

On the return trip, the first sight of the College across the fields is the clock-tower, with its beacon, 'Winking Willy', flashing every three seconds. Mark finds it reassuring – he knows what the rules are here.

Others can't bear the sight of it. One lad, a Scot from Nairn Academy, has already thought better of it and reports back to the 'C' Squadron Flight Commander in order to pack it all in. The entry is down to fifty-four souls.

***

The navigation trips continue, the Valetta ('the Pig') supplemented by the slightly more user-friendly Varsity ('the Super-Pig'). Over the distinctive way-markers on the North Sea coast, such as Spurn Head, the tyros get to plot some positional fixes.

John amasses six hours and ten minutes in three ear-blasting trips – two in the Valetta and one in the Varsity. In the latter there's a navigator's observation window under the nose where the lucky ones, including John, get to stretch out and doze as the Lincs landscape slips lazily by below.

Despite constantly incipient nausea, Mark finds navigation enthralling, writing home:

> The trick is to find what the wind is doing up there. In the Varsity there's a device you can look through to estimate the drift of the aircraft. A viewfinder is permanently lined up with the aircraft's centreline while a revolving grid can be twisted round to line up with the track being made good over the ground. The angle between is measured off on a scale and bingo – that's your drift. Once you've got that, you have control.
>
> It's a bit trickier over the sea, though. There, the thing to do is line up the grid with the waves, if there are any.

***

Officer pattern Number One uniforms are to be issued. Messrs RE City have the contract and fitting sessions with them allow the lads, just for a while, to imagine themselves as officers.

They've already been kitted out with a College blazer – dark blue, with the Cranwell Crest on the pocket and a light-blue stripe edging the collar. 'They're probably there,' Chris reckons, 'to make sure nobody wears the thing off the station.'

College blazer badge. (*RAF College*)

But it's the civilian clothing that's the problem for Mark. Suits are compulsory on weekday evenings, save for Wednesday when a blazer or sports jacket is the prescribed rig. He confides in Sid:

> It's all very well for the well-funded chaps, especially those of normal size who can make do with off-the-peg clobber. Tall blokes like you and me though, we have to have stuff made-to-measure and just now, financially, that's not an option for me.
>
> Cooped up here, with so much time spent in uniform and sports gear, I can manage with my old suit, sports jacket and flannels, plus the blazer. It'll be different next term, when we can escape to the pubs and clubs – Lincoln, Grantham, Nottingham!

John writes home about the same problem:

> These first months have been much more expensive than expected. After just three weeks, my mess bill came to close-on a fiver and that's not counting the cleaning equipment I've had to buy. I've also needed a new pair of rugger boots – that's cost me a further £2.
>
> I'll try to keep it down for the rest of the year but next term will be a different matter – we'll be allowed out. I need a sports

suit quickly and can get one made here by R E City in six weeks for sixteen guineas. Then, I ought to be thinking about a new sports jacket and trousers.

And, I'll need to bring the car up here – that'll cost.

The basics of financial management are learnt pretty quickly. There's a Flight Cadets' Bank on site, a single-story building not far from the Junior Mess, at which all are provided with a personal account and a chequebook. Pay is deposited automatically on the last Thursday of the month. Mess bills appear in Junior Mess pigeon holes as regular as clockwork three days into the next and have to be paid latest on the tenth. This leads to some heart-in-mouth juggling of spend in NAAFI and bar to make sure the mess bill cheque's covered.

'Bouncing cheques and not paying your bills on time are considered criminal offences,' say the Flight Commanders. 'If you can't manage your finances, you're unlikely to manage as an officer.'

As a result, the tyros learn fast. For a start, there's the writing of a cheque, which the majority haven't done before. Mac tells Mark:

> When our chequebooks arrived, I flipped through and saw no problem. Very short while later, we're all in the hut having to write out our first ones to pay the mess bill. Vernon, comes round and quite openly takes a look at how we're doing. I think, 'Cheeky tart,' but say nowt.
>
> 'I'd try that again,' says he to me, 'and that, and that.'
>
> Three mistakes! How could anyone make three mistakes on one cheque? Well, I'd managed to do it. Nothing for it but to put them right and say thanks to Vernon.
>
> Turns out his father's a bank manager.

There's much resorting to help. In extremis, there might be some spare cash among the more affluent of the entry – but embarrassing to ask for and usually in short supply. Rescue can come in the form of postal orders hastily sent by generous relatives, in response to emergency calls from the pay telephone in the Junior Mess lobby (money in slot, dial, press button 'A' if answered – 'B' if not).

***

There's a continuing schedule of inter-squadron competitions at the College, and in their first term, 81 Entry find themselves competing in the Knocker

Cup, for Physical Training. This makes further demands on the beleaguered Junior Entry, with many hours spent climbing ropes and wall-bars, vaulting horses and pressing up.

With clipboard in hand, hawk-eyed PTIs note down all individual performances against the clock, allocate them to squadron totals and in due course come up with an overall champion. It's all done for the good of individual bodily fitness, not to forget team spirit within the squadron.

The inter-squadron competitions are miracles of organisation by the staff. In this first term, as well as the Knocker, there is also the Chimay Cup, for games. In that, the three squadrons take on each other at rugby, soccer, fencing, badminton and shooting.

For Senior Mess entries, all this has to fit in with an all-consuming drill competition, the Ferris Trophy. The 81 Entry lads are not yet ready for that, but they're warned that in Term Two they'll have their own Junior Entries parade contest.

The navigational flying pauses at the end of November and is rounded off with a test on 7th December. Despite having managed to spend the bulk of his time at the navigator's table covertly writing letters home, Chris finds he's done rather well.

A general discussion in the FGS concludes that so far, they appear to be at a Sports Academy, with serious drill, some officer-training and a few vomit-trips thrown in just for the record.

There's a variation for all when a Geography tutor takes the entry on a visit to a local coalmine, Annesley Pit, north of Nottingham. It's old, deep and dank, as the lads find when they're winched down to the depths before lying prone on self-propelled trolleys to explore the narrowest of seams. The art-deco pit-head baths are memorable, as well as welcome.

The experience puts the trials of the Flight Cadet into perspective when compared with the life of a miner.

***

Mark is surprised to find himself in London, not once, but three times. The first occasion is to be fitted out with a fast-track Number One uniform. He'll need this earlier than the rest as he's been most unexpectedly detailed to travel back to Kingston for the school prize-giving, as ADC to the Commandant. Air Commodore Spotswood is presenting the prizes and Mark's been awarded the one for English.

Flight Lieutenant Gilliatt has briefed him well on the boss's preferences, which include 'Craven A' corked-tipped cigarettes. Fortunately, the Flight Lieutenant has duty-free boxes of the brand lurking in his cupboard and when Commandant collects Crow at Kingston railway station in the staff car ('Can't miss it – it's big and black with a silver star on the front') there's a packet ready to hand.

All goes well. The Air Commodore's speech is well received and the acting, unpaid ADC collects his copy of the *Oxford Book of English Verse* while doing his level best to sell the idea of Cranwell to the sixth-form boys. He enjoys the day out and the new Number One uniform does great things for his self-confidence – but it's just as well there's not time to contact his pacifist girlfriend...

He does look her up on the next occasion, when he travels down the A1 with the RAF College hockey team to fulfil a fixture with his old school. They're currently top dog in the London hockey-playing scene and find the Flight Cadets easy meat.

Mark tells Sally:

> Our centre-forward and captain, having decided to motor leisurely down in the old MG Roadster, is 'unavoidably' delayed. By the time he arrives, hot and breathless, we're already three goals down.
>
> He might just as well not have bothered – he didn't make much difference. Final score – zero for us and twelve for them. Just a bit embarrassing.
>
> Another coffee?

***

On the Strikers front, one 'C' Squadron chap, David, gains notoriety by being put on a charge for having 'valuables unlocked' (copper coins to the value of 1½d) in his locker drawer.

David seems a good bloke to know. Educated at King Edward VI Grammar School, Stafford, he'd taken, and passed A-levels in French, English, Art and Architecture, together with General Studies. An Air Cadet, he'd cycle seven miles each way to parades. With the Air Training Corps he got into gliding aged sixteen, before winning a Flying Scholarship and an RAF Scholarship but at Cranwell he's getting the reputation among the staff for being a bit 'bolshie'. He persists in wearing a flat cap until Flight Lieutenant Gilliatt takes him aside, saying, 'A cap is not a hat.'

He has an easy, laid-back attitude, confiding to Mark that he sees crowing as just a public-school throw-back. 'As with so many things here at Cranwell, I reckon it's safe to assume it's part of the system and get on with it.'

Mark wonders if in that, he includes the draconian system of discipline. One who reckons he's going to make it unscathed to the end of this first term is James, the lad who turned up on the first day without a hat. As he has no military background or experience of the public-school ethos, he reckons the Drill Sergeants are going easy on him. It's a vain hope – the system gets him in the end. In the very last Church Parade of the term, he hears the hoarse whisper behind his neck, 'See me after!' He's on a charge for 'idle marching'.

Mid-Winter Leave 1959/60

Before the first term ends, Mark receives a totally unexpected financial helping-hand. It seems that the mother of a Flight Cadet, her son a casualty of the War, had granted a bursary in his memory, aimed at assisting those with limited means in meeting the expenses of cadetship. Mark finds himself a beneficiary, with a grant of no less than £50, specifically to finance civilian clothing.

Thus, immediately following the Passing Out Parade of 76 Entry on 15th December (the new boys officiating as stewards in their new Number Ones) he begins the three-week break with a shopping list. His second stop, after saying hallo to his mum, is at the local tailor's.

Over the three weeks, recalling all the experiences he's had and official writings he's read since arriving at Cranwell, one sentence sticks particularly firmly in his mind. In an early report to Churchill some forty years ago, Trenchard stated his objective for the new Royal Air Force:

> To make an air service which will encourage and develop airmanship, or better still the air spirit, like the naval spirit, and to make it a force that will profoundly alter the strategy of the future.

He and his colleagues are now invited to share in that sort of spirit and the new academic syllabus provides just the sort of challenge needed to do so.

At home, reunited with family and friends, he finds a mismatch with the demanding experiences of his new life.

Somewhat to his surprise, it's a toss-up which of the two worlds he prefers.

Chapter 4

A Step up the Ladder

Term 2: 5th Jan-5th Apr 1960

January 1960 is the month when Her Majesty the Queen graciously assumes the role of Commandant-in-Chief of the Royal Air Force College. It also sees 81 Entry moving out of the South Brick Lines to one of the Junior Mess's two-storey accommodation blocks, and rooms of their own. This leads to a reorientation of identity.

A room of one's own. (*JGL*)

In a letter, Mark considers the new state of play:

> In our term in the South Brick Lines, the focus of our loyalty
> has been the hut. Four or five new boys, from assorted
> backgrounds and of differing character, we've all been through
> the grinder of bull, boots and bullying. Sid and I both felt it
> when our two hut-mates, one with a broken leg and another
> with sinus problems fell so far behind the syllabus that they
> had to be re-coursed to 82 Entry, just arrived.
>
> The rest of us, fifty-two in number, have been knocked off
> our perches and reduced to the lowest of Air Force ranks but
> now, we've our own rooms, our own living-space. That's the
> first step towards what, I suppose, is now expected of us –
> progress towards becoming fully-fledged officers.
>
> Our rooms are on squadron corridors so the new focus has
> to be the squadron. Another part of the plan – individuals but
> obeying the squadron's rules.
>
> But the big thing is – we're no longer Junior Entry
> Crows!

Better than that, they now have 82 Entry taking that lowly place – for two
terms, until the autumn. There's a decision to make – whether or not to go
crowing. Some go for the idea, but many more don't, and their decision is
respected by their mates. In any event, what does take place is much on the
lines of Mike's 'banter and sending-up'.

However, as is the norm, a good number of 81 Entry have been detailed
to stay on in the South Brick Lines, as mentors to the new boys for their first
term. Chris (just eighteen-and-a-half years old) and John (not much more
than a year older) are on the 'B' Squadron mentor roster for the first half of
the term. They both find it 'an early opportunity to get some experience of
leadership'. But there are snags.

John writes home:

> I have to show the new entry how to do their boots and check
> all that they do. If they do anything wrong, I have to carry the
> can. On top of all that, I have to do all the normal work on the
> 'A' Stream curriculum.
>
> Being a mentor makes one's life a very full call.

***

In general conversation the 'lads' have become 'chaps' – another rung up the status ladder. They find themselves more at home in their batman-valeted uniforms and admit to feeling less self-conscious as they march around the station alone, in pairs or in platoons.

That's something else that has altered the balance – the new academic programme has kicked in and although they still get together for GST, GDT, Airmanship, Navigation, PT and twice-weekly drill, the 81 Entry working world is for much of the time one of streams and sets.

The 'A' Stream, some three-dozen strong, continues to form pretty much a squad, as perhaps does the 'B', with its nineteen scientists. But the Humanities students of 'C' have sets comprising anything from one single cadet (Mark, for Economics) to seven (Robert and his colleagues for Geography). They can all march together to arrive for the 0830 start at the West Site but thereafter go their own ways. All this has reorientated the chaps' points of focus from hut and entry, to set, stream and squadron, in that order.

At the same time, there has been a massive shift in emphasis in favour of academics for all streams. The timetable has all but doubled the number of classroom hours, at the expense of non-academic subjects. All Private Study periods are now combined, taking the whole of Friday afternoons when there's no Navigation Flying, and Saturday mornings when there isn't a parade. Work to be completed outside the classroom has ballooned.

The week starts off at 0800 with an hour of drill, followed by six periods of an hour each, covering a mix of subjects from Gym, Pure Maths, Physics and Airmanship (which includes learning and practising Morse Code) for all, with specialist subjects for the 'B' and 'C' Streams.

Tuesday is much the same, but without the drill and with the addition of a couple of hours' GST from 1500 hours. Wednesday is also drill-less and the afternoon is sport for all. Thursday has three hours of specialist subjects from 0800, followed by an hour's PT. After lunch, an airlock appears in the form of Private Study from 1400.

Friday brings more drill, plus two of Airmanship, two of GST and in the afternoon, three periods of Navigation, including occasional Pig flights.

That's thirty hours out of a forty-hour week, on top of which come Saturday and Sunday morning parades, plus, for 'C' Stream, out-of-hours Latin studies (English Lit for Robert). The General Streamers' syllabus is no cakewalk, requiring a Current Affairs essay to be submitted by each term end. The students really need those half-a-dozen hours allocated to Private Study – just to keep up with the work.

It's about now that the word 'gonking' makes its appearance – the act of falling uncontrollably asleep on the bed, leaving tell-tale 'gonk-marks' on the side of the face.

***

Two in the 'C' Stream, Pete and Michael, have opted for English as one of their chosen subjects (alongside War Studies and French) and are surprised to find that there's an Anglo-Saxon module involved.

Kraut and David, together with other selected students in the 'A' Stream, are tasked with launching College learning in yet another new direction – the study of Russian. This will entail taking O-level Russian in the autumn of 1960, and A-level at the end of the following year. A sweetener is the prospect of visits to the Services Language School at RAF Tangmere for oral practice but for now, they grapple with the intricacies of the Cyrillic alphabet on the Humanities Site.

In addition, David is joining the degree group French set, for their stab at Civil Service Linguist and Interpreter qualifications.

***

One Friday night in January, the heavens open and on Saturday morning, the cadets wake up to two feet of snow outside. What an opportunity! The chaps of 81 'B' Squadron forsake the intellectual challenges of Private Study for a more enjoyable, if risky project – building a life-size snowman on the Junior Parade Ground.

Hoping the sergeants don't spot them, a squad sets to with a will. Shovels are found in the coke bunkers, fire-buckets are pressed into service and in no time at all a defiant figure begins to take shape, right outside the front door of the Mess. It's a symmetrically satisfying site, and out of sight of the Orderly Room at the rear. It's a provocative one too, being visible from the Senior Mess across Cranwell Avenue.

In no more than half-an-hour, the snowman's the tallest chap in the group. He has buttons, mouth, nose and eyes made of coke and on his head perches a bright-red fire bucket hat. Grinning widely, the well-satisfied construction team poses for a photograph, willing to record their subversive moment for posterity.

Hugh, one of those captured by the camera, can be forgiven for his somewhat concerned expression. He's been railroaded into the scheme just a couple of weeks into joining 81B from 80 Entry and knows that building snowmen in Private Study periods just isn't done. There could be hell to pay.

College in the snow. (*RAF College Journal*)

'B' Squadron snowman. (*JGL*)

Hugh's been educated in the spiritual atmosphere of the Benedictine Downside School in deepest Somerset:

> There, I was never academically inclined – I pursued a general syllabus of some eight O-levels and eventually two non-scientific A-levels. I did join the RAF Section of the CCF and

71

was keen enough to be in charge during my last year. I passed the pilot and Cranwell selection without trouble.

I also took and passed the Civil Service exam which gave me the minimum qualification for a Pilot Cadetship here. I arrived a year ago, a month after my eighteenth birthday. But I never studied Physics or Chemistry at school, and for my three terms with 80 Entry, I have found Aerodynamics, Thermodynamics, and such, rather baffling.

Fortunately, the authorities have decided that a repeat year should allow me to grasp these subjects, and here I am – bolshily building a snowman rather than studying privately. Quite a risk, don't you think?

I don't, by the way, blame the monks for my lack of sciences – just for an over-developed guilt complex!

Hugh, increasing the number in 81 Entry to fifty-two, has no need to worry. The Drill Sergeants see the joke and the snowman reigns supreme on the Junior Square for a few days – before an unexpected thaw, with the help of a few discreet shovels, consigns him to glorious memory. The fire bucket and coke regain their proper positions in the South Brick Lines.

***

Among themselves, some nick-names are now firmly established. Bill (of the glasses) is 'Blind Bill', and 'Kiwi' doesn't answer to anything else. Brian, the soccer player, is now 'Brawn', and Dave of the AFRAeS group, unfazed by most turn-ups, is on occasion 'Dauntless'.

But the biggest social change for the chaps is that from now on, they're allowed off-base at weekends and can explore the local pubs. Further afield, there's the Co-op dance hall in Lincoln (introduced to them by 80 Entry as 'the Coop'), the Dancing Slipper in Nottingham (or even better a 'do' at the University) and the night spots of Doncaster.

'However,' they are firmly told, 'Sleaford remains out-of-bounds to all College cadets, at all times.' Apparently, that's where the airmen drink and this could lead to unseemly encounters with Other Ranks.

To go out anywhere at all, wheels are essential. Having a car at the College requires permission, requested in a 'Formal Official Letter'. This needs to be written by hand according to an exacting format, but it's worth the effort. Those among the entry with access to the necessary cash, immediately take advantage.

A STEP UP THE LADDER

One of the old North Airfield hangars serves as the Cadets' Garage, where there's already a wide selection of vehicles and motor-cycles, from sleek saloons to old bangers badged Morris and Austin. Some have been left behind by previous entries and the garage is on its way to becoming a treasure-trove for collectors. Robert parks his sleek 1.5 litre Riley alongside John's 'very second-hand' Ford Anglia which lines up against Andy's pre-war Morris 8.

There's a number of high-decibel motorbikes, among which Sid's Lambretta scooter begins to look somewhat out of place. One frosty night he falls off the machine on the icy level-crossing in Sleaford – and trades it in for a 250cc P&M Panther.

There are enough vehicles to take most of a squadron entry, if required, to the pubs within range. 'A' Squadron has soon established squatters' rights to the Duke of Wellington in Leasingham to the east and 'C' are frequent visitors to the Houblon Arms at Oasby to the south.

PERSONAL TIME TABLE

	1 8·00 - 900	2 9.5 - 10.5	3 10.25 - 11.25	4 11.30 - 12.30	5 1400 - 1500		6 1505 - 1605	7 1610 - 1710
MON.	DRILL	PHYSICS HEAT. FLT. JOHNSON S.R.1	M.S S/L. WALSH	Hi EVE HISTORY	MATHS S/L. HARRIS · S.R.2	PURE	AIRMANSHIP	P.S
TUES.	PHYSICS FLT JOHNSON NAV ROOM	MATHS PURE S/L ...	H2 GEOGRAPHY	Hi HISTORY ENGLISH FLT ADAMS	PHYSICS ELECTRICITY FLT COOPER · H504.		G·S·T	
WED.	H2	M.S.	Air	MATHS. APPLIED. SR3	SPORT		—	—
THU.	H2 GEOG.	H1 HISTORY ENGLISH	M.S.	P.T.	P.S.		P.S.	P.S.
FRI.	DRILL	PHYSICS (ELECT) H.504	MATHS APPLIED	E.L. or P.S.	FLYING or		P.S	P.S
SAT.	P.S	P.S	P.S.	P.S.	SPORT		—	.

'C' Stream member's calendar, Spring Term 1960. (*RO'B*)

Those who'd like to have a go at chatting up landlords' daughters simply don't have the time. The new syllabus has hit them full in the face, calling on every academic and physical reserve. It's also a logistical challenge.

Five minutes are allowed for transfer between classrooms and sites – it's always touch and go and in bad weather, even more so.

Sid, in the AFRAeS group, has additional doubts about the situation:

The lectures have started without anybody outlining the aims and content of the syllabus. It's just begun – with arcane details of fluid flow of gases.

Already it looks as though it's been designed for engineers, not pilots – except perhaps test pilots. The lecturers are transferees from the RAF Technical Cadet College at Henlow, and it shows – equations on the blackboard and all that. It's like being back at school.

I'm beginning to think perhaps I should have opted out of the Science stream from the start – on the other hand, it would've been very difficult, as a junior cadet, to do that.

Peter, another 'B' Streamer, agrees:

Working out a syllabus for us is one thing – it's something else to put it into practice. There's a shortage of adequate equipment as well as qualified instructors. You could say that a certain degree of confusion exists as to what to teach us and how to do it. Unfortunate – but probably, in the circumstances difficult to avoid.

Mark, on his own with the Economics tutor, has a better experience:

He's a great chap, Squadron Leader Nabarro. Wings and DFC on his chest and he's open-minded – treats you like an adult. He seems to know his stuff and has the knack of putting the laws of supply and demand into plain English for a layman like me. The problem is – the bloomin' dog.

She's a large, very large, black Labrador – excessively friendly. When I arrive – it's a very small, claustrophobic office – she comes nuzzling up. Cold, wet nose in the groin and all that – not good at any time but when it's hosing it down outside and she's still soaking after her walk, it doesn't do a lot for your dignity – let alone the trousers.

Then, she gets under my chair for a nap. I can just about ignore the way she smells and snores – it's when she wakes up that we have a real problem. Up she gets, under the chair, and just about pitches me off.

Happens every time.

The other thing is, he's editor of the College Journal and he's tried talking me into going on the staff of that as a Cadet Sub-editor, alongside Kiwi – he's already there. But when would I do it – in my non-existent spare time?

There's praise from all for the War Studies team. One's an RAF Squadron Leader, another an army major (who served with the Gurkhas in Burma), and the third, a major in the United States Air Force. The latter seems to embrace his overseas deployment with particular enthusiasm and this raises his students' interest level no end.

In fact, all three show a professionalism which stands out from the majority. Mac reckons:

> Just perhaps, there's something to be said for military training after all. I like the way an army officer can find it possible to lead an amusing discussion on almost anything. Such as, the proper term for describing a 'diminished group of light artillery' in Marlborough's Army.

John is soon forced by logistical problems to give up belonging to both 'B' and 'C' Streams. He writes home:

> It's turned out to be totally untenable. The timings don't work. Humanities Site and the Sciences Huts aren't reachable in the time available, even at the fastest walking pace. The authorities have agreed and now it's the General stream for me.
>
> I'm really quite pleased. I'll now be able to take part in a few more of the activities available here – rugger is just the start.
>
> Then, it's very clear that the key to passing out from Cranwell with merit is doing well in pilot training. I've got a head start with over sixty hours already in my logbook, thanks to the Flying Scholarship – and Aunt Marion and her Hornet Moth. I fully intend to keep at the head of the pack.
>
> I'm not expecting the General stream syllabus to be a cakewalk but there must be less work to do than in the other two. I'll make sure there is – flying's the name of my game.

His colleagues in the 'A' Stream include Nigel, of a similar frame of mind:

> I'm surprised, given my A-level subjects that I'm not in the 'B' Stream, but for this relief, I now give thanks. It allows me to participate fully in what's available.
>
> I'm playing soccer and squash and looking forward to cricket – and I'm keen to join the Photographic and Film societies.

John and Nigel's position vis-à-vis non-academic activities is the source of some envy from 'B' and 'C' Stream members, who are beginning to be dimly aware that there's an outfit known as the College Society.

College Societies & Activities. (*RAF College Journal*)

Set up in 1947, it promotes and supports a host of extra-curricular indoor and outdoor recreational pursuits. Kiwi and Phil had become involved straight away, and over the Christmas break, together with a dozen other Flight Cadets, have enjoyed a two-week subsidized skiing trip to Zermatt, organized by the RAF Ski Club.

The College Society offers every activity a Flight Cadet, with energy and time to spare could want. Early in this second term, there had been two Society meetings, one for the 'Outdoor Group' and one for the 'Indoor'. At those meetings, the participants would have learnt that this term, the Society is to move into accommodation of its own in a block near the Junior Mess giving homes for the first time to Fine Arts, Photography, Radio, Engineering and Aeromodelling. Alongside that, the Printing Section is to move into new premises in the old Station Defence building, to be joined by Graduation Ball Decorations and Folk Music.

The Society is the umbrella that allows activities to flourish, ranging from potholing to mountaineering, and travel to foreign lands, taking in gliding and leisure flying on the way. There is even a flourishing ballroom dancing school in the Junior Mess (under a professional instructor who brings a car full of girls from Lincoln) and a Debating Section in both Messes (the one debate per term in the Junior Mess is compulsory).

The Society arranges insurance for College property employed on activities and in return requires properly formulated proposals with aims and objectives spelled out, diaries kept and completion reports presented post-trip.

Many 81 Entry chaps make full use of the Society's offerings but for some of those grappling with the new syllabus, finding the time and energy to take advantage of those is a challenge.

The saving grace is that every Wednesday afternoon is Sports Afternoon – where non-participation would be sure to mean a black mark in their record. They perforce find time for games and are happy to do so.

***

Everyone on the entry is eager to start pilot or navigator training, but understands that military schooling of the mind and body must come first. However, it gets around the grapevine that the plan is to delay them getting seriously airborne until January next year.

Flight Commanders confirm that's the case. There has been a delay in delivery of Cranwell's new Jet Provosts because Flying Wing have insisted they need all their JPs in one shipment, enough to accommodate all four-score pilots starting their training together. As a result, they've been put at the back of the queue at Luton, behind all other RAF Flying Training Schools' allocations.

THE
ROYAL AIR FORCE
PRIMARY
AND
BASIC
TRAINER

Jet Provost

Powered by the Bristol Siddeley Viper

Also available equipped for arma-
ment training and for use as a tactical
weapon. Rugged construction and
simple maintenance ensure high utili-
sation under the most demanding
conditions

HUNTING AIRCRAFT LIMITED

Member Company of British Aircraft Corporation
Luton Airport, Bedfordshire, England

Above: Piston Provost.
(*RAF College Journal*)

Left: Jet Provost, the new
trainer. (*RAF College
Journal*)

On top of that, the number of hours required for the new academic syllabus leaves no time for anything other than a pilot's or a navigator's basic training course while they're at Cranwell. They'll be awarded their Wings or Navigator's Flying Badge at the College, but then they'll go off for the final stage at an advanced training base somewhere else.

Can it be so? None of this was in the brochure, either.

Also not best pleased by the delay are the pilots of 80 Entry. Originally down to begin on the JP in their Term Four, they've now been told they'll be on the Piston Provost, followed by Vampires and Meteors, after all. But, disgruntled as both entries are, as with so many other things, the chaps can only grin and bear it.

For now, getting airborne for 81 Entry means making do with trips, on Fridays this term, in the Flying Classrooms. But throughout February, the Varsities and Valettas are grounded through snow or low cloud.

Spirits are not at their highest. The three-and-a-half day mid-term break can't come soon enough. Noon on Friday 19th February sees much rubber laid down on Ermine Street.

***

On the first Thursday back, the Junior Mess hosts a further Dining-in Night, this time an occasion for 81 Entry to get to know the new boys of 82. Peter, now sporting Interim Mess Dress (the relative chic of a Number One, but still with white wing collar behind black bow tie) has the luxury of watching another lad in his Hairy-Mary suffer the embarrassments of Mister Vice's chair.

Mark gets talking to Jim the Nav, who with his navigator oppos has now joined the pilots for a couple of backward-facing Valetta trips. They're billed as an introduction to map-reading but Jim confesses to finding little value in them:

> One trip a month – no continuity, no net gain. In any event, I'm learning more of the underlying maps and nav skills through my new hobby – motor rallying. Jock needed a navigator and I was happy to give it a go. Sitting in a Mini, bucketing through seriously lumpy country such as the Pennines or the Lake District, and from Saturday night to Sunday morning – now that's a real buzz.
>
> Map-reading at high speed, under pressure to plan a route along roads and tracks seldom straight and flat and having

to maintain accurate timing on the move – surely I couldn't wish for better lead-in training for future flying tours. Time well-spent.

On the academics side, Economics just isn't clicking with me. So, with the help of our Physics tutor I've been signed up for the City and Guilds of London Institute's Technology Certificate. It's highly-regarded and it looks like I've already covered the first three years of what's a four-year course while at Archbishop Holgate's Grammar School in York, and then over the excellent three years at Locking.

I've joined the College Choral Society, too. They put on an annual Gilbert and Sullivan show on the Longcroft Room stage – that's going to be fun.

Mark's also making a musical contribution. He's put his name down for the C of E Church Choir. He quite enjoys singing, and it gets him out of the parade part of Church Parades into the bargain.

As he's a newcomer to Economics, his tutor is keen for him to 'read around the subject' as much as possible, saying, 'You'll find everything you need, including the Economist magazine, in the College Library'.

In the West Site NAAFI break, he hears from Mac that he too is keen to get to the Library, in his case for Geography and History reference books, together with War Studies analyses by generals and others. Before long, a Saturday morning period of Private Study finds them marching as smartly as they know how, up into 'enemy territory', the north side of Cranwell Avenue.

Along the corridor from the east end, they hoof it up the stairs alongside the Founders' Gallery and into the Library, where they're almost overwhelmed with the range of choice.

In the College Library. (*RAF College*)

80

A STEP UP THE LADDER

Mark soon loses patience with *The Economist*, with its turgid prose and endless statistics and sidles across to the well-thumbed tomes which chronicle the origins of the RAF and the College's place in all that. He wants to learn more about this place he's committed himself to for three years.

By the time of the Great War armistice in November 1918, the RFC had downed over 7,000 enemy aircraft at the cost of well over 9,000 of its own airmen. Its 280 squadrons had won eleven Victoria Crosses. But with peace declared, what had been seen by the public as an age of heroic air battles came to an end. Anti-war feeling became widespread and demobilisation was swift and brutal.

RAF manpower had reached a peak of one million, making it the largest air force in the world. Now the number of its squadrons was being slashed from 280 down to thirty. The WRAF, created during the hostilities to provide an essential support resource, was summarily disbanded. As a result, the new RAF became understaffed and ill-equipped with obsolescent biplanes. Continuing attempts to take back their air arms from the nascent RAF were made by the Army and the Navy. They saw a unified air force as no more than a wartime expedient. Prime Minister Lloyd George was inclined to back them, but Churchill was a staunch RAF supporter. He appointed Major General Trenchard as Chief of the Air Staff, who channelled his drive into saving the Service's independence.

Trenchard (promoted Air Marshal in the summer of 1919, when the new RAF ranks were introduced) and his staff, many of whom were wartime heroes, had a great deal of work in front of them. As a first step, Trenchard proposed the foundation of three training establishments: an Engineering/Technical College, with an Apprenticeship scheme, at RAF Halton, a Staff College for senior officers and, to create a future backbone of quality junior officers, an Air Academy. They would provide a cadre of officers and men with sufficient expertise and leadership skills to support others whenever a crisis arose. Churchill agreed the plans.

To be the home of the Royal Air Force (Cadet) College, the world's first Air Academy, Trenchard chose RAF Cranwell. He is quoted as saying that by surmounting the challenges of Lincolnshire isolation, weather and a strict regime, the cadets would prove they had the qualities to lead his air force of the future.

By this time, RAF Cranwell had its own branch railway from Sleaford, as well as two airfields, both of grass. To the north of the

Sleaford Road, the field was for airships and balloons. To the south, fast-developing and of reinforced grass, were runways for biplane aircraft. Accommodation and services huts and hangars were springing up in both West and East Camps.

Driven by Trenchard, the new Officer College was operational in time to welcome the fifty-two members of No.1 Flight Cadet Entry on the fifth day of a cold February 1920. The entry included two Sub-Lieutenants and fifteen Midshipmen transferred from Dartmouth. The balance comprised the first School Entry, boys aged between seventeen-and-a-half and nineteen, destined for a stay of two years. They had taken and passed a written exam (in English, Maths, Geography and a modern language) arranged by the Civil Service Commission.

In 1919 a Parliamentary committee under Lord Hugh Cecil stated that the RAF should select for Cranwell training 'boys who possessed not a particular degree of wealth or social position but a certain character, the quality of a gentleman'.

The first Commandant, Air Commodore Charles Longcroft, one of Trenchard's squadron commanders in the RFC, was ex-Charterhouse and a man who rode to hounds. One of his first actions in post at the College was to invite the local hunt to foregather on the Orange. Another was to form a pack of beagles.

The ethos was thus set.

The Cranwell Beagles 1920-21. (*RAF College Journal*)

A STEP UP THE LADDER

Mark wishes to find out more about those early 'trainee-gentlemen'. A friendly and helpful librarian shows him the Library archive of the twice-, often thrice-yearly College Journals, dating from 1920 and the start of operations. Scanning the early issues, he notes some details of Entry No. 1:

Naval cadets, in uniform with war ribbons, had a course of twelve months – School Entry boys two years. Parents had to pay – a whacking £125 a year. Lads got five bob a day in first year and ten in the second, plus a bob for rations.

Boot camp stage eerily the same – five to a hut, built then in corrugated-iron but with the same coal stove. Until uniforms were ready, wore suits, and bowler hats. One chap 'did appear in breeches, stockings and trilby hat, but not for long'.

Weeks of bull, boots and drill. One change – those days, batmen made the beds and cleaned boots. Another – full mess kit the rule five nights a week.

From the start, College organised as Flying School and Ground School. Entry No. 1 did more in workshops – fitting and rigging, plus metal and woodwork – made all the station's toilet-roll boxes. Not allowed cars or motorbikes – monastic existence. But four weeks leave at Christmas and in summer, with ten days for Easter.

Studied English, Science and Maths, Airmanship and Navigation, with periodical exams. Games and exercise encouraged, alongside running with beagles and hunting. For those with the money, horsemanship's promoted – develops sensitivity in hands, essential for flying.

Pilot training (no Observers on course) not until second year but two familiarisation flights a week scheduled for first twelve months. First flight within fortnight but targeted two seldom achieved. Much excitement on first flight – not surprising, 'despite advances spurred by the needs of the Great War, aviation was still very much in its infancy and known to a privileged few'.

Principles of flight only barely understood and world of RNAS and RFC one of open-cockpit biplanes. Monoplanes did exist – Blériot's cross-Channel aircraft a monoplane – but lacked stability and torsional strength. Biplanes strong and stable, save when pushed past limits into necessary spins and nosedives of combat. Pilots very wary when approaching stalling speed.

At Cranwell just a North Airfield – no runways, parachutes or flying control. Pupils solo after ten to fifteen hours – after that, flew alone, save for occasional check by instructor. Self-taught aerobatics! Solo cross-countries to Lincoln and back, and further – landmark of airship hangar a godsend.

Flying not for faint hearted. Up to twenty biplanes of varying speed – Avro 504Ks, Sopwith Snipes, Bristol Fighters and DH9As – at any one time milling over station at various heights. Despite that, for Entry No.1, although engine-failure forced-landings regular occurrence, just the one crash. Round-out too high, stall, splat – no one hurt.

Average of just forty-five hours flying for the School Entry.

Exterior of the Cadet College, 1920. (*RAF College Journal*)

Naval wooden huts. (*RAF College*)

Belvoir Hunt at Cranwell 1931, passing Lynx Avro 504N. (*CGW*)

Flight Cadets, 1923. (*RAF College*)

Graduation Parade 1934. (*RAF College*)

Twenty-seven out of the thirty-three are commissioned – just the three prizes: Abdy Gerrard Fellowes for Science and Mathematics, Groves Memorial for flying and Sword of Honour for cadet at top of Order of Merit.

Following graduation, those who stay in UK go to conversion squadrons but fair proportion go to overseas Commands – in Egypt there's a flying school but for those posted to India and Mesopotamia, operational squadrons have to do it – strain on squadron but none of the 'keep the new boy in his place' common in other two services.

Meanwhile, Mac's engrossed in books from the War Studies shelves and discovers more on the background to the first years of the RAF College.

The anti-war sentiment prevalent since the armistice meant that early Cranwell entries were joining an under-funded air force. Trenchard himself had a hand in that. He accepted a Treasury ruling that all military budgeting should be driven by a running assumption that there would be no major conflict in each subsequent period of ten years. This resulted in close on two decades of under-investment in the defence industry.

Nevertheless, against continuing opposition from both Army and Navy, Trenchard and his staff managed to keep up the fight to retain the RAF's independence. In this, he continued to have the welcome support of Secretary of State Churchill. In the first edition of the College Magazine, Winston had addressed the Officer Cadets thus:

> *Nothing that has ever happened in the world before has offered to man such an opportunity for individual personal prowess as the air-fighting of the Great War. Fiction has never portrayed such extraordinary combats, such hairbreadth escapes, such an absolute superiority to risk, such dazzling personal triumphs.*
>
> *It is to rival, and no doubt to excel these feats of your forerunners in the Service that you are training. I look forward with confidence to the day when you will make the name of the Royal Air Force feared and respected throughout the world.*

Stirring words indeed – a demanding challenge for Numbers 1 and 81 Entries both. Mark vows to try to remember them during the *longueurs* of French literature lessons and the intricacies of Economics.

Over lunch, Mac and Mark continue to talk. Subjects range from Prime Minister Macmillan's February 'Wind of Change' speech before the South African Parliament in Cape Town, to the rumoured plans to cancel Britain's 'Blue Streak' missile project.

***

On Friday 11th March, Mark travels down south again with the Hockey XI to do battle with Sandhurst. Alongside him in the bus are Kiwi and Peter, Sid and Jim the Nav, together with Andy – they're in the fencing, basketball and squash teams respectively.

At a Guest Night that evening in the atmospheric surroundings of the Old College, food, drink and conversation are all good. It appears that life at both Sandhurst and Cranwell have much in common, the main difference being that the army chaps belong to a Regiment while they are in training (for two years rather than three, with the emphasis on military training) and therefore know precisely where they are going on graduation. But from their description of early cadet life, it's obvious where Lord Trenchard got the ideas for Cranwell from.

On instruction from their escorting officers, the visiting sportsmen from Cranwell take it easy with the copious amounts of wine and port on offer – which is more than can be said for those escorting officers.

The next day, the weather's fine, the hockey pitch is fast and despite going one man down with a broken jaw Cranwell come away with a two-nil victory. Great celebrations for the men in blue.

After building up a twelve-six lead, Kiwi and the duellists need only two victories in the sabres to give them the match for the first time in some years. The sabrists then proceed to strike dread into the hearts of all Cranwell supporters by losing their first seven assaults by some margin – before pulling together and winning the final two. Game and match, by one – more celebrations.

The basketballers can't quite match the regimental brawn, but 'gain a valuable experience' nonetheless. Andy, going at Number One against the hosts' best, has a torrid time of it, as do all but one of his fellow squash players.

Spirits however are far from dampened. With thanks to the hosts, off they go to Camberley station with the prospect in view of the panelled nooks of the 'Captain's Cabin' (just off the Haymarket, and where a 'Party Directory' for the benefit of Cranwell cadets is lodged) and a night in London Town.

***

A further member of 81 Entry, a Kentish man, is unable to come to terms with the flatlands of Lincolnshire, coupled with the remoteness and intensity of College life. He applies for a voluntary discharge from service. Again it's a 'C' Squadron man who leaves – the entry's now down to fifty-three and 81 'C' Flight's original eighteen recruits are reduced to fifteen.

***

Training starts for the Cairngorms Winter Survival Camp in the Easter leave. On 8th March, there's a fitting-out session in the Survival Stores followed by a seven-mile route-march to test out kit and muscles. The following week, there's a trial-and-error session with the tents that'll be their home for ten days in the mountains, before a night exercise around a five-leg route using a compass.

Navigation trips resume, but the weather limits their usefulness as well as comfort. It also restricts the other way Flight Cadets can get into the air – from the North Airfield, in one of the College's gliders.

North Airfield glider. (*RAF College*)

Most have brought experience from their time in the ATC and CCF. Dauntless Dave's one who gets airborne any weekend he can, and Chris is another. The latter was solo just a few weeks after arrival, and found it 'a fantastic escape. Looking down on the College and Parade Grounds from a glider puts things back into perspective'. He managed twenty-five flights in the first term, all at weekends, and this term he's racked up no fewer than fifteen already, including his first solo sorties in the aerobatic Prefect. 'I've also enjoyed my first solo land-away, to the satellite airfield at RAF Spitalgate, near Grantham, as well as my first experience of an aero-tow – behind a Chipmunk'.

Masters of Junior Parade Square. (*RAF College Journal*)

Junior Entries Drill Competition. (*RAF College Journal*)

The second term winds down with a further Dining-in Night in the Junior Mess, a production in the Lecture Theatre of the 'Mikado' (in which Jim the Nav takes the title role to great acclaim) and, to round things off, that inter-squadron Drill Competition (in which 'B' Squadron takes the laurels).

But there's no freedom for 81 Entry, yet. They're off to Scotland to enjoy the dubious delights of 'an exercise in testing resourcefulness and endurance under unfamiliar and challenging conditions', organised by the College's RAF Regiment team.

Easter Leave 1960

Members of the RAF Regiment are known as 'Rock Apes', but regardless of that disrespectful soubriquet, the Regiment's a formidable force with a proud history of service since their establishment in the Second World War. Their exploits in airfield defence during the Burma Campaign became the stuff of legend. From GDT and drill, the tyros of 81 Entry have learnt to treat them with respect.

So it is that when the rest of the College hare off for three weeks' Easter leave on Tuesday 5th April, 81 Entry are packing their full winter-survival rig.

The issue is heavy-duty khaki parka, trousers and anklets. Underneath, they'll sport the woolliest of sweaters (the forecast mentions snow and ice) as well as winter underclothes, worn with the regulation blue officer-pattern shirt and tie, all held together with a webbing belt. Everything is surmounted by a beret with its white-rimmed cadet badge, and feet are protected by studded survival boots – 'cobbly-wobblies'.

They'll travel in battledress with parka, boots and beret. The rest goes into a heavy-duty backpack, together with knife, fork, spoon, mess tin and mug, bedroll and wellington boots. By late evening, cadets and escorts succeed in hauling baggage and themselves aboard 3-Tonners for the dozen miles to Grantham station and the midnight train to Edinburgh.

With kit stacked in the guard's van, the chaps get what sleep they can, sitting up like rows of nodding rag dolls, rocking to the rhythm of the wheels.

Breakfast at Waverley Station. (*JGL*)

Ready to go. (*JGL*)

Early morning on Wednesday 6th April sees a bleary-eyed crew in the café of Waverley station, falling on platefuls of breakfast before picking up their connection north to Aviemore. Another small fleet of 3-Tonners carries them over 'B' roads that are scarcely more than tracks, to the Base Camp between Loch Morlich and Loch an Eilean, on the western edge of the Cairngorms.

The tented camp has been set up by Regiment men under the watchful eye of the Officer Commanding the Cranwell Unit, Squadron Leader 'Shudders' Hudson, and his deputy Flight Lieutenant D.D. ('Deedie') Anderson. At 1500 hours, they call the Flight Cadets for a briefing.

There are to be seven days of action. The first four are for training in living off the land, using both multi-man and single-person bivouacs, to be constructed by the cadets themselves out of parachute silk, and other materials provided by Mother Nature. The following three will comprise an Escape and Evasion exercise – being chased (and possibly caught and bothered) by the Regiment, reinforced by zealous toughs from the Seaforth Highlanders.

The chaps are split up into two Flights of four Sections each, the latter comprising ten cadets together with an escorting officer. The remainder of the daylight hours are spent setting up tented bivouacs, one per Section in a location of choice, before the Headquarters staff serve up a surprisingly good meal.

Home from Home. (*JGL*)

That night, they're straight into action. A patrol, from 2230 to 0100 hours, loosens up cobbly-wobblies and muscles, as well as testing ability to keep awake. Back at the bivouacs, after groping their way into sleeping bags the blokes fall into an exhausted sleep.

***

The following morning, Thursday 7th, the campers find that the night temperature had dropped to twenty-two degrees of frost. There's thick ice in the fire buckets to prove it. The Rock Apes tell the gentlemen not to worry – the day's to be spent in warming-up exercises.

One includes practice in building a one-man A-frame from locally-sourced timber and strings of ivy. 'Take good care – you'll be sleeping in them tonight.'

The afternoon sees what Chris's diary describes as, 'a pleasant ten-mile hike in good weather at a modest pace'. That evening, after a mug of soup and a crust of good Scottish bread, Sid muses, 'As kids, we'd spend days out in the woods, building bridges, dams and dens and all that. So far this camp's not that different.'

Mark stretches out in his sleeping bag to see whether his A-frame effort passes muster. It doesn't. His excuse is that there aren't many six-foot-six lengths of timber lying around. In the end, a groundsheet and parachute silk have to do.

Friday 8th sees more serious route-marching. After breakfast, they're deposited at the foot of the first of three summits, each well over 2,000 feet high. Forming a triangle, the distances between them total a dozen miles from start to finish. Map-reading shouldn't be too testing – most of the ridged route can be seen the whole way round – but just in case, the phalanx of cadets is escorted by Rock Apes, together with Flight Commanders.

Among the latter is a Flight Lieutenant Vampire instructor, who turns up from a hotel in Aviemore in an immaculate bright-red Aston Martin, which seemingly shrugs off Cairngorm mud. In his passenger seat sits Flight Lieutenant I'Anson, a Provost instructor, known to all as 'Chunky', for obvious reasons. He's braving the rocky paths in flying boots.

Off they stride into the magnificent Highland scenery. The way gets steep, the path rocky and the air increasingly chilly. There's not much talking from anyone. These hills, so beautiful from train and lorry, are cruelly challenging from soggy glen to windswept crag and peak.

It's a much-subdued entry of Flight Cadets that gets back to base, where the only sustenance on offer today is the issued iron-rations lunch. The Flight Lieutenant 'Doc', up here from Cranwell Sick Quarters, does a roaring trade in blister plasters in the medical tent.

Small comforts. (*JGL*)

Saturday 9th begins with a timed team-race over a bleak Scottish road for close on a dozen miles. Shudders explains, 'On this march, each section will be hefting one of these lengths of timber on their shoulders,' whipping a groundsheet off a stack of pine logs, each ten feet long.

He tells them they'll be following a loop in the network of so-called 'Military Roads', built under the command of General Wade in the attempt to bring the Jacobite Rebellion to order in 1715. Mark feels some sympathy for Jacobites and general both, but keeps most for his section as thighs, knees, arms and backs cry out for mercy.

All make it within the allotted time. Then Shudders, making his early evening rounds of the bivouacs announces, 'Right, Gentlemen. Get your boots ready again. Night march. Muster at HQ Tent, 2200 sharp.'

Again, they find their way along further Military Roads. They're not difficult to follow, but tension is high. A rumour's afoot that there's to be harrying by Seaforth Highlanders on this one. This has the cadets taking cover at every perceived alarm.

The march totals fifteen miles, and the chaps totter back into camp in the early hours of Sunday 10th. After a short recuperation, an eight-mile evening route-march begins. 'To stretch your legs,' says Shudders. The heavens open and on their return, the bivouacs are flooded. Flight Sergeant Pawson, an engaging chap from the West Country and everyone's favourite Regiment instructor, kindly arranges for everyone to sleep in the HQ tent. There's little food on offer, but somebody manages to get a gas stove going and there's tea and corned beef.

***

In the morning of Monday 11th, Regiment instructors give a convincing demonstration of Movement in the Field. They're followed by an army captain, an expert in avoiding and surviving capture – rough and tough stuff in preparation for tonight's Escape and Evasion exercise.

A cooking competition is to be judged this evening by no less a personage than the Commandant, arrived to take stock of the morale of his charges.

Muscles ache and blisters throb. The weather's cold and damp. Rations are getting debilitatingly short. Morale is creaking but the chaps have to put on the best show they can for the Air Commodore.

Right: Commandant's coming - look smart! (*JGL*)

Below: Hope he liked the 'lentils'. (*JGL*)

Sid's group prepares pine-cone soup with handfuls of grass for garnish. Another team has managed to catch, kill and dress an unfortunate hedgehog for the pot. Sam and his section set out an Arabian Café-style offering based on what he calls 'lentils'. Andy is his group's head waiter – he has the cleanest hands.

The Commandant is able to see that the cadets have indeed tried their best and declares the result an honourable draw.

***

Shudders briefs on the E&E exercise. It's designed to represent a situation that RAF aviators might face after baling out of an aircraft over hostile territory, without exact knowledge of their whereabouts. At drop-off points, the escapers are to be given the coordinates of the first of three Rendezvous Points (RVs) widely spread around an area within an approximate twenty-five-mile radius of Base Camp. At the first RV, the location of the second will be revealed, and at the second, the third. The leader of each group is given a sealed envelope with the coordinates of the final RV, to be opened only in dire emergency.

The aim of the exercise is to make each of the RVs in turn, before the cut-off time for the last at 2300 on Wednesday. Anyone captured, must expect to be interrogated 'in a forthright manner'.

In the dark of the evening, in groups of three, faces smeared with mud for camouflage, it's time to go. Pocketing the last of the survival rations, they clamber back into 3-Tonners to face forty-eight hours in the unknown.

At varying times and locations, groups scramble over the tailboard, and set about finding ways to identify their position. Apart from inch-to-the-mile Ordnance Survey maps, their only navigational aids are hand-held compasses.

By Thursday morning, they should have exciting tales to tell.

***

Chris writes:

> We couldn't fix our position on the OS map – nothing fitted. So I crept to a telephone box near the drop-off point and tore the map out of the directory. We were at Bridge of Brown, on the River Spey and just off the OS map.
> We walked ten miles or so until the early hours of Tuesday, sleeping in a wood before sneaking up to the RV, checking in with the Rock Ape there and picking up the location of RV2.

Then, we got some sleep in a cold barn until eleven – when the farmer's wife gave us some porridge for breakfast.

We had a narrow escape crossing a road then continued all day to RV2 and picked up the details of RV3 – Boat of Garten. We were bounced by the Highlanders again but managed to scoot off, find a farm and slept for fourteen hours until dawn on Wednesday.

Mark, Sid and David are the last to be dropped:

We're by a bridge and road junction but can't find it on the map. No lights anywhere – no signposts or doors to knock on. The North Star's visible and we reckon a westerly heading might get us back on the map. So, into the hills we bravely go.

Before long, skies close in, stars disappear, and it's snowing. After several hours' march, we're huddling together in a gully, thanking Shudders for the parachute silk. Come dawn, we find a signpost – 'Tomintoul 3 miles'. No idea how we got here – must have gone round in circle – but we've finally got our bearings. Set off towards first RV, arriving late afternoon. Of course, it's abandoned – no chance of directions to the next.

No option but to open the envelope for the final RV.

Chris's group walks to Grantown-on-Spey:

From there we hitch a lift in a lorry to near Aviemore where we approach a farm and they kindly give us tea. After this, two of us go out to check the lie of the land and we're captured. We're taken in a Regiment Land Rover for questioning and then released again into heavy rain.

We get to the garage which is RV3 – deserted. We get out of the rain in a barn and late in the evening, the farmer comes in and tells us there's a bloke in a truck looking for us. It's Deedie Anderson, who tells us the exercise has been called off through bad weather and everyone's being rustled up.

The lorry fills up with soaking wet Flight Cadets and a fellow escapee has to sit on my lap for the journey. I'm grateful for the warmth.

Meantime, Mark and chums are making their way to Boat of Garten:

> Shouldn't have taken the road route. We're vigorously interrogated by Rock Apes before being loaded into a Land Rover and taken out to re-join the exercise. For endgame, we're told, all stragglers have to cross a finish line on the outskirts of Grantown.
>
> Off again, in freezing rain, not too bothered if we do get caught.
>
> Find sympathetic farmer and hay-barn, and finally get some kip. In the afternoon, angelic farmer's wife brings tea and oatcakes.
>
> Late evening, we're back on the road, and Shudders scoops us up in a Land Rover.

***

Back at Base Camp, Flight Sergeant Pawson excels himself. In the relative comfort of the HQ tent, he serves up a fortifying cauldron of sausage stew, heavily laced with the chaps' 'hard-lying' rum ration. Good for him!

Andy has a tale to tell:

> We weren't sure where we were from the start. By the first morning, on the hills, in snow, and lost, we put our safety first. We followed a stream downhill and knocked on a farmhouse door.
>
> A charming lady insisted we had some breakfast and told us we were near Tomintoul. We were miles off course, with no hope of getting to other than the final RV. I opened the envelope – we somehow had to get to Boat of Garten, some twenty miles away.
>
> We decided to try for the final RV but to play our own game. We bussed it from Tomintoul back to Aviemore. Another bus took us to the outskirts of Boat of Garten where we holed up overnight before scrounging another breakfast. Then, after more sleep, we walked, triumphantly, into the final rendezvous – bang on time.
>
> Nobody seemed concerned to know where we'd been or what we'd been up to. But we'd survived, avoided interrogation and enjoyed a couple of good meals along the way!

Another group has had a hidden advantage. In their number is Mike, the Yorkshire man, who explains:

Prior to pitching up at College last summer, I walked from Aberdeen to Fort William, through the Lairig Gru Pass. So the territory on the north side of the Cairngorms is fairly familiar.

However, overconfidence is the devil, and whilst striding out confidently under cover of darkness, along comes the duty Rock Ape Land Rover... And so we're all off to the defaulters' restart point!

Tim, a Lancastrian, has ploughed a lonely furrow:

I started the exercise limping, with huge blisters on both heels. I was soon on my own – it took me until dawn to get near the first RV. Then I spotted a squad of Highlanders down below, coming my way.

I dived into the forest and collapsed behind a fallen tree. All quiet – I fell asleep. When I woke up, with the help of a friendly lorry driver I made my way back to Base Camp, hoping for some tender loving care. But Shudders drove me and a couple of others back out to find and cross that finish line.

I was soon on my own again. The sleet was by now so heavy that the enemy couldn't see me, and I finally crossed the finishing line – I think.

I was very cold, very wet and very, very tired. I'd lost track of time. I saw a large puddle – looked like velvet. All I wanted to do was lie down on it – and sleep! Most likely would've died.

I was saved by the pick-up lorry, and the whisky-laced coffee in the back. Bliss.

A late-comer arrives – Robert, looking concerned:

Terry's still out there, somewhere.

We were down to just the two of us and doing pretty well. We were closing in on the final RV and needing to cross the Spey. We kept watch on a railway bridge with a footpath that would take us over. All seemed quiet.

I go forward first, climb the embankment, and just start to cross when I'm pounced on by this big Rock Ape and bundled into the railwayman's hut. Some minutes later, the door opens and Terry's pushed in with me.

The Regiment bloke decides to take us back to his base but it's two of us and only one of him and that gives us a chance. We make a break for it but the Rock Ape fells Terry with his rifle butt. I scarper.

I hope Terry's OK – he was certainly knocked to the ground.

As the bivouacs are now flooded out, the survivors under instruction are allowed to retrieve their sleeping bags and get what sleep they can in the Headquarters tents. It's another bitter night and they're glad of the remains of the rum.

***

Come the morning of Thursday 14th, the adventurers are hard at work packing up the camp. Jock, with a few of the more impulsive chaps, reckon they stink so badly they should strip off and jump into the icy shallows of the nearby loch. 'We jumped out quicker than we jumped in!'

Time for reflection. (*JGL*)

A STEP UP THE LADDER

There's a cold half-hour waiting at Aviemore railway station to catch a train south, during which the story quickly spreads that the Highlanders had been told where the RVs were, so that all the cadets could be caught and interrogated – for experience!

Huddled on the platform, Mark asks, 'What do we reckon to all that then?'

Robert draws his conclusions. 'They wanted to see how we'd cope. They'll have been marking us up on a score-sheet the whole time. Kiwi and Phil will be somewhere near the top, for sure – they know the rules of the game. And probably Andy and his team too – for reaching the final RV in some style.'

Mark wonders whether it's possible in fact to be marked down for living off the generosity of sympathetic farmers' wives.

Despite many of the chaps having to stretch out on the carriage and corridor floors for lack of seats, the overnight train ride back south from Edinburgh provides a much-needed wind-down from a challenging second term as well as the time in the Cairngorms.

There's further chat about the E and E.

Jock and his group are others who have enjoyed Scottish hospitality. 'We holed up under a chicken house for warmth. In the morning we wake up the chickens – farmer's wife comes out to see what all the racket's about. She takes us in and gives us porridge!'

Danny protests. 'We're hearing all about this ducking and diving and lucky breaks. What about blokes like James and me? Played it all by the rules, got put in the bag twice, but made all the RVs, on time. Let's hear it for us!'

Sam picks up the story:

> I am with Danny at the end – in pigsty, huddled in straw and muck to keep from freezing.
>
> I start off as leader of three. I send one of the guys off to find road sign – he not come back. Then other fellow sprains ankle and surrenders. I march on alone – get to first RV second evening and join up with gang of blokes. We're bounced by Highlanders and scatter. I drop flat in long grass and get away – but on own again, and soaking wet.
>
> I march on compass bearing, find cattle barn and sleep. Later, I'm woken – big hairy nose in face. Yellow eyes and horns – is it Devil? I get going again and at dawn I see cadets in distance. Spirits lift, but when I hail them they start running, me in hot pursuit. I start shouting and swearing – in Arabic. They stop.

They think I'm one of chasers, but my Jordanian colleague, Mahmoud, with them, says, 'Nobody in Scotland curse like that in Arabic – except Sam!'

My happiness only short-lived – caught that morning, put back on road and meet up with Danny. That's when we bed down with pigs – and me, a Muslim!

The train rattles on, its rhythmic wheels soporific. Blind Bill sleepily hopes that he's come sufficiently up to scratch to avoid having to do it all over again with 82 Entry. Peter sums it all up as he mutters, 'So they put us through all that to see how we'd react under pressure. Now they know what...' before falling fast asleep.

***

On the morning of 15th April, Good Friday, after a spectacular fried breakfast in the RAF Cranwell Officers' Mess (the College kitchens are closed) the cadets go their various ways with both body (except, for many, the feet) and mind at rest.

Robert conveys Danny and Mark down south to the Thames Valley in the comfort of the Riley. Travelling with them is Kiwi, who's to be Mark's house guest for the remaining dozen days of the Easter vacation.

Chris braves the A1 on his newly-acquired Matchless motor cycle. On the pillion, released from Rock Apes and Scottish medics both, and bound for his family home in Tooting, is the missing Terry.

Chapter 5

On Parade

Term 3: 27th Apr-26th Jul 1960

Kiwi proves a perfect house guest. While Mark hobbles for the whole of the break, the New Zealander strides about – he doesn't do blisters.

So far he's been a revelation to everyone at College – those three years at Halton have served him well. He's not in a specialist degree-level stream, but he's in pretty much everything else. Pentathlon, fencing, gliding, gymnastics and drill, he's excelling in them all. According to other 'A' Streamers, he doesn't fall asleep in lectures. Is he hell-bent on emulating his brother and winning the Sword? Why not?

He's also turned out to be a pretty good carouser. He has a head like a rock when it comes to beer. It's the same in the pubs and clubs of North Surrey – he beats all comers with the yard of ale. His Maori *haka* immediately tops every bill, closely followed by various monologues of increasingly risqué nature. However, he carries all this off with a

Kiwi. (*FM*)

103

modest charm that makes him a hit with both girls and blokes. Mark's mum invites him to come back anytime.

For ideological reasons (he inclines to the Right Wing) he declines an invitation from his host to join him on Easter Monday, when Sally has suggested that the two aspiring military men accompany her on the now traditional 'Ban the Bomb' rally in Trafalgar Square.

Leaving Kiwi to a ten-mile run, Mark, defying blisters, makes it to London, where he and Sally join more than 60,000 people. They're all keen to hear Michael Foot speak, in what is billed as a 'Democratic Protest against Military Dictatorship'. The majority of those gathered under Nelson's Column have walked the fifty-plus miles from the AWR Establishment at Aldermaston, west of Reading.

The marchers are certainly not rabble and have their sincere reasons for protesting against government policy. The experience makes Mark think long and hard about the ethics and effectiveness of the independent nuclear deterrent.

After three too-short weeks, the two Flight Cadets are on the bus to Kingston, where Robert and Danny scoop them up in the Riley and onwards up the A1. Kiwi says he's thoroughly enjoyed the convivial company in the saloon bars of Surrey, Mark reports that he's successfully remembered to watch his language in the maternal house, while Robert remarks that he's 'been on leave in an Army camp – no easing up on military disciplines there!'

The journey's a race against the clock. Will they make it to the College by midnight? Later than that, they'll be a cert for a week's Strikers.

They pass the roundabout at Norman Cross, the turning for Peterborough, at eleven o'clock and make the deadline – just. 'Norman Cross at eleven' is engraved on their mental roadmap for the duration.

***

Her Majesty the Queen is to present a new Colour to the College at No. 77 Entry's Passing Out Parade in July. To swell the ranks, 81 Entry are being fast-tracked on to Senior Parades a term earlier than usual.

Still-developing drilling abilities are sorely tested by exposure to the combined tender mercies of the College Warrant Officer and the Senior Mess Flight Sergeants. The former is an impressive figure of a man, with responsibility for discipline across the whole of the Cranwell RAF Station. For the cadets of the Junior Entries, he's from the realms of the gods and when he barks, 'Number nine – back up!' up you back, sharpish.

For their Senior Mess Flight Sergeant, 'C' Squadron has the formidable Flight Sergeant Jack Holt, known among themselves as 'Bogbrush', on account of his bristling ginger moustache. A substantial Yorkshireman of the old school (a stalwart of the Station Rugby XV) Flight Sergeant Holt was awarded the BEM in the 1959 New Year's Honours List. He's soon down at the Junior Mess, knocking the young blighters of 81 Entry into shape.

Mac and Mark, and others in the degree studies contingent have met him already. Mac gets the attention of all in the FGS when he tells the story:

> I'm on the way from the gym to get to the Humanities for extra Latin with the Wingco, when I meet Mark and Brawn coming up from the Junior Mess. We form a trio.
>
> We're late – so we decide to jog. At the double – in step, naturally.
>
> Soon, there's the creak of a very old bicycle doing its best, coming up behind us. With some yards to go, we hear, 'Gentlemen. You are running. An Officer Cadet does not run.'
>
> Then, as he pulls past us, 'Why are you running? Because you are late, Gentlemen. You're all on a charge. See me later!'

After a while, the majority of the entry come to respect Bogbrush, even like him, but from the start, he fixes on a couple of the less coordinated members of the group – and makes their lives hell.

But these challenges come second to the problem of webbing belts. The chaps have now been issued with a second belt, the original one still to be blancoed blue, the new one to be blancoed white for ceremonial parades. But the underlying colour of the new one is still blue and applying sufficient white blanco is a bind. Then there's a problem when it rains – white streaks on the Number Ones. It's all a bloody chore.

***

On the academics front, there's a replacement Director of Studies – for Mr Antony Constant MA, read John A. Boyes MA. Mr Constant, in post since January 1953 and much involved in restructuring the syllabus, has left to serve as an adviser to the Air Minister in Whitehall. Mr Boyes, a Rugby School pupil and master, has the not inconsiderable task of making a success of his predecessor's innovations.

***

For the 'C' Stream, the War Studies curriculum reaches the inter-war years. Mark continues to find the College Library and Journals a generous source of Cranwell detail.

This seems to imply that Lord Hugh Cecil's 1919 aim of selecting for elite training at Cranwell, boys of the 'right stuff' from society as a whole, wasn't being fully achieved. Testimony from early entries suggests an ethos and atmosphere that was 'muscular and public school'. Did this reflect the 'gentlemanly qualities' that Lord Cecil's committee was looking for in recruits?

It appears that promising boys from 'ordinary' families could, and did apply. However, Air Ministry recruiting officers seemed inclined to select the applicants who most resembled themselves. Does this chap look and talk like an officer? Which school did he attend and what does his headmaster say about him? In other words, is he one of us?

In any event, families with modest incomes were unlikely to be able to afford the fees: £45 payment prior to entry, £75 per year plus £30 at the start of the second year towards uniform and books – tidy sums of money in those days. The result of all that was that in the inter-war years Cranwell entrants and graduates were overwhelmingly from the upper-middle and upper classes.

But, almost from the start, there have been further routes to Cranwell open to the RAF Apprentice schools. Annually, three outstanding graduates from each of Halton and Locking have been able to apply for a cadetship. Having successfully completed three years of military study and exams, they have tended to prosper at Cranwell.

This chimes with 81 Entry's experience so far.

***

In Term 3, a real bonus for the aspiring 81 Entry pilots is that the vomit-inducing navigation sorties are a thing of the past. They are looking forward to some dual instruction on the de Havilland Chipmunk Flight, newly set up on the North Airfield.

According to the Flight Commanders, the entry are to be the first at Cranwell to be exposed to 'short air experience exercises' in the single-engine monoplane. Three days into the term, the trainee pilots and navigators come back to their rooms to find their 'bone-dome' protective helmets sitting on their beds, ready for the flying to start next Friday.

By the end of May, 'B' Squadron, as confirmed by Mac, 'have had more than the usual share of flights in the Chipmunk. This has been down to our Flight Commander wanting to keep his hours up'. The Flight Commanders of 'B' and 'A' Squadron are Qualified Flying Instructors (QFIs) and the chaps soon twig that they're the ones to fly with if you want some proper instruction.

De Havilland Chipmunks arrive. (*RAF College Journal*)

Chipmunk flight briefing. (*RAF College*)   Satisfied customer. (*RAF College*)

By month's end, Chris has managed five sorties, chalking up three-and-a quarter hours. During that time he's practised circuits, spinning and some aeros, as well as map-reading exercises. His only disappointment is that they've all been logged as 'passenger' flying, even though on one of the flights he sat in the front seat, the student's position in a Chipmunk.

Mark is at the other end of the spectrum. He gets just the two Chippie flights and on one of those he sits as an immobile and nauseous passenger in the back seat, fretting about an essay that's overdue, watching while a Master Pilot short of hours enjoys himself. It's the day of Princess Margaret's wedding to

Anthony Armstrong-Jones in Westminster Abbey and take-offs and landings are verboten until the happy couple are safely indoors at Buck House.

The time spent in the Chipmunk Flight Hut waiting not to fly has been frustrating but at least it has also given him the chance to meet a few more 81 Entry colleagues from other squadrons. Adrian, a Man of Kent from 'B' Squadron, is one of them:

> I was born a few months after the declaration of the Second World War and grew up as an Air Force brat. Grandfather served in the RFC and father was an RAF pilot. I also had four uncles in the RAF, one an armaments officer and the other three pilots, one of whom flew me in a Hunter on a CCF camp at Chivenor. Surrounded, I was a cert for the RAF, looking to fly.
>
> At seventeen, with the Hornchurch and Daedalus tests successfully negotiated, I flew Tiger Moths at Rochester on a Flying Scholarship. In the Sixth Form at St Lawrence School in Ramsgate I was supported by the £290 a year of an RAF Scholarship. Mind you, this was repayable in the event I pulled out of going to Cranwell.
>
> But I was never going to do that. For me, it was always Cranwell – didn't consider any other method of entry into the RAF.
>
> Not so sure I'm hooked on this Chipmunk-flying bit though – it vibrates, stinks of fuel oil and it's all pointless. Just flying around to keep some bloke's hours up.

Kraut, an RAF Scholarship and Flying Scholarship man who trained to PPL standard on Tiger Moths at Cambridge, is another who's not happy with the Chipmunk exercise and the lack of flying training:

> I had a schoolmate in 80 Entry – a great ally to have in the South Brick Lines days. Anyway, he's now left – re-mustered as Direct Entry. He's now enjoying the Jet Provost at Syerston.
>
> Gave me the same idea. I went to talk it over with Dave Moffat, who sent me home – just down the road – to have a chat with my parents. They of course are all for my staying and seeing it through. Don't want to have to pay that scholarship money back.
>
> I've now seen the Assistant Commandant and at least they're moving me from the AFRAeS stream to the General. We'll see how it goes.

Kraut's colleague in 'A' Squadron, Robin, is similarly frustrated by the Chipmunk non-flying:

> I've not got into the air yet! A pity. All that exciting business of the Flying Scholarship – opening that cardboard box with all the kit in it, stalling and spinning in the Tiger Moth – it's all being lost in these endless hours of waiting for a pilot to turn up and take us up just for drudge passenger flying, Lincs weather permitting.
>
> It's a far cry from the world of Biggles, the Dambusters or Neville Shute that I discovered in the Pokesdown branch of the Bournemouth Library. Or all those grainy black and white pictures of War in the Air that I watched on a nine-inch TV for the price of one cup of coffee-bar sludge. Is it for this that my mother took waitressing jobs to keep me at grammar school?
>
> Mustn't complain though. Head down, don't make waves – that's me.

Robert is also not best pleased:

> On one of the few trips I've done this term, I was a passenger to a Vampire QFI who did nothing but aeros. I was sick in an aircraft for the very first time. The whole thing is ill-prepared, and success depends on whom you're lucky enough to fly with. There's been no pre-flight briefing and only a minimum of dual.

A rare positive review for the Chipmunk experiment comes from Jim the Nav:

> I've had six flights – thoroughly enjoyed them all. Not having previously controlled any flying machine, I found it satisfying to manage it in the Chippie. That was down mostly to my instructor, a Master Pilot QFI who treated me as an adult, with none of that divisive 'Bloggs' and 'Sir' attitude we get on the ground.
>
> Evidently, I showed some promise. After my last flight, my instructor suggested I might like to consider 'retreading' as a pilot. Now, I'd been asked that at Locking but had declined – I was fascinated by the whole art of navigation. Again I said, 'Thanks but no thanks.'

Some use the contact with College QFIs to make their own luck. Guy explains, 'We non-academics have sufficient leeway in our diaries to scrounge early-morning trips in the Vampires that do the weather checks. I've already managed two – one with Dave Moffat.'

***

The last week of May 1960 sees the start of first-year interviews with Flight and Squadron Commanders. People generally seem to be getting along all right, the only apparent exceptions being Kraut, together with the Group Captain's son from Whitgift who lets everyone know this wasn't his idea and he'd rather be at Brasenose College Oxford, where they're 'keeping a place warm' for him. The languid manner of one of the public school men keeps him in the Drill Sergeants' sights, as is the case with the Liverpudlian attributes of Zak, from Quarry Bank High School.

As a result of his interview with Flight Lieutenant Moffat, Robin is having to re-think his Wednesday afternoons:

> He said I had to raise my profile, do more, in order, as he put it, 'to stay out of my office'. I've taken him seriously – have to, fear of the chop and all that. Can't risk being thrown off the course – nowhere to go to!
>
> So, I'm having a go at equestrianism. I've noticed that it's popular with the officer classes here – some of their style might rub off onto me. I've borrowed some jodhpurs and a riding hat and taken my first few nervous practice rides.
>
> I'm also exploring mountaineering. There's a regular group that goes to Stanage Edge, in Yorkshire. But I'm not sure – I'm terrified of heights.
>
> And I've been invited to join the potholing fellows for a weekend. I'm thinking about that. But there again, I'm not good at handling claustrophobia.

***

During this term, the Flight Cadets of 81 Entry are being rationed to one weekend off, subject to a successful submission to the Flight Commander, in a Formal Official Letter.

The 'Formal Official' is required to be on foolscap paper, in best long-hand, with line-spacings and indentations measured to the inch. It must begin with, 'I have the honour to request…' and terminate with, 'I have the honour to be, Sir, your obedient servant, J.S. Bloggs, Flight Cadet'. It's almost enough to put a fellow off even asking.

From time to time, stories of unofficial escapes get around, and not just at weekends. John makes it down to London on a Tuesday in May for the white-tie Queen Charlotte's Ball at the Grosvenor:

> As private study starts, I 'go out riding', in civvies, and sprint the hundred yards from the stables to the garage, where the Ford Anglia awaits, full fig in the boot. By half-past six, I'm tying my bow in the Gents of the King's Cross Hotel and ninety minutes later, I'm strolling into the Grosvenor, to be greeted by Aunt Mary and party.
>
> After a champagne dinner and then the two-o'clock in the morning last waltz, I tear myself away to hoof it back to the car in Portland Place. Some three and a half hours later, despite being stopped by police outside London – 'Routine check, Sir' – I'm marching smartly back from the garage to the Junior Mess. Unwittingly assisted by a dozy Duty Cadet, I've made it. There's just time to grab an hour's sleep before the day starts at seven.
>
> Great wheeze!

Sadly for John, he's brought down to earth at the morning parade – getting charged for having his hair too long.

***

The first half of the term is turning out as busy on the sports fields as any term before it.

For all, there's the Knocker Cup to endure – this term it's athletics. There's practice, by squadron, every evening, lasting from thirty to ninety minutes. For 81 Entry, the competition takes place on the evening of 10th May.

For John, the less strenuous sport of sailing is part of his relaxation. He has managed to make the College team and is looking forward to summer matches on the briny – with Dartmouth off the Devon coast, and with Sandhurst at Thorney Island. Andy and others are founder members of a College golf team and Mark gets to open the bowling for the cricket XI and takes the occasional wicket while David's a star on the athletics track. He runs in first in the Knocker Cup mile – earning him points with spectating Staff officers. Robert is king of the tennis courts and Chris is outdoing all comers over the hurdles.

Cricket on the Orange... (*RAF College*)

...sailing on the Trent. (*RAF College*)

The mounted part of the sport. (*RAF College Journal*)

Sid's a key member of the basketball squad, and he's been joined by Jim the Nav who says he's been 'intent on avoiding rugby at all costs as it almost did for me at school. Basketball's non-contact and all-year-round. Suits me fine and shouldn't affect my hard-won medical category.'

Adrian's principal interest is rifle shooting. There's an active College Shooting Club which uses the .22 range alongside the Science Site and the .303 range over the North Airfield. They compete with the universities, as well as Sandhurst and Dartmouth. Jock's speciality is also shooting. He says, 'I enjoy the chance to get out on the rugby field and have my face rubbed into the cow-pats by the local yobbos, but I was captain of the shooting team at Epsom and won good money from prizes at Bisley'. Kraut has also 'played some gentle rugby', and 'tried a little riding' and is a fixture on the swimming and water polo teams to boot.

Kiwi, Peter and Guy outdo the lot with their modern pentathlon. Introduced by Baron de Coubertin at the Stockholm Games in 1912, this sport comprises pistol shooting, swimming, fencing, horse riding and running. It was the baron's belief that this event would test 'a man's moral qualities as much as his physical resources and skills, producing thereby a complete athlete'. Of course it also gives them five events from which to earn Order of Merit points.

The North Airfield gliders continue to do good business. On a sunny Saturday in May, Chris gains his 'C' certificate. With 'CJ' from Campbell College, Belfast (also known as 'Boy', being one of the younger lads) and others, he's working on plans to inaugurate an RAF Cranwell Flying Club. They're aiming at wangling a space in a North Airfield hangar and getting hold of a couple of light aircraft.

***

Before the mid-term break arrives, each cadet must decide which two guests he'd like to invite to the Royal Parade to be held on the last day of term. There's some manipulation of the ticket allocation – Kiwi, Phil, Sam and Mahmoud are not likely to be inviting guests, are they?

The break is scheduled from midday on Friday 3rd to Tuesday 7th June – the Whitsun weekend. Spirits are high – before a tragic event casts everyone down.

80 Entry is pursuing the old syllabus, with basic flying training in their Term Four, on the Piston Provost at Barkston Heath. Just now, however, Barkston's runways are being strengthened to accommodate the Jet Provost expected this autumn, so 80 Entry Piston Provosts are operating from the grass airfield at RAF Spitalgate.

In the late afternoon of the last day of May, there spreads around the College a chilling piece of news. A West Country lad and a well-liked and respected member of 80 'B', has been killed on a solo flight at Spitalgate.

It seems that he was in the circuit when he lost the engine – ploughed in one-and-a-half miles north-east of the airfield. The aircraft caught fire and the fire truck got to him too late.

Anthony, of 80 Entry and a one-time mentor to 'C' Squadron, says, 'I knew the chap well – he was the scrum half in the College rugby team and I'm the hooker. And we boxed against each other in first term.'

Mac recalls, 'He'd missed the Escape and Evasion with 80 Entry, so he did a couple of days on our team in the Cairngorms.' He speaks for all when he says, 'One of the best. Great shame.'

Just three days later, as Robert drives Mark and Danny down Ermine Street to London for the break, their holiday mood changes when they see the ring of burnt grass where the Piston Provost and its pilot bought it.

***

Mark manages a couple of weekend games of cricket in North Surrey before Robert's Riley whisks him back to the world of study, Strikers, and drill.

In the first week of the second half there's a Junior Mess Guest Night, at which the main subject of discussion for 81 Entry is their forthcoming participation in the Ferris Drill Competition, to be held just two short weeks away at the end of June.

The following month sees the whole entry coming together for Queen's Parade practice, to be given the once-over by their old adversary, 'Shudders' Hudson. His often repeated, 'Not good enough – go round again' becomes shriller and shriller as Her Majesty's visit looms closer and closer.

Mark's mum will be coming – she's bought a new hat – with her brother-in-law as escort. He's well placed in the YMCA hierarchy and they've secured lodgings in the camp hostel. Just as well – naturally the hotels in the area are filling up. It's to be a grand occasion.

Flight Sergeant Holt and his colleagues are supremely zealous in searching out the smallest deficiency in drill kit – invitations to 'See me after!' increase in frequency.

***

In the classroom, the pressure also increases. Examinations, for the Latin, Russian, Anglo-Saxon and English Literature O-levels, as well as for Part

114

1 of the AFRAeS qualification, are just a few months away. In addition, language students are being put in for Civil Service Linguist and Interpreter certificates.

The majority of 'B' Stream members are finding the AFRAeS studies, with their concentration on Theoretical Physics, hard going, but half a dozen, those who breezed through A-levels at school, are finding their way through. One of these is Peter, and another is Dave:

> It's turned out that I've studied most of the first year's syllabus already, and not just at A-level. All that detailed instruction I got in the ATC helps, not forgetting four summer camps at RAF Stations.
>
> As a result I'm well-grounded in basic Aerodynamics, Meteorology, airframe structures, piston and jet engines, radio, radar and navigation aids. So I'm enjoying the AFRAeS course.

In the 'C' Stream, the Latin studies continue, mostly in the evenings at Wingco Watt's married quarter, along Lighter-than-Air Road, north of the North Airfield. Mark has discovered from the Journals that Watts was awarded the OBE in the 1959 Birthday Honours List for dedication to the cause of raising Cranwell's academic standards. The Latin scholars have no reason to doubt his determination to see the job through to success, with a few BA General Certificates to show for it. Under his tutelage, Mark for one is beginning to find Virgil's *Aeneid* quite enthralling and the patterns of Latin declensions and conjugations increasingly make sense. In any event, it adds variety to the military round.

In the interests of English Lit, Robert and two others have a day out at Stratford:

> We went to see the Merchant of Venice, travelling in our tutor's Morris Oxford.
>
> It was a long day and driving back in the dark he falls asleep at the wheel. The car lurches down the camber, which luckily wakes him up – just in time. There's a screech of brakes and he gets the thing back under control.
>
> It was a close-run thing. Biggest scare we've had so far up here.

In all the academic lectures, there's frequently a struggle to stay awake. One Aerodynamics student notes:

> This last week, our Rhodesian chum Phil climbed out of the window when the lecturer had his back turned, writing on the board. Several moments later, Phil knocked on the door and came back in, apologising for being late. He was told not to be late again and to sit down and pay attention.
>
> A quarter of an hour later, Phil repeated this procedure, with the same result – although there was a slightly puzzled frown on the lecturer's brow this time.
>
> The penny only dropped when Phil did it for the third time!

The degree course members have no problems with tedium when the bright officers of the War Studies team cover the inter-war years.

The RAF's role in the 1920s and most of the 1930s was one of policing, across the Empire. The areas concerned were vast and required huge numbers of troops and enormous expense. The nascent RAF's aircraft showed they could take on the task with far fewer assets at a fraction of the cost, much to the delight of the politicians and the fury of the Army.

India, in particular, saw RAF squadrons participating extensively in joint ground-air exercises and operations and from 1921 to 1930, under a League of Nations Mandate, the RAF famously administered the occupation of Transjordan, Iraq and Palestine. At a time when the RAF's two sister services were making every effort to scrap the independent Air Force and divide the spoils, political necessity saved Trenchard's baby.

In a time of post-war stringency, mechanics were drawn to the RAF by the prospect of paid employment but there remained the difficulties of recruiting, and training, officers and pilots. The Air Board knew that through the 1920s and on, it needed many more competent officers and pilots than could be supplied by the RAF College. Partly to answer that need, new classes of pilot training were offered.

From 1921, technicians from the ranks were offered transfers as Sergeant Pilots for five years as aircrew, following which they would return to their own trades. This helped, but sourced never more than 1% of RAF flying school trainees.

From 1924, 500 Short Service aircrew Commissions, comprising six years in service, with four years in the Reserve, were offered to British subjects. These were snapped up, often by ex-Great War pilots unable to find work in civilian aviation.

Also extremely popular was the Auxiliary Air Force (AAF), established in 1925. Equivalent in status to the new Territorial Units of the Army, these squadrons were manned by air and ground-crew volunteers, operating RAF-owned and -maintained aircraft. These units set out to foster a local flavour, with a view to raising the status of the RAF in the eyes of the public.

The same year, University Air Squadrons (UAS) formed in Cambridge and then in Oxford and London, offered elementary flying training to undergraduates, in the hope of encouraging them to join the RAF. Those proved a fertile recruiting ground for the AAF and Cranwell both. In 1936, Trenchard championed the creation of a 'Citizens' Air Force', the RAF Volunteer Reserve.

Alongside these initiatives, air displays at RAF Hendon were hugely popular with the public and excellent recruitment PR. Unfortunately, the reality was that the far-flung policing role was ill-served by an underfunded supply chain, and the same under-funding led to navigation training being neglected and the prevalence of the biplane.

Naval aviation was largely neglected by the Air Board and suffered even more than the RAF from being starved of resources. In 1936, with conflict looming on three continents, the RNAS was returned to the Royal Navy as the Fleet Air Arm – with a paltry 232 aircraft on strength. It was to be many years before naval aviation was rebuilt.

Despite the fiscal restraints, the RAF College had by 1929 graduated forty-four entries, logging some 32,000 flying hours, and was on course to have supplied over 1,000 officers for RAF service by the end of the 1930s.

Bristol Bulldog, RAF 1930s frontline fighter.
(*Aeroplane Photo in RAF College Journal*)

However, flying in the RAF and the Navy largely remained the preserve of officers from moneyed classes. It was going to take some kind of world cataclysm for the RAF to gain the level of investment that would enable it to achieve one of Trenchard's stated aims – to open up the Service to the breadth of British society and thus improve its effectiveness and image.

Mark and his fellow students know full well that by the late 1930s, just around the corner was such a cataclysm – one that, although young children at the time, they've experienced. They're looking forward to hearing the official line about those years.

***

On Monday 9th July, 'A' Stream members start a week of Year One exams, a series of three-hour papers in Military Studies, Physics, Electronics, Maths pure and applied, Economics and English. The papers are reportedly not too challenging but as they are taken at the same time as the drilling intensifies with the build-up to the royal visit, they are testing days.

In the event, no one is declared a failure in any of the subjects and all members of 81 Entry join College and Station in concentrating on making Her Majesty welcome.

Kerbstones are painted white, all grass is mown and trees are trimmed into submission. A new pathway is created, to be inaugurated by the Queen herself.

This requires the demolition of the Post Office, which has stood for many decades on Cranwell Avenue, over the road from the main College Gates, so that the pathway can lead directly down to the Junior Mess Parade Ground. Holes are dug, one either side of the path, where the Queen and the Duke will be invited to plant trees in commemoration of the opening of this 'Queen's Avenue'. Meanwhile, a replacement Post Office is being built on the far side of East Camp.

On either side of the Reviewing Base, across more than half the width of the Orange, spring up seven raked rows of seating. A large number of spectators will be watching the hour-long parade, marking both the graduation of 77 Entry and the presentation of a new Queen's Colour.

For the Flight Cadets, the final week sees both studies and flying taking a back seat as parade rehearsals become intense. In the Junior Mess, Mr Riley's scissors ensure that no hairline attracts the Drill Sergeants' disapproval. However, there's a moratorium on charges – 'Can't have the fellows spending time on Strikers at this stage of proceedings!'

Up at the Parade Ground, the College Warrant Officer, with pace-stick, records every measurement possible – spaces between squadrons and ranks, the length of an individual's stride, the distance of the marchers from the Receiving Base and even the line-up on the steps of the College Band.

There's a surge in bulling fervour. Boots are given a rejuvenating layer of Kiwi black, button-sticks and Brasso get to work on anything shiny and belts are re-blancoed a brilliant white. Rifles and bayonets gleam and wooden parts are loosened, so as to maximise the crack of the 'Preeesent – Arms!'

On Friday 22nd July, there's a wet-weather rehearsal in the standby hangar, with much slipping and sliding. This is followed the next day by a full outdoor run-through.

By Sunday 24th, many parents and other loved-ones have arrived in the Cranwell area. A good number of them attend the Church Parade and, at the end of the march back to College hear the departing SUO of 77 Entry issue the order, 'Parade to remove head-dress. Remove – Head-dress!' He then calls for 'Three cheers for 77 Entry!' Hats are raised and the cheers ring out.

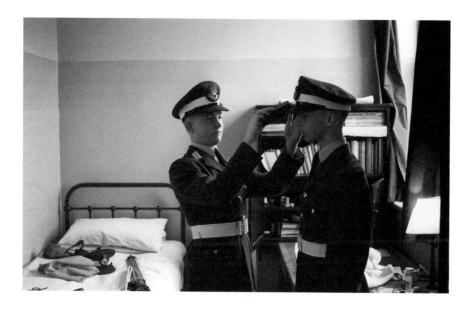

Above: Flight Cadets – the final adjustments. (*JGL*)

Left: A ceremonial boot – the final product. (*JGL*)

With extended arms the parade waits for the order, 'Replace – Head-dress!' No order comes. Parade and spectators are left bemused as the SUO and his colleagues march off gleefully. Jolly good jape chaps, what!

The 81'C' Flight Cadets take their guests off for lunch at a favourite local, the seventeenth century Red Lion inn, just a couple of miles west of the College, in Caythorpe. Mark's mum, a primary school teacher, finds an immediate rapport with Terry's dad, a Post Office Telephones engineer from

Tooting. Single mum and single dad from the outskirts of London, they are joined by the Group Captain father of the wannabe Brasenose man.

In the classic opening gambit, the officer asks, 'And what do you do, Sir?' To which the response is, 'Well actually, I'm in phones.'

Mark's mum warms even more to Terry's dad. Barriers are broken all round and the lunch is a great success.

***

The same can be said of the next day, as far as the Flight Cadets can see. Booted, polished and close-shaven ('Do not use a new blade, Gentlemen – any nicks and it'll be "See me after!" ') they proudly march onto the College Parade Ground to the strains of the *RAF College Quick March* and form up in line.

Then, the Parade Commander, the SUO of the term's Sovereign's Squadron gives the order, 'Preeesent – Arms!' as the Queen's Colour is marched on, to *The Lincolnshire Poacher*.

Out of the corner of their eyes, the ranks are aware of the arrival of the royal party. Her Majesty, escorted by the Commandant, smiles in the sunshine. The Duke of Edinburgh walks a pace or two behind in Air Marshal's dress uniform, escorted by other dignitaries.

Queen and Commandant.   Advanced Flying Wing Fly-past.
(*RAF College Journal*)   (*RAF College Journal*)

Her Majesty inspects the ranks. (*RAF College Journal*)

March Past in slow and quick time. (*RAF College Journal*)

As the Queen moves to the dais, jet trainers roar overhead in a fly-past, College trumpeters sound a rousing fanfare and chests swell with pride. The parade again presents arms and the band strikes up *The Royal Salute*.

Leaving the dais, escorted by Under Officers, Her Majesty inspects the ranks. Under strict instructions not to meet the Monarch's eye, the cadets remain rigidly at attention, weight on the balls of their feet to avoid cramp, or worse still, 'doing a Guards' and fainting. The experience of being so close to their sovereign, is one never to be forgotten.

The cadets march past immaculately in slow time, and return in quick time, before the old Colour is marched off for laying up in the chapel. Her Majesty then presents a new Colour, which is slow-marched to take its place among the ranks.

As Commandant-in-Chief, she then addresses the parade. After acknowledging her close links with the College and the RAF, 'guardians of the nation', she stresses the significance of the Colour:

> It embodies the traditions of the College and the Royal Air Force, traditions of steadfastness and devotion, courage and skill, intelligence and inventiveness. At this time of challenge and uncertainty, these qualities are more important than ever. Conditions may alter from day to day. But it was these qualities of spirit which made the Royal Air Force, and it is they which will sustain it in the future.

The Commandant thanks Her Majesty for the confidence which she places in the College, which will 'provide us all with inspiration for the future'. The parade advances in Review Order for a second Royal Salute, before the Queen presents the Sword of Honour and Queen's Medal to their respective winners. The new Colour is marched off up the College steps and the Graduating 77 Entry follows, disappearing one-by-one through the College doors to the plaintive notes of *Auld Lang Syne*.

The Commandant-in-Chief, the Duke, and the party of dignitaries make their way down Queen's Avenue for the tree-planting, before being driven back up to the College for a formal lunch, with doubtless plenty of further ceremony, in the grand Dining Hall.

***

Left: The Queen presents the new Colour. (*RAF College Journal*)

Below: Formal luncheon with Her Majesty. (*RAF College Journal*)

The Queen and the Duke review the Flying Wing. (*RAF College Journal*)

81 Entry are marched down to the rather less grand ambience of the Junior Mess, where they are reunited with family and friends, all dressed up as if for a Royal Garden Party. There's much chat – everyone's delighted their lads made the grade on the Parade Square.

Mark congratulates his mother on choosing a hat almost identical to Her Majesty's and she embarrasses him by telling Sergeant Ross how much her son enjoys drill. 'Not surprising,' she says. 'As a boy, he was so good at dancing round the maypole.'

Blind Bill professes, 'It was almost as exciting for me as the Coronation', while Andy comments, 'For me, it's been the highlight of the term. It's the first time that I've seen Her Majesty in person and I swear that as she passed by on the inspection, I caught her eye.'

Sergeant McDill takes note.

***

The night after the parade, Flight Lieutenant Moffat has organized for his 'A' Squadron chaps a glorious 'hooley' in a disused hangar on the satellite RAF airfield at Fulbeck.

The party is to celebrate their leaving the Junior Mess and on the morning after, 'A' Squadron, always ready to thumb their noses at protocol, arrive for breakfast in pyjamas and dressing gowns, brandishing their trade-mark collection of walking sticks. These they've been steadily accumulating over this first year, some of them innocent canes, others quite lethal swordsticks which would be impounded in other circumstances. Robin entertains his mates with the outcome of his Wednesday afternoon efforts:

> I'm off to spend the summer leave with my grandparents in Bournemouth. Whatever I decide to do there, it won't involve equestrianism. At the gymkhana, neither the horse nor I managed a single jump. The horse declined and simply off-loaded me each time. No officer charisma absorbed there.
>
> I've done much better with the mountaineering – Stanage Edge, right from the bottom, up to the top, and down again on the abseil rope in a joyful rush. And I've gone down a pothole.
>
> You get into it by jumping into a muddy sump which works on the principle of a flush toilet – struggle down and around a u-bend, and there you are, popping up into the start of a cave system. Out again through the sump at the finish.
>
> Next term, I'm signed up for dinghy sailing, on the River Trent. Ship ahoy, Flight Commander!

***

The chaps of 81 Entry depart for the 1960 summer leave happy in the knowledge that they've come successfully through their first year. On return they'll all be moving up to the College building. The fourth wing is now

If at first...   ...you don't succeed...
(*RAF College Journal*)   (*RAF College Journal*)

...send for the Flight Sergeant. (*RAF College Journal*)

complete, the connecting wall having been sledge-hammered through in the spring by the formidable Flight Sergeant Holt, before being opened just yesterday by Her Majesty.

This makes room for that fourth squadron. A selection of cadets has been told that they are being siphoned off to man the ranks of the new 'D'. They spend the final hours of Term 3 moving their kit to the north-east wing and commissioning their batmen to change their gorget cords to the new squadron's green.

Summer Leave 1960

Various officer-training group activities, ranging from caving in France to safari in Africa, are planned for the six weeks of leave.

The day after the Queen's Parade, Chris and Andy, in the latter's Morris 8, drive to RAF West Raynham in Norfolk and one day later, they take turns as passenger in a two-seat Hawker Hunter T7. They fly to 42,000 feet, experience a Mach 1.05 dive, as well as aerobatics, and finish with fast and low flying at 250 feet.

The following day, they drive to RAF Coltishall, in Norfolk, where they take a look at the English Electric Lightning supersonic interceptor, before watching a 111 Squadron Hunter display.

On the Friday, Chris's brother arrives in a Gloster Meteor NF 14 from RAF Bovingdon and Andy drives off in the Morris, while Chris hitches a lift in the Meteor back to Bovingdon.

After the weekend, Chris, Martin and Boy set off for a nine-day gliding camp at Netheravon. For this, one of the Cranwell gliders has been towed over there behind a College Chipmunk while the other two are hauled by road.

Chris reports, 'I managed twenty-one glider flights including solo thermal flying in cloud, first solo loops, and first solo in the high-performance Olympia.'

Finally, Chris is taken by his brother in the Bovingdon Anson to Guernsey, where he relaxes for a week – on holiday with school pals.

Dauntless Dave continues the holiday job he had in his schooldays and also gets into the air.

'I've spent a lot of the leave with my old friends at the Hampshire Flying Club, looking after their fleet of aircraft including a two-seat Spitfire. I've cadged many a flight too. Some aircraft owners need someone just to hold the maps during cross-countries.'

By the end of the month, Chris and others return to the College early for pre-arranged Chipmunk sorties but this venture turns out to be a damp squib – terrible weather, acute shortage of Flying Wing pilots. So Chris hitches yet another ride in the Anson, this time to Holland.

When Mark hears all this, he realises that this level of enthusiasm could carry these chaps on to great things in the RAF. He wonders how much weight a pass in a BA General Degree will carry, compared with that kind of determination to get airborne and, in the words of the cadets' motto, 'Seek the Highest'.

Chapter 6

The Senior Mess

Term 4: 7th Sep-13th Dec 1960

The men of 81 Entry can now luxuriate in the comparative opulence and tradition evident in the Senior College building. John writes home:

> Now that we have moved up into the College, life is much more pleasant. There is almost a London club atmosphere about the anterooms – leather armchairs, newspapers and valuable oil-paintings looking down on us. And having everything under one roof – meals, lecture hall and library – makes a difference.

Again, it's single rooms for all but they're able to mix with other entries, including the senior. Although each has its separately allocated anteroom, open to all are the Dining Hall, billiard room, and Library, as is the FGS.

The latter hosts an early get-together of the 81 Entry chaps, to hear tales of derring-do over the summer leave. Naturally the flying features strongly, but stories of the 'C' Squadron expedition to France for a fortnight's caving in the challenging *Grotte de la Cigalière* in Provence capture the most attention.

Mentored by 'C' Squadron's SUO, Terry, Danny, Kiwi and Blind Bill have crawled through parts of the subterranean world where man has seldom, if ever, crawled before. On knees and elbows, with no space to crouch in, let alone stand up straight, they've squeezed through 'syphons', with a three-inch breathing-space between rock and water. Going without daylight for as much as forty hours at a stretch, they've seen stalactites and stalagmites, caverns and cascades, as well as prehistoric cave drawings reckoned to be some 15,000 years old.

No one can top that, but the gathering turns to listen when Mac introduces a thoughtful note:

After forty hours in the dark. (*RAF College Journal*)

May I propose a toast to the Junior Year Drill Sergeants? Against seemingly impossible odds, they've turned a gaggle of civilian schoolboys into a smart military unit, fit to look at a Queen – don't y'know. They made us feel we were all in it together, didn't they?

Here's to them!

Mac's motion's passed unanimously.

There's then a more formal discussion about 81 Entry matters. Chris is somehow elected as Complaints Representative. 'Seems a poisoned chalice, whatever I do,' is his reaction.

The chaps then file out, to change for a Knocker Cup practice. This autumn it's athletics, which entails, among other exertions, a four-mile cross-country race around the perimeter of the North Airfield. The competition also includes a tug-of-war and the bigger blokes in 'C' Squadron soon find themselves up-close and personal with their coach – none other than the formidable 'Bogbrush' Holt. He brings the rope, they bring themselves, in the heaviest of boots. He ties the rope around one of the famous lime trees and sets about getting the fellows to do their best to pull it down – for a back-breaking hour.

When it comes to the event, the 'C' team wins – that's the usual Bogbrush way.

***

On the academic front, despite Blind Bill and others passing the summer A-level Maths exams (Bill enhancing his grade to a triumphant 'C') the authorities appear to have decided that 'A' Stream students aren't doing enough work. So they're giving them another nine hours a week in the classroom as well as out-of-classroom work calculated to fill their Private Study time. This hugely discomforts Kraut, who's just moved from the 'C' Stream to 'A' for an easier time. 'It turns out we're going to have to submit an essay every term – reckon I'll let them have a few thoughts about our first year at this place.'

For pilots and navigators both, this racking up of the mind work coincides with the start of the ground school phase of training – Aerodynamics, Meteorology and other professional subjects. However, both 'A' and 'B' Streams are disappointed to find the syllabus apparently disconnected from their sciences curricula.

***

On the Battle of Britain weekend, the chaps are treated to a reminder of airborne excitements to come. On the Saturday afternoon, around four o'clock, a low-flying Vampire zooms over the rugby pitch, the College and the Orange, before disappearing at treetop height, to make a low-level run-in and break for landing on the South Airfield.

Nigel of 'A' Squadron has the info:

> The man flying that Vampire was Dave Moffat – our erstwhile Flight Commander down in the Junior Mess. He was just back from thrilling the crowds at an air display somewhere over the horizon.
>
> Five-foot five-inches short, with huge G-tolerance, he's an aerobatic ace – even won the Flying Training Command trophy for aerobatics, the coveted Wright Jubilee. They say he's managed a low-level three-sixty turn within the perimeter of the College grounds.

There's further cause for wonder when, from time to time, a stream of four Vulcan V-Bombers roars out on a V-Force scramble from nearby RAF Waddington, each with four Bristol Olympus jet engines tearing the air apart. Is this a practice, or is it for real – the start of the third, and final, World War?

Avro Vulcans, together with Vickers Valiants and Handley-Page Victors, developed in the 1950s when Britain led the world in aviation, are the ones that carry the British Independent Nuclear Deterrent. That subject has been in the forefront of Mark's mind since Easter, and that CND rally in Trafalgar Square.

As well as the Vulcans, there's a sight to be seen from the A1, not far south of Grantham, at RAF Woolfox Lodge, where ranks of Bristol Bloodhound ground-to-air missiles, the latest and most lethal in the armoury, stand with their warheads pointing menacingly eastwards. They are there as a second line of defence should any Russian bombers escape the first wave of Lightning interceptors.

The sight of those Bloodhounds, ready to fire, together with the thunderous howl of the Vulcans, convince Mark to make Nuclear Deterrence the basis of his next War Studies essay. He writes that he finds it difficult to buy the arguments behind the government's support for the UK having its own nuclear weapons – the school of thought that goes, 'Make your sword as big, if not bigger than your enemy's and you'll be safe'. Is it not ingenuous to have a bombing strategy which relies on the premise that the awful and atrocious effect of nuclear blast and radiation means no one will ever use the weapon? The thing is, they have already been used – by the Americans against Japan just sixteen years ago, with the loss of an estimated quarter of a million lives – the vast majority civilians.

Plans are afoot to lease the Americans a nuclear submarine base, to be built in Scotland's Holy Loch, in exchange for a supply of Polaris nuclear-armed missiles for Britain's own submarine fleet. In October, HMQ will be in Barrow, launching *Dreadnought,* the first of those nuclear subs. Submarines and V-Bombers – a terrifying arsenal.

Meanwhile, it's been made clear to the Flight Cadets that the RAF's solemn duty is to train the crews of the V-Bombers, over a period of five years at a cost of about £100,000 for a Vulcan captain. Mark, although certainly too tall for V-Force cockpits, is expected to toe the official line.

So it's probably just as well that the shrewd RAF tutor on the War Studies team gives him an 'A' for effort, before quietly filing the essay at the back of the deepest cabinet he can find.

***

The Chipmunk flying programme continues its stuttering progress, dogged by strong winds for days and weeks, followed by autumn mists, as well as heavy rain. In the first week of October, the Meteorology lecturer (known to all as 'Cu-Nim Jim') reports that a notable flood has occurred two-score miles to the north-east in Horncastle. The town has entered the record books with the highest three-hour total rainfall measured in the area, at seven inches.

In the clearer spells, some progress can be made, but this Chipmunk initiative is turning out to be a kind of jolly for the staff officer pilots. The Flying Club, which now has its hoped-for hangar space, together with a clubhouse hut, continues to be a flying lifeline for its members. They have acquired their first aircraft – a Tiger Moth (including a spare Gypsy Major engine) bought for £300, alongside two Turbulents, on loan from the Tiger Club at Redhill and powered by VW Beetle engines. Club members make sure they make the most of any clear weather, as does the glider fraternity. But it's only at weekends now – long summer evenings are a fading memory.

The weather hasn't held Robin back in his determined quest to impress his Flight Commander. Despite, or perhaps because of the wind, the sailing's gone well:

> We tackle the River Trent up near Newark. It's on the bit where Staythorpe power station's on the far bank. The dinghies are kept at RAF Syerston.
>
> The power station's coal-fired but as long as the wind's blowing the smoke away, all's well. The trick is to stay away from the weir – large, fierce and no way back. It's also a good idea not to fall in – the Trent's not known for being particularly wholesome.
>
> And I think my perseverance has been noticed – I've been allowed the honour of going down to Bournemouth as ADC to the Inspecting Officer for my school's Annual Review.
>
> So far, so good. Now my staying the course all depends on the flying next term.

Nigel has his own, weatherproof way of relaxing:

> I'm whiling away a few spare hours with the grand piano in the anteroom just off the Rotunda. To be allowed to play it, I've had to be auditioned by no less a personage than the College Secretary, Group Captain Nuttall himself. Fortunately, he's given me the tick in the box.
>
> All are very welcome to come along and listen. I'm not shy.

Nigel has also become a Staff Member on the College Journal, along with Jim the Nav and Kiwi, who are Sub-Editors, for Sports and Articles respectively. Jock and David have been recruited as cartoonists. Whatever the weather, there's always something to do at Cranwell.

***

The weather doesn't keep the GDT instructors idle. A highlight is a demonstration of anti-gas procedures. The routine involves Flight Sergeant Pawson, a tear-gas canister and gas masks. The whole thing kicks off with his memorable cry of 'Gas – Gas – Gas!' before the hissing canister spews choking gas and the life-saving masks give relief. It's an extremely effective way of showing the protection that could be provided from more sinister gasses – should an enemy choose to deliver them in anger.

An equally convincing routine is demonstrated when a travelling decompression chamber visits from the School of Aviation Medicine base at RAF North Luffenham, in nearby Rutland. In that, small groups of cadets experience an atmosphere equivalent to that at 30,000 feet together with the effects of anoxia (lack of oxygen). A rapid descent then tests the robustness of eardrums and Eustachian tubes. Despite the occasional difficulty (popping eardrums and shaky writing) the vast majority suffer no adverse outcome.

There's one exception. The set-up is that there are two chambers – the inner one where the trainees sit and ascend to simulated altitude as the air's pumped out, and an outer one that acts as an air-lock.

Adrian relates:

> I'm in there with Jock and others and we're pumped up to 30,000 feet. First exercise is to reduce the oxygen coming through our masks. Before long our writing, which we're told to do so as to monitor the effect, becomes all wobbly. That's as expected but then one chap becomes almost hysterical – starts throwing himself about.
>
> Those in charge decide a doctor's required. One's on hand but there's finger-trouble with the air-lock doors. We get far more than we bargained for – down from 30,000 feet in five seconds!
>
> Excruciating pain. Sinuses filled with blood and mucous. So it's into Nocton Hall RAF Hospital for an op to flush out the sinuses and we're kept there for a week to

guard against infection. Bloke in charge of the mechanics is up for court-martial.

How do we feel about it? I suppose it's another step nearer the real flying experience – albeit a pretty drastic one.

***

Their progress to the skies is also helped by the ground schooling. A highlight is the introduction to pilot navigation. The tutor, a hard-bitten Aussie Flight Lieutenant, is a long-service professional single-engine pilot, both piston and jet. He presents the art of finding the way around the countryside through mental dead reckoning, fair weather or foul, with an almost religious fervour. He teaches ways and means of complete reliance on self, with no need of a navigator.

He shows how a pilot can hold mental images of the data and manipulate those to find drift, before calculating headings to get back onto required track, with timings into the bargain, all while safely flying the aeroplane.

His method works. It's magic! In one test, a chap comes up with an answer using the computer. Our man doesn't like that answer, and says so.

'But I did it on the computer, Sir.'

Full of scorn, the Aussie growls, 'Then your computer's wrong.'

***

The mid-term break weekend arrives after work on Friday 21st October and Saturday afternoon sees Mark and Sally in a Kenya Coffee Bar in the Finchley Road. He expounds on life as a fourth-term Cranwell cadet:

> Now we're up in the Senior Mess, everything down there south of Cranwell Avenue seems very much 'junior'. We're up a rank and feeling pretty good about it. Of course, that's what it's all about – having us climb the ladder, step by step to a commission.
>
> We take all our meals in the grand Dining Hall and on formal Dining-in and Guest Nights, we dress up in black tie and Number Ones and there's a good deal of pomp and circumstance. Over the port and cigars, the band's lead trumpeter plays the Post Horn Gallop – we beat the time on the table and give him three cheers.
>
> If the speeches go on too long, we've got all sorts of tricks to relieve the tedium – a good one is crawling under the table and tying a bloke's shoelaces together. The meals they dish up

are enormous – my mate Danny from Kingston put on a show by demolishing a whole dish of sprouts, all by himself.

When the President leaves the top table with the dignitaries, it's back to our squadron anteroom to let off steam with mess games – Tunnel of Love, Mess Rugby, Human Pyramid, Ring-a-Ring-o'-Roses – that kind of thing. In the main corridor, there's jousting on bicycles – dustbin lids for shields and mops for lances – but that's for the Senior Entry, they're the only ones issued with bikes.

Mind you, after a Monday Dining-in night, we all have to file into the Longcroft Room to watch a War Studies film – 'War in the Air', 'Victory at Sea' and so forth. Sunday nights there's a film too but that's art club stuff – last week we had Brigitte Bardot and the hall was packed.

There's still plenty of drill but now it's on the College Parade Ground. When all the entries are together, it somehow seems more to the point. It even makes the Strikers' Parade a bit more bearable – you get a privileged view of the College tower and the flag-raising ceremony but most times, it's a punishing run around the Orange, with a rifle held in both hands in front of your chest.

Then, there's the Fancy Goods Store – bar, bar billiards and darts – and the billiards room itself. Studies permitting, of course – they're racking up.

And the Cadets' Garage – that's filling up with 81 Entry cars. Chris has bought himself a 1935 Singer 9 at Pevensey for £22-10s – he's very pleased with that.

There's enough wheels now to take the whole squadron entry out for pub-crawls, or into Lincoln and the dance halls. We sink bitter by the gallon but the drivers have got away with it, so far.

And Sid's now letting me ride his motorbike, solo. Last Saturday, I took it into Nottingham for an evening at the 'Trip to Jerusalem'. Smashing pub – reckons it's the oldest in England. Carved into the sandstone under the castle – darts, and great beer.

He suddenly stops – he can see Sally's not impressed.

'So,' she asks, with a straight look and a raised eyebrow, 'you're not doing much flying then?'

136

Deflated, Mark grabs her hand and takes her off to the cinema, where there's a newly-released film showing. *Saturday Night and Sunday Morning* is billed as a ground-breaking 'socio-realist' effort. It's certainly realist – Albert Finney, as Arthur Seaton, doing his gritty northern best, to confront society's conventions and restraints.

It makes Mark think. He could do well to go easy on all that Cranwell malarkey. Back at the Coffee House, he asks about Sally's Drama College and London life. He keeps off the subject of the RAF and pays her some serious attention – Arthur Seaton style.

***

Back at 'Sleaford Tech' (the name bestowed by Dartmouth matelots) Mark discovers that Andy is another making a fourth-term self-assessment:

> By the summer break, I'd been having serious doubts about whether I wanted to stay at Cranwell – the thought of another two years was getting me down. I went so far as to discuss this with my parents and the City Livery Master I'm apprenticed to. He advised me to get back to the College and keep my head down. 'Officers don't give up at the first hurdle,' was what he said. I have come back – with my tail firmly between my legs.
>
> This term, the move to 'D' Squadron has lifted my spirits – a roomier corner room in a new building and 'Pop' Amies, the same batman I had in the Junior Mess. He's a real character – colourful vocabulary to say the least but he brings a cheerful morning cuppa and is Mister Reliable for shoe cleaning and valeting.
>
> But this fourth term's a problem. We should have been flying Piston Provosts by now, but instead, it's this extra term with just masses of academics. I realise that the disorganisation is down to the sudden imposition on staff of a revolutionary academic programme, together with the delay with the Jet Provost but even so, it's a bore.
>
> So, I've made a strategic decision to stay the course and turn over a new leaf. I'm going to be more accommodating towards the drill and academic instructors and I've vowed to get more involved with the general life of the College.
>
> I've made a start – cemented my place at Number One in the squash team!

Chris has also had a Term Four dip:

> It was good to buy a car and move up to the College, but with so much seemingly pointless academics, Knocker runs, parades, and almost no Chipmunk flying, I became disillusioned with everything. It was so frustrating and seemed rather aimless. I kept sane with gliding, running around the airfield and playing squash. But I'd become careless, and was getting put on Strikers again.
>
> However, during the half-term break I've decided to try harder. I'm paying better attention at academics and being more polite to the instructors – showing them what I'm capable of.
>
> As a result, things are improving a little. I'm sure I'm regaining my keenness.

'Keep going, Chaps,' is the message from tutors and Flight Commanders. 'Only two months and the flying starts!'

***

It's now that the 'C' Stream syllabus reaches the serious business of the build-up to the Second World War.

> *With the barbarous bombing of Shanghai by the Japanese in 1932, politicians and public around the world woke up to the extent of damage to people and property possible in total war. Newsreels in cinemas showed aircraft dispassionately targeting civilians and towns alongside military targets and causing death and destruction. A global moral panic ensued, no more so than in London where, in November, during a disarmament debate, the Prime Minister Stanley Baldwin declared:*
>
> > *I think it is as well for the man in the street to realise that there is no power on earth that prevents him being bombed. Whatever people may tell him, the bomber will always get through.*
> >
> > *The only defence is offence, which means you will have to kill more women and children more quickly than the enemy if you want to save yourselves.*

These were far from reassuring words for the electorate but Baldwin was simply stating the Air Ministry's strategy of the time which was one based on 'strategic' bombing. It was dubbed by the Press 'Arming for Armageddon' and was, in essence, 'Get your knock-out blow in first'.

By 1933, and the coming to power in Germany of Adolf Hitler, both the bombing lobby and the fighter boys found themselves pushing on an open door. The government's perception of the British armed forces changed. Alongside the Foreign Office's strenuous efforts to continue peace talks, the Treasury's ten-year rule was shelved and military investment rocketed. From 1934 to '39 the name of the RAF's game was 'Parity with Germany'.

This meant a switch from dozens of wood and canvas biplanes bought for pennies to metal monoplanes, Hurricanes and Spitfires, in their hundreds at £20K each. Technological investment was sharply increased, led by that in radar and navigation aids.

The number of home-based RAF squadrons was set to increase from fifty-two to sixty-four, of which twenty-five were fighter squadrons. At the same time, funds were provided for the development of a heavy 'knock-out' bomber.

Extra, and newer aircraft, meant that the provision of more pilots was now a matter of immediate national security and in 1939, all the reservists were called up. The 'Citizens' Air Force' now had 2,500 under training. It was a notable exercise in opening up the RAF's officer class to a wider social world.

Sitting in their classroom on the West Site, appropriately enough, in what were wartime huts, the 81 Entry 'C' Stream students learn that when on September 3rd 1939, a Sunday, the Prime Minister, Neville Chamberlain finally took to the airwaves, the cadets at Cranwell gathered in their anterooms to listen. On the announcement that 'this country is at war with Germany', their cheering was loud and long.

That goes down well with today's chaps but it gives them pause when they reflect on how many, too many, of those cheering cadets were to figure in RAF casualty lists by the war's end, some six years later. However, by then, many airmen would have seen their days of glory and by the end of hostilities the RAF would have found its place of honour with citizens of Great Britain, the Commonwealth and worldwide.

***

West (Humanities) Site huts. (*RAF College Journal*)

Examinations for 81 Entry 'A' Stream start in November, when they face Military History and English Essay tests, together with a three-hour Maths paper.

December sees O-level Latin study reaching its climax – the Senior Tutor has done his job well and all pass. Robert gets his English Literature O-level certificate. In the Science stream, all candidates pass their Intermediate AFRAeS exams.

The party is somewhat spoilt for the College Academics staff by all candidates in the O-level Russian exams, apart from David, sinking *en bloc*.

***

Chris, over a pre-Christmas noggin in the FGS, observes, 'That's the fourth term just about over then, and I'm glad to see the back of it. We've been mostly marking time with little if anything achieved.'

Andy agrees, and adds, 'I haven't exactly put my back into this Cranwell course for the first four terms but when the flying starts in a few weeks I've steeled myself to set to with a will. By the time we come back in January, I've promised myself to have the JP checklists off by heart.'

Sid has some stern criticism of the course so far, concluding, 'We've passed stage one OK, but I still reckon that the AFRAeS studies are unlikely to have any practical use for me. And so much of the rest has been concerned with turning us into officers and gentlemen by what seems some process of osmosis – do as I do, sort of thing.'

On the flying side, it's generally agreed that the Chipmunk experiment, no doubt well intentioned, has generally done more harm than good. Just a couple of sorties in a whole term doesn't exactly get a fellow into the swing of the thing.

However, there have been exceptions – in a late-term boost with a proper Master-Pilot instructor, Jock has managed no fewer than three times to go solo, making forty minutes on his own, within a total of just over seven hours. Not quite the results that had been promised to all at the start, but better than most.

Peter also has a good word for the Chippie Flight. 'I managed fifteen flights between May and December. These were all a bit of a bonus for me, complementing my hours under the Flying Scholarship scheme. I feel ready for the JP now.'

Mid-Winter Leave 1960/61

Just in time for the twenty-six day break, the tyros have been issued with brand-new copies of Pilot's Notes for the Jet Provost Mk3. For Mark, it was a special moment, opening the stiff card cover, in RAF blue, and turning the pages to see for the first time the instruction manual for the new toy that's coming their way after Christmas. He's determined to read it from end to end over the break. He might even ask Sally to help him get the take-off and landing checks off pat.

'That'll show her I mean business in January – won't it?'

Chapter 7

Jet Jockeys

First-half Term 5: 9th Jan-24th Feb 1961

It's Monday 9th January 1961. The weather in Lincolnshire is just what's hoped for at this time of year. There had been snowfall over Yuletide but today, it's dry. However with high pressure and a clear blue sky it's freezing cold. The countryside is gleaming white with snow. These, say those who know these things, are perfect conditions for flying jet aircraft.

The GD/Pilot trainees of 81 Entry have been brought back from leave a couple of days before the Spring Term begins, to cover administration elements of their flying training. After breakfast, again in the Officers' Mess as the College kitchens are not yet fired up, all thirty-four of the wannabe pilots are being bussed down Ermine Street en route the satellite airfield of Barkston Heath.

Mark, Mike, Danny and Chris are sharing the back seat.

'So, this is it,' enthuses Mark. 'Never mind all that drill and dining stuff – not to mention the dress and decorum, it's the flying that counts.'

Danny has more down-to-earth matters on his mind. 'That's all well and good but how about the news in the paper last week? National Service came to an end, for everyone, on New Year's Eve. Maybe now, if any of us get chopped, they'll let us off the rest of those five years we signed up for.'

'Flight Lieutenant Moffat'll be pleased,' says Mike, with a broad grin. 'He reckons that once all the National Service blokes have gone, the RAF can get back to being a professional service.'

Mark looks thoughtful. 'Chop – there's a thing. How many of the chaps sitting in this bus won't make it through to the Easter leave?'

Chris chimes in, 'This bus driver must reckon he's Fangio – hope he knows what he's doing on all this ice. Yesterday I spun the Singer off the A1 in no uncertain fashion. No one hurt – fortunately car not bent.'

'Fangio', with no further alarums, drives up the hill out of Ancaster before swinging the bus right, through the High Dyke gates onto the perimeter road of RAF Barkston Heath.

***

The chaps have been briefed that it's one of the Second World War airfields imposed on Lincolnshire's farm and wood land in the later years of the 1930s when Hitler's aims became crystal clear. Its role was as a Bomber Command training airfield before becoming in late 1943 a base for the USAAF Douglas C-47 Skytrain squadrons involved in the D-Day landings.

The collection of wooden huts just inside the gate and alongside Ermine Street again reminds Mark and Danny of the Biggles books and wartime stories that inspired them as boys. One of the huts houses the Barkston Flying Wing Headquarters, where, in the main Briefing Room, are pinned up the lists allocating students to the two Flying Wing squadrons. No. 1 Squadron, which will be operating from Cranwell's South Airfield, takes the cadets from 'A' and 'B' Squadrons while 'C' and 'D' go to No. 2, which will be based at Barkston.

Seated at the rows of desks, the student pilots are called to order with the arrival of the Flying Wing's Chief Flying Instructor, Wing Commander Green who immediately commands their full attention.

After a few words of welcome to the Wing, he outlines the current situation. There are now two-dozen serviceable Jet Provosts Mark 3 on the Cranwell establishment, ready for 81 to be the first Cranwell entry to embark on all-through jet flying training. The aim for the trainees is to complete the course, a total of 180 hours flying, and be awarded Wings on their Graduation in July next year. However, in contrast with the programme currently in operation they will not have completed the Advanced Flying stage.

For that, they'll progress, according to aptitude as well as Air Force needs, to either the new Folland Gnat jets at RAF Valley in Anglesey or the twin-piston engine training offered on the Vickers Varsities at RAF Oakington, Cambridgeshire.

The Flying Wing are aware that 81 Entry is taking the academic side of the course in brave new directions and they intend to work with science and humanities tutors to manage the cadets' time in the best way possible. That management, it appears, starts right now – the numbers of Jet Provosts as well as qualified instructors to fly them are not yet up to full strength and in addition, the contractors haven't yet finished with Barkston Heath.

The tarmac runways and taxiways are fine – the problem lies with the extensive new concrete dispersal, recently laid to accommodate the jets. In the arctic weather, it seems that the concrete has not yet 'gone off', and can't bear the weight of the fuel bowsers, let alone the heat of jet-wash.

Barkston can still be made available for limited numbers of Jet Provosts by making use of the half-dozen 'panhandle' dispersals of the taxiway but to allow the programme to commence, a good deal of flexing in the flying roster will be required. Until at least early February, the students will on occasion be required to move themselves and their flying-gear up and down Ermine Street. The good news is that Flying Wing staff aim to start getting 81 Entry into the air when the South Airfield opens up this week.

The Wing Commander, a forthright Canadian, then concludes the briefing with a few words of the wisdom he's gained over the years. The chaps remember them as being, 'For the first fifty hours of jet flying, you're likely to feel exhilarated. When you've got through the next five hundred, you'll probably reckon you know it all. Then you might chalk up another five thousand, realizing that you'll never, ever know it all.'

They are then advised never to forget that they're being trained to be front-line military pilots. Anyone who is not happy with that, should consider opting out now, before flying training starts.

Otherwise, they should bring their flying-gear with them on Thursday, making sure all's in order before stowing in the lockers.

With best wishes to all the new boys, the briefing ends.

**

A number of instructors are introduced. Not all on the Flying Wing's strength are present – they're still on leave – but it's clear that they're a mixture of officer and Master Pilot QFIs, many with last-war experience. A good number come from Barkston's Piston Provost operation and many of those are only just getting checked out on Hunting-Percival's new jet-powered machine.

The chaps agree that some of the instructors seem to reckon the JP's just a bit too easy to handle. Others say it's certainly vice-free but that makes for a stable platform and that's a very good thing. It results in less stress for

Hunting Percival Jet Provost T3s arrive at Cranwell. (*RAF College Journal*)

the student and allows fuller attention to the development of all-important airmanship skills.

***

The trainees' crew rooms are situated at the ends of the two squadron huts flanking the Wing HQ. In each, recently vacated by 80 Entry, there's a rudimentary coffee-bar, with chairs and three or four tables. Down the corridor are offices for the Squadron and Flight Commanders, together with instructors' crew room, briefing cubicles and locker rooms for flying gear.

The cadets are mightily pleased to find waiting for them in the crew rooms boxes of 'Flying Rations' – all the 'nutty' (chocolate bars and biscuits), coffee, sugar and evaporated milk they could wish for, and all free of charge. It's one of the perks offered to aircrew, the only snag being that the amount depends on hours flown. This first feast is there through the generosity of the instructors themselves.

In the afternoon, there are briefings on emergency drills and airmanship and for some, practice in the JP emergencies simulator.

There's a Martin-Baker Ejection Seat tethered-rig in the dead area behind the HQ hut – a half-power ride up a ramp. Mark and Sid take a look but decide against, having been advised that at their height, there's still the outside chance of compression injury to the spine.

For homework that evening, the chaps are tasked with reading through briefing papers on the workings of the fuel system. Fangio then whisks everyone back to College in the winter gloaming for a very welcome Officers' Mess tea.

The conversation on the back seat is subdued – the Wingco's words have given food for thought.

***

Come Tuesday morning, the mood's upbeat again as the pilot trainees heave into the bus their nav-bags crammed with pilot's notes, logbooks and now well-thumbed details of the fuel system.

There's a quiz on the fuel system, followed by an introduction to the hydraulics on the JP and a lecture on air traffic control disciplines at Barkston and Cranwell. Into the programme are fitted trips to the Tower, Met Office and Fire Section among the station buildings over on the southern edge of the airfield. Any spare time is filled with familiarisation with start-up, taxi and take-off checks. Thursday could see them being used.

***

For the first week of term, 81 Entry is staying with Flying Wing. The chaps spend the Wednesday morning at ground school work before moving to the sports fields for the afternoon. There's an evening session in the FGS, when attention's drawn to the new entry down in the South Brick Lines – No. 84, thirty-eight lads. 'Shall we go crowing?'

The vote's unanimous. 'No, we shan't. Let's get back to those take-off drills.'

***

Thursday 12th January 1961 is a red-letter day for some of 81 Entry's pilots. After five terms' long wait, flying training proper finally begins. 'A' and 'B' Squadrons march from West Wing, kitbags bulging with flying gear, down to the Flights in the hangars at Cranwell, while 'C' and 'D', having drawn their packed lunches from the Mess kitchens, muster outside East Wing for Fangio's Barkston bus. At both airfields, with flying-gear safely stowed away, they file into the main briefing-rooms for met and operational briefing – beginning to feel like real jet pilots.

Flight Lines at Barkston. (*RAF College*)

The Met Men forecast that the weather should stay fine for the whole day and the Ops Officers brief on any unusual activities planned, such as Royal Flights – there are none notified.

Before long, the Cranwell air is filled with the roar of jet engines. To the familiar howl of the Vampire's de Havilland Goblin and the throatier note of the Meteor's twin Rolls-Royce Derwents is added the ear-splitting blast of the Jet Provost's Armstrong Siddeley Viper.

The Basic Flying Wing Staff have made ready a dozen JPs, with the same number of instructors currently qualified. At both airfields they've set out a roster of sorties covering Exercises 1-4: Familiarisation with Aircraft; Preparations for and Actions after Flight; Air Experience; Effect of Controls.

By the afternoon, the lucky ones with their names on the Barkston Ops Room Chinagraph boards include Mark. He's down to fly at 1400 with his allocated instructor, Master Pilot Good, a man with considerable experience on all types, which is reassuring.

Out of his battle-dress jacket and into his flying-suit and boots, he mixes himself a cup of coffee, sits down in the functionally furnished crew room, and waits. He takes out his Pilot's Notes and tries to concentrate on running through the checks. That doesn't work so he picks up a copy of *Flight* magazine – and finds himself reading the same paragraph time and again. Mr Good comes in and tells him their flight's been delayed for an hour to 1500 – a bit close to the 1600 shut-down for comfort.

It's all a test of a bloke's patience. Not a bad thing, Mark supposes. Best get used to it. Like the fighter pilots in the Battle of Britain, waiting for the 'phone to ring – or those bomber crews in their Vulcans at Waddington, sitting at the end of the runway for hours to start World War Three.

Then, there's a shake of his shoulder. 'Wake up Mark, our JP's waiting.' Quick nervous pee (otherwise known as QNP), check of the pockets – Flight Reference Cards, Chinagraph pencil, sick bag, handkerchief. Grab chamois-leather flying gloves, helmet and oxygen mask, bone-dome. Okay – hot to trot!

On the walk over the grass to the panhandle dispersal and the aircraft, Mister Good runs through the mission objectives.

> You've not flown a jet before, have you? All Tiger Moth and Chipmunk so far? Thought so. Tiger some time ago, and Chippie just a couple of hours? Well the main difference is going to be the quiet – no noisy prop or engine up front so the noise is left behind for the good folk of Lincolnshire to enjoy. The second thing is the lack of propeller torque. You'll soon get used to both of those.
>
> In this trip, the aim is to get you a little more familiar with the aircraft, with wearing an oxygen mask and bone-dome, together with preparations for and action after flight. We'll make a start on showing you the effects of the flying controls. There, it's much the same as with a Tiger or a Chippie, but faster and higher, with the addition of airbrakes.

The shiny silver Jet Provost Mk. 3 stands ready – the crew chief tells the skipper she's been flown in from Cranwell just this morning. A socket under the nose is connected by cable to what looks like a bright yellow wheelbarrow – a Houchin power-pack. The red warning panels of a training aircraft glow on nose, rear fuselage, wingtips and tip-tanks. Mark notes the fleet number, 12, unmissable in black either side of the nose, alongside the cranes of the RAF College Arms. Around the rear fuselage is the distinctive RAF College blue-painted sash, but most evocative, behind the wings, are the red, white and blue roundels of the RAF – icons of British aviation history.

Mister Good conducts a tour of the aeroplane, pointing out the pitot head and air-intakes that should be uncovered and checking that everything, from the aerials to the ailerons, and the tyres to the tail pipe, is in good condition and ready for flight.

The cockpit is reached via a walkway at the rear of the wing-root, close to the fuselage, avoiding the flaps – pupil to port, instructor to starboard. Having checked that the ejection-seat and canopy-jettison safety pins are in position, it's into the cockpit – for Mark, a highly significant step.

JP3 cockpit from above… (*Hunting Aircraft Ltd*)

…and from right-hand side. (*Hunting Aircraft Ltd*)

Helmets on, they begin the strapping-in process. The harness business is designed to be quite straightforward, but it's a cramped cockpit with two up, and Mark can see it's going to take some practice to make it quick and slick. The instructor is patient.

The new, lanky student makes sure the adjustable seat is at the bottom of its travel and that the rudder pedals are at maximum reach. He plugs the intercom lead into its socket and connects the oxygen hose to the main supply. He's read all about it in the Flight Reference Cards but it's much more of a test, getting it all right for real.

On command from Mister Good, the ground-handler removes the safety-pins from the face-screen seat firing-handle and the canopy-jettison gun before showing them to the pilots and stowing them away in fixings on the cockpit walls. Student and instructor remove their individual seat-pan firing handle pins and they too are stowed. Then it's bone-domes on and time to close the canopy with the winding handle on the student's side of the cockpit wall.

Mister Good calls out the checks as he makes them, from 'Flap selector lever – Up', through 'Elevator trim – Neutral, Starting master switch – On', to 'Fuel cocks – Open'. With a thumbs-up to the ground-crewman it's, 'Press and release starter button'.

There's a whirring noise aft of the cockpit – the electric starter winding up the compressor and the turbine. At 10 per cent RPM on the gauge, the combustion chambers on the engine should light up – they do, with a deep-throated rumble that becomes a roar down the back, where the hot gases meet the air. The Viper, although originally designed for a pilotless target drone, has been developed to deliver 1,750lbs of thrust. 'Pretty good for a trainer,' says Mr Good.

He asks Mark to note the Jet Pipe Temperature gauge – it shouldn't exceed 750 degrees Centigrade. All goes well and, as the Viper's now generating their electrical power the handler's instructed to remove the external power supply. 'Chocks away!' and the JP's now ready to go.

'Follow me through on everything I do.'

Save for the fuel cocks and undercarriage selector on the central pedestal, most of the instruments and controls are dualled-up and with left hand lightly on throttle, and feet gently on rudder bar, Mark can feel the forward movement to ease the aircraft off the stops, the double toe pressure to check the brakes and then the further light touches left and right to steer the aircraft away. Mister Good calls the Control Tower for take-off clearance, and gets it before instructing Mark to 'Set flaps to Take-off, please'.

'Roger.'

Mark grasps the flap control-lever on his left-hand side and moves it down to the TAKE-OFF position, glancing back from the cockpit to confirm, 'Flaps set to take-off'. His first control movement in a JP! As the instructor lines the aircraft up on the centre-line with, 'Controls – Full and free movement', the pupil has his right hand lightly grasping the control column.

Calmly, and just loud enough to be heard, Mister Good has been talking Mark through all this. Now, he raises his voice a decibel or two as he pushes the throttle through to the stops. 'Fire warning light – Out, Wheelbrakes – Holding, RPM – 100 per cent, Jet Pipe Temp – below 725, Oil pressure – Okay. Let's go!'

Kick in the back from the jet engine behind. Tarmac rushing by at seventy miles-per-hour, smooth as you like. What a difference a nose-wheel makes – can see everything in front! Moments later, they're airborne. Up into the wide blue yonder - although a light mist's gathering as the JP soars away.

'Wheelbrakes – On momentarily, Undercarriage – Up, 100 feet and 100 knots, Flaps – Up.'

Quiet and smooth? Sure is. Comfortable? Good secure seat, all-round fishbowl visibility, instruments, switches and levers in easy reach – feels grand. Powerful? Just four minutes to 5,000 feet – can see for ever.

Up front, under helmet and bone-dome, the absence of noise is surreal. Still following through as Mr Good turns left and right, it seems that the control response is immediate.

Straight and level and it's, 'You have control.'

'Roger. I have control.'

'Keep her straight and keep her level.'

What a moment for the new boy. Absolutely bloody wonderful!

'Try a turn to port.'

No one out there to the left – stick over a bit, and a bit more. Round she goes – no torque, unlike the Tiger and Chippie.

'That's good. Straighten up. Now to starboard.'

Just the same.

'Now ease back on the stick – up goes the nose, down goes the speed. Now forward – down goes the nose, up goes the speed. Right-ho – level off – and move the throttle firmly forward.'

Mark notes the increased rumble from behind his seat as the engine burns more fuel and the revs increase – but the effect's not as instant as with a prop-driven aircraft and it takes a moment or two for the turbine to wind up to its new setting.

But now, the JP's really moving. Coming up to 300 knots, it's, 'Now, bring the throttle smoothly back.' Again, the delay in deceleration is noticeable – the JP continues to whistle along. But across the landscape, the light's beginning to dim.

'Time to go home. I have control. Airbrakes going out.'

Mister Good thumbs the airbrakes rocker switch on the throttle. Looking out, Mark notes the upper-wing gate sitting in the slipstream. Down she slides, smooth as you like. As Barkston's runways come into view, car headlights are beginning to appear on Ermine Street.

'Follow me through. Coming overhead on the dead side at fifteen-hundred feet – no other traffic – letting down to circuit height, one thousand feet. Turning downwind – airbrakes in – fuel, flaps, harness all as required – speed below one-fifty knots, undercarriage down please, Mark.'

Feeling immortal, he presses the button. There are three reassuring thumps from below and three greens light up on the instrument panel.

'Three greens.'

'Roger, Mark.'

This is going like clockwork – what a great partnership.

'Feet off the brakes,' cuts through Mark's thoughts. Whoops!

Mister Good brings the jet over the threshold at ninety knots and eases the machine down onto the main wheels. As the speed drops off, the nose-wheel sinks onto the runway.

Rolling down the freshly-laid tarmac, Mark hears, 'You have control.'

'I have control.'

'Bring the aircraft to a halt. That's it, gently on the brakes. Now, go forward and turn left onto the crosswind runway. Flaps up. We're going to take Number Twelve back to the Ermine Street gates, ready for her night's lodgings. She's staying here now.'

Control Tower at Barkston Heath. (*controltowers.co.uk*)

Over to starboard, can be seen the Barkston Control Tower, with its all-round glass viewing windows giving it a classic Second World War shape. The Signals Square shows the Barkston Heath airfield identifier, two large white letters, BA – 'Bravo Alpha' on the radio.

'That's it, nice and smooth – a little more power in the turn. Now, take her right the way down to the end.'

This is a moment to remember. He's never driven a car but here he is, driving a jet. Can those motorists on Ermine Street see us? Look, over here! A shiny Air Force aeroplane and I'm in control. How about that?

'Turn to port here on the taxiway.' Whoops again! Mark very nearly gives in to the urge to give a bootful of rudder to turn corners, as in Tiger and Chippie.

A minute or two more and it's, 'Parking brake – On, Throttle – Closed, Flaps – Take-off, Fuel – Off.' Everything winds down to silence. Mister Good locks the flying controls and ground-handlers surround the aircraft. With chocks in position, it's 'Parking brake – Off'.

Hood open and, with all safety pins inserted, oxygen hose and intercom lead disconnected, the pilots climb out of their harnesses and clamber back down to the ground. The ground-crew hitch Number 12 to a tractor for towing across Ermine Street to the hangar and Master Pilot and pupil walk back to the Ops Room in the rapidly-fading light.

'There we are Mark. What did you think of that?'

'Unreal. Half-an-hour out of this world. More please?'

'More it shall certainly be. When you've come down to earth a bit, find time to go through your Pilot's Notes and Flight Reference Cards to cement in your mind some of what we've just done. Looks like the bus has left already – like a lift back to the College?'

'Yes please, Mister Good.'

'Right you are, Mister Mark.'

The news back at College is that Dauntless Dave's had fifty outstanding minutes in his first JP flight. Robert's had three-quarters of an hour while Danny's had thirty-five minutes. Mark's had just thirty minutes but he tells them all about it, just the same.

Chris, disappointed to have missed out on flying today, has made the rounds. 'Just about half the squadrons have had their first JP flight today. They all seem greatly impressed, is all I can say. Heigh-ho. Roll on next time.'

***

But the weather gods aren't feeling helpful and on Friday 13th, azure skies are replaced by an occluded front, with thick rain cloud from 1,000 to 30,000 feet – not conditions for first experience flights. The chaps are bussed down to Barkston for more ground school work. Chris takes the opportunity to run over his checks with his instructor, Flight Lieutenant 'Red' Sankey, an experienced pilot with a background in the maritime anti-submarine Shackletons of Coastal Command.

As the back seat quartet meets for the teatime bus ride back to the College, Chris lets it be known that he's already written his diary entry for today: 'A useful and enjoyable day but disappointed not to fly. Interesting lectures at Barkston in afternoon.'

***

Alongside the start of pilot training for 81 Entry, January 1961 also sees the start of the Basic Course for the navigators. The two originals, Jim the Nav from Locking and his colleague from Lutterworth Grammar are joined by Anthony, a retread from 80 Entry. He's the same Anthony who was a mentor to 81 Entry back in the South Brick Lines, and a man from Hampshire with an unusual journey through his four years of service life to date:

> At Portsmouth Grammar I'd been a keen member of the RAF Section of the CCF, and had tried unsuccessfully for an RAF Scholarship at the age of sixteen. So when National Service loomed for me in 1956, I applied to Hornchurch – just going there would get me two weeks off my two years' commitment.
>
> There were forty others from a variety of backgrounds and after two weeks of selection procedures, just two of us were offered National Service Commissions. The other chap went to Canada for pilot training and I accepted the offer of a commission in the Secretarial Branch. I graduated from 104 OCTU Course at Jurby on the Isle of Man in June 1957, still eighteen years old.
>
> I was posted to Hemswell, a Bomber Command station just north of Lincoln, as Assistant Administration Officer, on a three-year Short Service Commission. I was the youngest in the Officers' Mess, a prime candidate for Mr Vice on Guest Nights. I decided that I should try for a career in the RAF and with help from my bosses, applied for Cranwell – I was still young enough, the age limit being twenty-and-a-half. At Daedalus House I was accepted, so I resigned my commission in January 1959, and started again – a crow on 80 Entry. I was

in 'C' Squadron and one of only two Secretarial Branch Flight Cadets on the course.

Eighteen months into my training, which included the Chartered Institute of Secretaries course, I too was becoming uncertain. By now, I'd spent time flying in both the Valetta and Varsity on rugby trips and I could see the attraction of a career in the General Duties Flying Branch.

So I consulted Pete Gilliatt, who, having confirmed that my Hornchurch aptitude results were still valid, put in an application for me to change to GD/Navigator. I learnt later that the Assistant Commandant had said to the staff something along the lines, 'If the man wants to fly, train him'.

In the autumn of 1960, Anthony was given a three-month intensive course (with much homework) in A-level Maths and Electronics with personal coaching by Wing Commander tutors to bring him up to speed. Now he's a member of 81 'D' Squadron, a mainstay at hooker in the College Rugby XV and clearly with high level support.

'With that determination and those connections,' asks Mark, 'how can you go wrong?'

'Don't know about that. I've really struggled with thermodynamics in the "A" Stream – the first few lessons I was completely at sea, but I'm now beginning to understand what it's all about.

'That said, I've always been fascinated with maps and navigation, right from those flights with the CCF. I should have made this move earlier – but then I'd not have had the pleasure of being among the intellectuals of 81 Entry!'

As with the pilots, the navigators' course contains a considerable ground school element, including classroom-based plotting exercises. 'Flying's not expected to start until mid-February. After all these months working up to it, I'm prepared to wait.'

***

After the excitements of the first week back, the entire entry is brought down to earth with the Saturday morning Drill Parade. Many minds are elsewhere and Chris is just one of those who's told, 'You – are idle! Watch it!' In the afternoon, Chris restores his equilibrium in the Olympia, with loops and spinning. 'Good for the soul.'

That parade's a rehearsal for a Ceremonial Church Parade scheduled for the next morning, at which the Queen's Colour is handed over from

'A' Squadron takes over the Queen's Colour. (*RAF College Journal*)

'C' to 'A' Squadron. In the afternoon, Chris again resorts to the North Airfield, where he's checked out for 'mutuals'. He can now take other Flight Cadets and Servicemen up with him, to experience the delights of gliding.

***

On Monday 16th January, the normal weekly timetable for 81 Entry resumes, with flying in the morning. Today, Chris is on the roster at Cranwell.

'After breakfast, we quick-march down to Flights, where we sit in eager anticipation. One by one, the others get off, but I don't – aircraft unserviceable.'

Chris is doing his best to manage his impatience. He whiles away the time skimming through a forty-page, foolscap-size stencilled document that's just been circulated throughout the College. Issued over an Introduction from the Assistant Commandant, dated January 1961, it's entitled, 'NOTES FOR THE GUIDANCE OF FLIGHT CADETS'. It's evidently been prepared 'in response to the many requests from cadets at Cranwell for an aide-memoire to help them in meeting their social responsibilities at the College and later as junior officers'. It's a challenging read – broad in scope and dense in detail.

The very first Section, 'The Requirements of an Officer', opens with a quotation from Confucius: 'When you see a good man, try to emulate him; when you see a bad man, search for his fault'. That sets the high-flown tone, and the section continues with: 'Officer Qualities cannot be defined as one quality or attribute and it is not necessarily something with which you are born. Nor can it just be assumed'. The qualities required are professional competence, concern for personal appearance, clarity of speech and conformance to a code of behaviour. The last of these is then explored at some length. Dress, both civilian and service, rules of and conduct in the Officers' Mess, through to saluting, and behaviour towards NCOs and airmen – it's all there. The Assistant Commandant believes 'there is no one who cannot learn something from these notes'.

Red Sankey appears with the welcome news that a JP's available and Chris's reading is cut short. His evening diary entry says it all: 'Short briefing from Red, and a very pleasant fifty-minute familiarisation flight with him, including a few aeros'. His JP flying is off and running at last, as is Andy's who reckons, 'The JP seems relatively easy to fly compared with a piston-engine trainer and the side-by-side seating makes the instruction process easier.'

A few sorties are scheduled for the afternoon of Tuesday 17th, but the day is mostly academics. The chaps are restless, they're Jet Jockeys now. But then come three days of solid fog – in pilots' parlance, it's 'black flag' weather, from the days when such a banner would fly on the signals square to signify 'No Flying'.

The entry's old chum from the Cairngorms, Chunky, now a JP instructor on 2 Squadron, takes the opportunity to give a lecture on 'The Aerodynamics of Spinning'. Having thoroughly confused almost everyone with the technical stuff, he grabs his audience's attention with, 'Having lost a considerable amount of height in the spin and seeing the ground coming up, you will need to pull a lot of G to recover – certainly enough to make your piles tingle!' Most of the chaps have only a vague idea of what piles might be exactly, but Kiwi's songs have given them a pretty good indication.

***

This is the week when for the 'A' Stream Maths Set, focus on flying is diverted by the need to spend two days down in Melton Mowbray school sitting the A-level exam. They've been given clearance to miss the 19th January Guest Night in order to revise, but they've been hard-pressed to concentrate. When the next day they're bussed to Melton, fog and black flag at Cranwell and Barkston mean at least no one's missing any flying today.

The paper's tough but spirits are high on adrenalin. A return to College for ceremonial kit work for the Saturday Assistant Commandant's Parade soon brings them back to earth. The fog turns to heavy rain, causing the parade to be moved inside the Drill Hangar. Boots sliding on stone floors, Quick and Slow Marches running out of room, Advance in Review Order squeezed at both ends – it's chaotic, and almost fun. But for most of the 81 Entry tyro pilots, nothing now beats flying.

There are always exceptions to every rule, however, and on the Monday morning, one 'A' Squadron chap from Llanelly Grammar Technical School, decides to approach Flight Lieutenant Moffat, requesting release from the course. He's a popular chap and his 'Chop Party' in the FGS, is well attended.

It's on the Monday evening, following a swimming competition for this term's Knocker Cup contest. Perhaps it's the relief of that being over, or maybe the flying adrenalin is running high off the scale but the party gets out of hand – so much so that on the Tuesday morning, the FGS is declared out of bounds to 81 Entry for two weeks.

The same day, the 'A' Streamers are back in Melton Mowbray for a further three-hour Maths paper – and this week, two Economics essays have to be handed in.

At the weekend, Chris and his colleagues drive into Lincoln, and Mark's invited to join them. It's made perfectly clear to him that 'it's not all plain sailing in the 'A' Stream'.

Chris also discloses that he's seen in his father's logbook that he flew a dual check on a Flying Officer Knocker in a Bristol Fighter in India in the 1920s, so it was probably the same chap. Drinks all round, and a toast to Flying Officer Knocker.

***

The month of January winds down to the end with bull (Assistant Commandant's Inspection every Wednesday at 1030 hours) drill, and intermittent flying (both affected by bad weather – wind, rain and on occasion both at once) with the ever-present background grind of academics. But the good news is that the new concrete of the dispersal at Barkston has finally gone off and the airfield's fully serviceable.

Thus, for light relief in the Lincolnshire murk, a clandestine poker school is inaugurated down at the satellite. For further escapism, there's always the weekend evening films in the Longcroft Room. Tom and Gerry cartoons are always popular, as are the documentaries – albeit the one on the final Sunday of the month tells the horrifying story of the Second World War concentration camps.

However, on the thirty-first the weather relents. David ensures that the month ends in triumph – he's the first in the entry to go solo on the JP. He's made it in under nine hours and says he owes it all to his instructor, Jack Jennings. Fortunately, the FGS comes on limits just in time and the carousing is loud and long.

This same evening, Dauntless Dave runs out of luck. Returning as one of two car passengers from Nottingham, where they'd been visiting girlfriends, his 80 Entry driver falls asleep and the vehicle runs full-tilt into a parked car. The driver, together with Dave and the other passenger end up in hospital to 'get stitched up', and on the first day in February, all three are incarcerated in Cranwell Station's Sick Quarters.

Dave's had nine trips with Mr Jackson and all's been going well – they've progressed to stalling and he's made his first approach and landing. The entry wishes him a speedy recovery.

***

Kraut welcomes February by being sent solo after the almost unbelievably short time of six hours, forty-five minutes. Adrian soon brings that down to a round six. Chris flies again, doing 'climbing and descending turns and stalling, also a spin which was faster than I expected. The first time I have spun in a jet'.

Tony is right up there with those going solo early and is enthralled with the whole flying experience. 'Love it. Can't get enough. I'm making flying my focus – low-level and head down with everything else. Not going to let the AFRAeS stuff stop me getting my Wings.'

The flying programme for all types is further disrupted by an outbreak of Asian 'flu, which results in a shortage of QFIs. A certain amount of shuffling's needed and Mark is brought up short when he finds that, after six sorties, totalling just four hours, he's having a change of instructor. For experienced Master Pilot Good, read first tourist out of Central Flying School, (CFS). However, Flying Officer 'Kipper' Kemball's a chap who's easy to get along with and he has local connections. He knows all the landmarks and helps Mark with the pronunciation of villages and towns. 'The City of Ely, is not to be pronounced as "Eli" – that's the chap in the Bible!' The changeover is hugely assisted by the allocation of five trips in three days – a piece of rare continuity that gets him into take-offs, stalls and landings, together with ten minutes instrument flying (I/F), by his twenty-first birthday.

That falls on the day before a handy Guest Night, when the occasion can be properly celebrated. The guests are a collection of headmasters, to whom the College is selling its credentials. What they think of the usual high jinks in the anterooms can only be guessed at.

The following day, during a cloudy and windy afternoon, the final flight of JPs is flown over from Cranwell to Barkston and Chris wangles a ride as passenger. 'We were four aircraft in formation as we flew over Cranwell and Barkston. Then three broke off, including mine, and had a bit of a dogfight. Good fun.'

That shows the advantage of having a jet-powered basic trainer – up through the murk and into the clear in no time. The wide blue yonder for stalls, spins and aerobatics.

That ferrying flight brings the establishment of JPs at Barkston up to its allocated twenty aircraft. The intended order is thus achieved.

***

Alongside pub crawls and rowdy twenty-first birthday celebrations, which are now coming thick and fast, sport continues to provide a much needed contrast to drill, academics and flying.

On Friday February 10th, squash player Andy, together with Mark and Vernon in the Hockey XI, Sid and Jim in the basketball team, and Kiwi, Peter and 'D' Squadron's Tim in the fencing squad, make their first visit to the Britannia Royal Naval College at Dartmouth.

They are impressed, right from the moment of arrival. The train from London runs along the wooded east bank of the river and there, on the further bank and dominating the scene, stands the Naval College – high on a bluff above the River Dart, a mile or two from the estuary and the English Channel.

At Kingswear station, two smart Midshipman Cadets are waiting, to lead them to the waterside and a ferry that's to carry them all across the river. Landfall is at a wharf which, their guides say, goes by the name of 'Sandquay'. Already moored are two immaculate forty-foot naval launches and on the shore stands a wide, white clapboard building, two-storeyed, with a distinctive green roof. Emblazoned across the front is 'Royal Navy Maritime Training Centre'. As they step ashore, the hosts welcome their guests 'aboard HMS *Britannia*'.

It's still a fair way to the College, through a picket gate and up a considerable flight of steps – 187 of them, they're told. From the top, the Dart estuary spreads out below while in front of them rise three storeys of red-brick, topped by a slate roof. Although even wider than the Cranwell

College façade, the two buildings are remarkably similar – tower at the west end, another at the east, and in the middle, a taller one with rotating beacon and four clock faces.

Sid remarks, 'You can see where Trenchard got the idea from.'

A Lieutenant Commander welcomes the Cranwell party before handing each of them a round box of fifty, full-strength, non-tipped cigarettes – the original 'coffin nails'. It seems that military visitors are entitled to the same privileges as the Dartmouth fellows while on board ship.

Inside, those who have not been here before, gawp at the magnificence of the décor and fittings. Built in 1903, when Britain ruled the waves, no expense appears to have been spared on its interior decoration. In the evening, the Cranwell chaps find themselves sitting at mahogany tables for a Guest Night, alongside panelled walls and below the magnificent, gold-painted timber of an arched roof.

Kiwi comments, 'We're sitting in an upturned man-o'-war.'

The ritual of the evening is much the same as at Cranwell, save that the loyal toast is made sitting down, as in the low-ceilinged wardrooms of all Navy ships. The band in the minstrels' gallery, which stretches from side to side across the full width of the place, plays a selection of tunes and marches. In recognition of their guests, they strike up the *Dambusters' March*.

The evening gives a chance to learn about the way of life for a Dartmouth Cadet. It turns out (not surprisingly, Trenchard again) that they are much the same as at Cranwell. It's razor haircuts for all, there are first-term mentors (known as 'Sea Daddies'), and a year's breaking down with drill, studies and absence of privileges. In the second year, Seamanship is taught down on the river and in the Channel in all types of small boats, including the picket boats moored at Sandquay. Cadets are here for just two years (they go to sea for another) and they have a town nearby. Dartmouth is a resort town, full, they say, of fascinating pubs, together with equally fascinating ladies.

After dinner, a group of midshipmen offer to escort the guests into town to see for themselves. Before long, there's a group of very happy RAF fledgling aviators in the warm embrace of a nautically-themed pub. Girls are smiling and sailors are singing – a special song for the Boys in Blue:

> They say in the Air Force, a landing's OK
> If the pilot gets up and can still walk away
> But in the Fleet Air Arm, the prospects are dim
> If the landing's piss poor – and the pilot can't swim.

As usual, Kiwi brings the house down with the *haka* and monologues – the girls are very good-humoured about it all. It's great fun and Sid confesses, 'I'll say it now and I expect I'll say it again – the best bits of Cranwell are definitely the extra-mural bits.'

The next morning, it's a bleary-eyed gaggle of Flight Cadets that totters down the 187 steps to Sandquay for a refreshing sea trip, out on the picket boats. There's a bit of a chop in the estuary and a creative session of high-speed cruising, in close formation, leaves not a few of the Cranwell contingent turning green. On the return, one of the helmsmen manages to crash his boat into the jetty – in front of the College Captain (an Admiral) too. That brings the colour back to Flight Cadet faces.

Strangely, there's been no sign of their hosts of the night before. There's no sign of them either on the fencing mat, hockey pitch or basketball court. The opposing teams are all fresh faces, allied to fit minds and bodies.

'It's an old trick, but it sometimes works,' observes Kiwi. He's a canny customer and has sensibly held back on the booze the night before as well as this lunchtime, and he wins his bouts, handsomely. Not so Mark and his mates. At the hockey pavilion there's a NAAFI bar serving Newcastle Brown Ale, and he and his team lose, decisively.

Sid's basketball match is so close as to be deemed by him almost a triumph. To celebrate, they overdo the carousing at the 'Floating Bridge Inn' and contrive to miss the last train to London. Sheepishly, they have to clamber back up the 187 steps to beg a 'cabin' for the night.

A veil shall be drawn over the exploits of Sid and his basketball chums' extra night in Dartmouth town but it can be said that, for all, the visit to the sister college on the Dart has gone with a bang.

***

On the train to Paddington, Mark falls into conversation with the 'D' Squadron fencer, Tim, whom he's scarcely met before. Their academic sets, sports and social activities at College just haven't overlapped and even in an entry numbering no more than fifty-three (just this month a further man has left of his own free will) that can mean invisibility.

Tim, ex-public-school boy from Lancashire, was to the forefront in the 'B' Squadron snowman team a year ago. Now, he's made his way into the team that's put the sailors to the sword.

What route did he take to Cranwell?

My father had been an RAF pilot since 1936 – flew Demons in Egypt. After flying Hurricanes in the Battle of Britain, he converted to Wellingtons, operating over France and Germany. Then he found himself caught up in the Burma Campaign, where, after his squadron had converted to Liberators, he became its OC and earned a DSO for gallantry under fire. It's been my Wing Commander father's example that's inspired me to try for Wings in the RAF.

I went the CCF, Hornchurch, Daedalus route. Despite getting involved in a bit of a hooley on the first evening at Hornchurch, I managed all right in the Officer Selection exercise. I took my father's advice and made up for my relative lack of inches by indulging in a bit of what they called 'vocal leadership' – got me noticed, served me well.

I'm all right with everything at Cranwell so far. I'm very proud to have taken that oath on our first day – something special, a contract with the Monarch.

Tim says he won an RAF Scholarship, which funded one-third of his school fees in the sixth form. At A-level, he studied History, French, German and Additional Maths, with passes in History and AS in French. In case this did not qualify him, he sat, and passed, the Civil Service Entry exam in Manchester.

Mark's puzzled, for despite those academic achievements, Tim's a faithful member of a job-lot of students in the 'A' Stream.

It suits me fine. We swan around somewhat but we still do Maths, Electronics, Aero and Thermodynamics, Radio and Radar, as well as Military History. Fills in the gaps in my education. The majority of the tutors are competent – National Servicemen, not concerned with RAF careers, non-pompous.

Oh, and I've added Russian Studies to the mix.

But none of that's going to divert me from the flying. My instructor says he'll be sending me solo this month – weather permitting, as always.

First solo – Exercise Fourteen in the logbook – same number it was when my father did it in 'thirty-six.

Mark's impressed. 'This fellow's got the balance right. Fencing – socially up near the top. Academic subjects – right in line with what an RAF pilot and officer needs. And Russian? Right in the Cold War slot. Now, he's up to snuff with the flying.

He's to be envied for his focus – relevant studies and Wings.

***

The clock tower bells ring reveille and Mark has to shake off any lingering dreams of Dartmouth exploits, sharpish. It's Monday 13th February, and the bus awaits.

The chaps like going down to Barkston. The journey's a chance to see a few miles of the outside world, together with, if lucky, a glimpse of girls in Ancaster. They enjoy the more relaxed atmosphere down at the satellite airbase, as well as its hutted last-war ambiance and the feeling of comradeship in the crew rooms.

This morning, Danny's waxing more than usually poetical on the bus. 'Look, look! The daffs are up – there'll be hosts of them soon, you'll see! And over there! Lambs – gambolling. Yippee!'

***

In the Ops Room, Mark is intrigued to see that Kipper has him slated for a run of two trips, both concentrating entirely on take-off and climb, approach and landing. That sets his pulse racing – others have told him that such a sequence usually signals the approach of a major milestone for trainee pilots, the First Solo.

He draws a deep breath. Now then – it might very well be the prelude to a chop-ride. Whichever, he makes a hasty trip to the gents before grabbing flying suit, boots, and kit from his locker, ready to meet Kipper in the briefing room.

The Met man, who comes round the airfield from his cubbyhole below the Control Tower to brief the pilots, says that the weather's holding fine for the whole day. 'Right,' says Kipper, 'Let's get those cockpit drills and start-up checks up to speed before polishing up your circuit patterns. We're in Number 24 today. Off you go and start the external checks.'

Mark strides out to the brand-new concrete dispersal for the first time. It's big all right – room for two lines of Jet Provosts, facing each other, two dozen in all. There's a concrete line hut on the northern edge, surrounded by a swarm of ground-crew in working overalls.

Number 24's at the top of the nearest line – that makes it the longest walk.

Time to concentrate. The aircraft's on an even keel – nothing wrong with the tyres. Plenty of room around it and a clear run to the taxiway. Up close –

all looks as it should, nothing hanging off or leaking out. No dents or cracks anywhere. Good look at the UHF aerial, pointing down under the belly – always at risk from a low-flying Dan Dare. Kipper's at the line hut, signing the Form 700 that gives him 'ownership' of the aircraft for this sortie and Mark waits until he arrives up at Number 24.

'Aircraft checked and ready for flight, Sir.'

The flight comprises forty-five minutes in the circuit, time enough for half-a-dozen roller landings and one full stop. Mark does them all. That time with Sally and the checklists was well-spent on getting the basics. Now in his seventh hour of doing it for real, he's beginning to remember his lines. From pre-take-off (Trim, Airbrakes, Fuel, Instruments, Oxygen, Hood, Harness, Hydraulics – easily remembered with TAFFIO-HHH) through to downwind for landing (Airbrakes, Undercarriage, Fuel, Flaps, Harness and Wheelbrakes – AUFFHW) they're beginning to become second nature.

At the debriefing, Kipper has just the one adverse criticism. 'Your lookout's not good enough. Remember, a danger seen is usually a danger averted. Keep that head swivelling. Avoid locking your eyes inside the cockpit. But you've got the knack of landing a tricycle undercarriage all right. Well done. See you in an hour. Same again.'

It's the longest hour of Mark's life. Kipper hasn't mentioned solo yet but he has praised his landings. That's key. There's half-a-dozen chaps who are having trouble with judging heights already, all facing chop-rides before the mid-term break if they don't hack it soon. He manages a cup of strong coffee and a nervous drag, before meeting Kipper at Number 24.

The same care is taken with the external check – it's been up again since their first trip and you never know… All is well, and right on schedule they're soaring away from Runway Two Four. Except they're not, not yet.

At 800 feet, Kipper closes the throttle. Mark knows the drill – practice engine failure after take-off. He pushes the stick forward to maintain speed and delivers the necessary patter: 'Speed below one sixty knots, land straight ahead if clear space available. No space available, speed above ninety knots, eject in level flight.'

'That should do it. Climb out on north, Mark.'

He does so, climbing at 1,000 feet a minute, head and eyes consciously swivelling, while his instructor changes from Local to Approach frequency on the UHF radio, for clearance to leave the airfield's controlled airspace. At 10,000 feet, well in the clear, Kipper says, 'Time for some stalling practice. Carry out the checks.'

The mnemonic for these is easily remembered – HASELL. Height (sufficient for recovery), Airframe (flaps and undercarriage as required, airbrakes test and in), Security (canopy closed, harnesses tight), Engine (temps and pressures within limits, fuel sufficient), Location (clear of controlled airspace and people), Lookout (for other aircraft, especially below, and clear of cloud).

'Take the aircraft into a stall, straight ahead, throttle closed.'

'Roger.'

He closes the throttle, while maintaining height. The speed rapidly falls away and an increasing amount of backward movement of the control column is needed to maintain altitude. It's not long before the tell-tale shudder in airframe and stick tells the pilot that the stall's imminent. Now, all lift is lost, the aircraft's dropping like a stone, but under directional control.

From the right-hand seat, 'Recover!'

Stick firmly and centrally forward, rudder bar neutral – don't want to flip over into a spin – pick up speed, throttle fully open and climb away. More swivelling – so far so good.

'Same again, this time with take-off flap.'

Similar recovery, this time with lifting up flap on the climb away, making sure it's before 150 knots.

'That went well. And now, with take-off flap and undercarriage down.'

A further look around and speed back to 150 knots before lowering flap and wheels. Recovery the same, although slower with the extra drag.

That's taken forty minutes and it's been hard work. Kipper takes control and does a max-rate descent back to the circuit while Mark takes a breather – remembering to swivel.

On the dead-side, control is handed back for Mark to join the circuit and land. Parked on the dispersal, with engine still running, the instructor then says the words that all student pilots hope to hear.

'Right, Mark. Here's where I get off. She's all yours. One take-off, one circuit and just the one landing, please. Okay?'

'Roger, Sir!'

Canopy open, Kipper inserts his ejector seat-pan pin, unstraps, stands up and inserts the top pin. He finally fastens the seat harness tight and, with a thumbs-up, leaves the aircraft.

A corporal, bearing clipboard, appears by Mark's shoulder and offers a Form 700 to sign. Now the twenty-one-year old with fewer than a dozen hours on type, has full responsibility for one of Her Majesty's shiny new jet trainers. Out of the corner of his eye, he sees Kipper jumping in a

Land Rover – off to the Tower to cross his fingers and watch? He draws breath, winds the canopy closed and checks RPM, temperatures, pressures and flaps, before pressing the transmit button on the throttle and calling the Tower:

'Romeo Alpha – Taxi.'

From Tower: 'Romeo Alpha – Clear taxi. Runway Two Four left, QFE 1012 surface wind 230/12 knots.'

Mark knows from ground school and air work that setting the altimeter with air-pressure level code-named QFE has the instrument showing height above touch-down point on the airfield, so he'll fly the downwind leg at 1,000 feet. This is a brand-new procedure, across the RAF. Previously QHN has been used, which sets the altimeter to show altitude above Mean Sea Level so that 81 Entry's first circuits have been flown at Barkston with the altimeter downwind reading 1,350 feet. All done for a good purpose – to show height above ground, but a puzzler for a new chap.

He dials up 1012 on the altimeter, checks his way is clear and waves away the ground-crewman. Then it's parking brake off, and off we go. The dispersal behind, the taxiways go past as if in a dream.

Wake up! Pre-take-off checks! TAFFIO-HHH before calling the Tower again:

'Romeo Alpha – Take off to remain in circuit.'

'Romeo Alpha – Clear take-off, surface wind 230/12 knots, one aircraft turning downwind.'

The moment has come. Line up, toe-brakes fully on, throttle fully open, warning lights out. 100 per cent power, JPT in limits. Brakes off!

The aircraft surges forwards. At 90 knots, Mark lifts the JP into the air. He touches the toe-brakes to stop the wheels spinning and brings the undercarriage up with three satisfying clunks.

110 knots, flaps up. All lights still out. JPT steady.

He climbs steadily ahead and careful to keep on the lookout, spots the other JP on the downwind leg. He's all clear to turn cross-wind to port.

Imagining things, or is she more responsive with only one bloke in the cockpit? Stop wondering and swivel – one joining over on the dead side. Okay, turning downwind – circuit height – throttle back to 85 per cent.

He calls the Tower: 'Romeo Alpha – Downwind – Full-Stop.'

In response: 'Romeo Alpha – Continue – One ahead on finals to roll.'

Downwind checks – AUFFHW, paying particular attention to the 'U'.

Three clunks – three bloody lovely green lights. Keep swivelling – where's that joiner? There he is – well clear.

End of downwind leg, take a good look at end of runway passing abeam and assess when to turn finals.

On the turn, and beginning to descend on base leg, call the Tower: 'Romeo Alpha – Finals – Three Greens.'

'Romeo Alpha – Clear land.'

Turning crosswind, sixty-five per cent RPM then full flap for landing. Nose tipping down, clearing line of vision.

Whoops! Overcooked turn a bit. Right aileron, slide back onto glide path. Runway clear ahead. Aiming just beyond runway threshold – height falling away nicely. Deathly quiet – miss the putter of the Tiger's prop. Concentrate, you fool! Ease back on the stick – power coming off – main wheels settling gently onto the ground. Rumble, rumble – nose-wheel down.

He lets the JP run along the tarmac, testing toe-brakes and bringing her gently to walking pace before turning off the runway with the call, 'Romeo Alpha – Clear complete'.

He stops to carry out the after-landing checks, then shouts at the top of his voice, 'Yes! Made it!'

Elated as never before, Mark again invites the passing motorists on Ermine Street to take a look at him, the world-famous Jet Jockey – who's just gone solo!

Having taxied to the dispersal, shut down the engine and everything else, put in the seat and canopy jettison pins and shaken the ground-handler's hand (resisting the urge to hug), he strides over to Ops to debrief with Kipper.

He's gone solo after just nine hours on type – just about par for the course.

***

Meanwhile, the formal basic-training course for the 81 Entry navigators has got under way, with just theoretical classroom work so far. As well as covering basic 'dead reckoning' techniques and the use of the Dalton computer and other navigation aids, the trainees have been introduced to the mysteries of magnetism and compasses (particularly the GIVB compass), maps and charts, time in all its navigational roles, aircraft instruments and the very basics of astronomical navigation ('astro').

But Wednesday 15th February sees the start of their Valetta and Varsity training flights (the three Valetta Model T and six Varsity T1s now operating out of Cranwell's South Airfield) and the navs are pleased to be able to tell the pilots all about it in the FGS.

'At last,' says Jim, 'we're getting to put the theoretical stuff into practice – not before time. Hands-on navigation and making good track.'

Anthony notes, 'Today's sortie in the Varsity turned out to be basically a map-reading exercise but we were also introduced to GEE, the radar-based position-finder of Bomber Command in the last war. In fact, we've been told that the navigation kit in the Varsity has much in common with the Lancaster's.'

It seems the only fly in the navigators' ointment is that they've no idea when their next flight might be.

***

The same might be said for Mark and many of his fellow academic students. On the day after going solo, he and the others in the French Studies set are on the afternoon train to London, where the following day, in the luxurious surroundings of Waterloo Place, they're to take the oral tests for Civil Service Linguist Certificates. They manage better than the tyro Russian speakers. Despite too much time being spent in the Captain's Cabin, David, Jock and Mark are among those who get their certificates.

An additional bonus is that while Mark's in London, he's able to pick up a copy of *Lady Chatterley's Lover* from Foyles. The book had sold over 200,000 copies on the first day of its release – it had been banned since 1928 – so he's the possessor of a story that's not only much in demand but also a sign of the fast-changing mores of British society.

Before catching the last train to Grantham, there's time for another coffee with Sally. He proudly shows her his Foyles purchase, asking her if she'd like to borrow it. 'No thanks,' she says. 'I've already read it.'

Collapse of stout party.

***

At Barkston, Sid, Peter and Andy go solo on the same day as Mark, but Chris doesn't. He's getting concerned – might he even miss out this side of the mid-term break, just ten days hence?

On Thursday 16th February, no fewer than five of the entry's other pilots go solo. These include Jock, Nigel and John, who reports to his 'B' Squadron colleagues, 'I didn't miss the instructor a bit. After all, we always repeat the checks out loud. Same on this trip. Didn't expect anyone to answer, that's all.'

The same day, Chris records 'a boring afternoon soldering joints in the Radio class – for two long hours'. The next day, fog leaves him 'nearly berserk with frustration'. Over the weekend, the weather is, of course cussedly fine. That means the Assistant Commandant's ceremonial parade finally goes ahead and after that, Chris and his friends can at least go gliding. But when Monday dawns with thick fog, there is much grinding of teeth.

There's hope when there's a sudden clearance in the afternoon, but the fog's lifted into low cloud. At least Red Sankey is able to get Chris up for a couple of circuits, before climbing up through the cloud for some extra-curricular aeros. But any hopes of going solo are dashed.

The fog continues until the end of the week, Friday 24th February, when the mid-term break begins at midday. 'That's it,' groans a disconsolate Chris. 'Going solo has to wait until March – thanks to Trenchard putting his Air Academy right in the middle of soggy Lincs!'

Mid-Term Break, Spring 1961

It's a short break, but Mark has to go home. It's only eight days since his milestone birthday and his mum's laying on a family celebration.

After hitching an exciting ride with Brawn down the Great North Road to London, he falls among thieves at the Railway Arms in his home town and arrives late to greet a roomful of relations. His defence, that the A1 was slow, quite rightly gets short shrift from his long-suffering mother and he's roundly harangued by aunts.

The high-flying Jet Jockey, now nominally an adult, is reduced to the pathetic young scamp that much of him still is. No one's impressed that he's mastered a jet-plane, well before most have learned to drive a motor car.

He's consoled by the thought that it should at least give him a great line to spin with Sally. But it turns out she's passed her driving test and is the proud owner of a drophead Model E Ford Coupé.

Trumped!

***

The break takes the rugby and fencing teams on a promising biennial four-day sporting excursion to the French version of Cranwell, l'Ecole de l'Air. Established in 1933 at the air-base of Salon-de-Provence, some forty kilometres north-west of Marseille, it's one of the top trips for College sportsmen.

Anthony, Mac and Michael are in the rugby team and Tim, Peter and Kiwi among the swordsmen. On Thursday 23rd February, they board aircraft of the RAF College's own airline – one Varsity and two Valettas of the Navigation Flight – for the four-hour, eardrum-pounding flight to Provence.

Anthony remembers the visit of two years ago, when he was a junior in 80 Entry:

> There were obvious differences in culture and approach to training but what I most clearly recall was what I suspected was a French ploy to deprive us of sleep before the matches. We had to queue up to collect straw palliasses to take to our stone-floored and spartan dormitory.
>
> All the matches were played out with the utmost enthusiasm and energy.

This time, although more comfortable, the accommodation is still very basic. Everything else cannot be faulted.

Again, the reporter is Anthony:

> The rugby matches were hard-fought. The playing of the National Anthems set the tone – our National Anthem majestic and solid, the Marseillaise stirring and flamboyant. We felt we were not just playing another team, we were playing the nation.
>
> Despite it being on a pitch dried out by the Mistral, we won the match. However, it was what followed that'll stick in my memory. We might have been foes on the pitch, but the already firm camaraderie between the Brits and the French was cemented at the Vin d'Honneur after the match. We then all set off, hosts and guests together, for a night out in the clubs of Marseilles – memorable for some but for one or two, perhaps better forgotten.

Tim continues:

> We lost the fencing match but the night in Marseille sampling the local wines and sea food made up for that. We were introduced to some of the hospitable local ladies. They rather fetchingly donned our service hats and marched us up and down the harbour wall – under the baleful eyes of the gendarmerie.

Our half-French fencing instructor got well and truly hammered with his French College counterpart before we were all discreetly seen home by the afore-mentioned gendarmes.

Anthony concludes:

A measure of our exhaustion after a whirlwind weekend is that on the flight home, we managed to catch up on our sleep – in a Super-Pig, for goodness sake!

Chapter 8

Airborne Highs and Lows

Second-half Term 5: 28th Feb-7th Apr 1961

Term 5 has just five weeks to run, during which there are questions to be answered. Dave's out of Sick Quarters – four weeks off flying, so how will he do? Chris is praying for some solo-friendly skies and half-a-dozen are fearfully awaiting the call for a chop-ride with Flight or Squadron Commanders. Will they make it through to Easter?

Dave's straight back into the air – forty minutes doing the collection of pre-solo exercises, but with a new instructor. Some do go solo in the morning but they include neither Dave nor Chris – the latter's down on the programme to fly in the afternoon, which is just when the gods decide to chuck sleet and snow down from the heavens.

The following day however, from the windows of Fangio's bus, the weather looks more promising, as a petulant Mark unloads his feelings to a patient Danny.

'Within the last month, I've logged eight trips, six hours dual and fifteen minutes solo. In the same time, I've spent three days at Dartmouth getting drunk, two in London speaking bad French and four days braving the aunts on a not terribly easy half-term. Then there's been the little matter of twenty hours a week in the classroom.

'I've worked it out – I've spent more time on the hockey field this month than in the air. It's been fifteen days since that first solo and no flying since. Well, we'll see what happens today – but it wouldn't be allowed at an FTS, where as I understand it, the minimum aimed for is twenty hours a month.'

In the event, the weather on the final day of the month allows three to go solo. Mark also flies – two forty-five-minute trips with Kipper which do little more than remind him what circuits, stalling and I/F are all about.

It's no secret that Welshman Frank, the lad from Tredegar, is having difficulty. He's clocked up fourteen hours so far, without going solo – but he's still aloft.

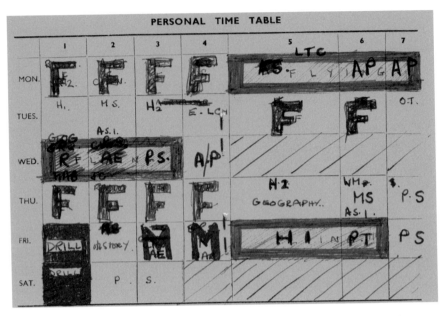

'C' Stream member's Personal Timetable, Spring Term, 1961. (*RO'B*)

Vernon however, has taken a ride with his Squadron Commander. Sadly, the flight shows that he's never going to be able to judge the distance between ground and cockpit and for his and everyone's safety, he's chopped. There's a macabre 'Chop Party' in the King's Arms and on the first day of March, he becomes the first 'Chop Pilot' to join Jim and his chums in the navigator group.

***

On the evening of the next day, 1st March, Chris is writing home, and enjoying it:

> The weather was unpromising this morning but we managed three dual circuits and I was, at last, sent off for a solo sortie. As I taxied out, I had my doubts whether I'd get off in time. The weather was closing in – would I be recalled?
>
> I radioed for take-off clearance as soon as I could and didn't hang around in getting airborne – a thrilling moment, the cockpit of a JP all my own at last.
>
> As I climbed away I heard on the radio the chap just behind me and one or two others in the queue being instructed to taxi back to the dispersal. I'd had my take-off clearance just in time!

As it was, I entered intermittent cloud at 800 feet. I found my way round, landed and taxied in, pleased as Punch.

Just a bit of I/F on first solo, how about that? I'd gone solo in a jet, at last. To celebrate, I got in two solo glider trips this afternoon. Super day.

The same day, after plenty of help and encouragement from his mates, Welshman Frank also flies round the circuit alone. Just as those milestone first solos are being chalked up, War Studies reach the heroic exploits of the RAF in its 'Finest Hour'.

As the skies darkened over Europe, cadet life was already changing as part of the modernising and re-equipping of the RAF itself, in preparation for possible war. The academic syllabus was being critically examined by His Majesty's Inspectors of Schools, to bring it more in line with future operational needs, and an Advanced Training Squadron was being established to bring the cadets up to the same standard as Service Flying Schools.

Cadets entering the College in the January and April intakes of 1939 had very little more than a concentrated flying training course. On the outbreak of war at the beginning of September, 931 of its graduates were on the active list, the graduation of 1,100 Officer Cadets having been achieved since February 1920.

The College closed while RAF Cranwell morphed into a Service Flying Training School for the duration. Research and experimentation in the RAF Cranwell Technical Wing continued throughout the war and on 15th May 1941, the world's first jet-powered flight took place from the South Airfield.

Enemy action had limited impact. German bombers launched several attacks on the College and RAF Cranwell but only succeeded in breaking one roof tile and cratering surrounding fields. The only damage inflicted on the College building was when the Whitley bomber plunged through the roof.

Peace and the College's first twenty-five years were both celebrated on 13th June 1945 in the presence of HM King George VI. By that time, RAF Fighter Command, re-equipped just in time with Hurricane and Spitfire monoplane fighters, had in 1940 triumphed in the Battle of Britain. Of the eighty-seven RAF College graduates who fought in that conflict, twenty-five lost their lives. Fighter Command also, by keeping the worst of the Luftwaffe at bay, made possible the evacuation at Dunkirk. By June 1944, Bomber Command had learned how to pound the German industrial areas with more ordnance in a day than had been dropped on London during the Blitz and Rommel was complaining that all roads up to 100 kilometres from the D-Day front were open to attack from the RAF.

Passing Out Parade at RAF Cranwell wartime Flying Training School.
(*RAF College Journal*)

Maiden flight of Gloster E28 at Cranwell, 15 May 1941.
(*RAF College Journal*)

The RAF had won enormous respect as well as an enduring place in the Nation's hearts. Those successes had come at a heavy cost, one shared by Old Cranwellians, of whom 430 had lost their lives in the conflict, a wastage rate of 46%. College graduates won a total of 600 medals, including one Victoria Cross, two George Crosses, eighty-two Distinguished Service Orders and 269 Distinguished Flying Crosses

For the two years 1958 and 1959, MRAF Dermot Boyle was to become CAS, the first Cranwell cadet to rise to that post. He made a very public statement that he was first purely because of the number of ex-cadets who had perished in service in the Second World War.

A significant effect on the RAF and subsequently the RAF College when it reopened in October 1946, was the democratisation of its ranks. In 1940 the RAFVR's reservists, recruited from many walks of life and racial origins, provided a quarter of the fighter pilots in the Battle of Britain. When the Lancaster bomber arrived, crewed by pilots, navigators, gunners, wireless operators and flight engineers, it was inevitable that more ground-staff would take to the skies. At the same time, at the peak of its wartime numbers, one-sixth were in the Women's Auxiliary Air Force (WAAF) and 400 of the overall headcount comprised West Indians.

At war's end, the elements were in place for a hierarchy based on merit rather than social standing. Might that influence the input, ethos and output of its Officer College?

For the first week of March 1961, Lincolnshire is allowed the luxury of a high-pressure area – lovely weather for flying and good numbers continue to go solo. On the sixth, it's the turn of Robert, who after his first dozen hours at the controls of an aircraft (he's one of the few not to have enjoyed a Flying Scholarship) has successfully flown on his own. As has Tim:

> The event has happened after just eleven hours instruction spread over two months. The problem is that just three half-days per week are allocated for flying, and if the weather isn't good enough, that's that. The syllabus doesn't allow any flexibility – the officer and brain training must go on.
>
> But finally, at the end of a morning of more circuits, my instructor climbs out and tells me the aircraft's all mine.

Off I go, keeping rigidly to the speeds and heights we've
been practising and make a perfectly reasonable landing.
Whoopee! What a great feeling of joy and achievement!

***

The Ferris drill competition is now not much more than a week away.
Practices begin – at a challenging 0600 hours, and back for more in
the evening – before the competition takes place on Saturday morning
11th March.

It's judged by a formidable team of Drill Sergeants and Officers from
Sandhurst. The man in charge is a tall and imposing Guards captain with
a droll sense of humour. He publicly asserts that the drill's been among
the best he and his colleagues have seen, even at Sandhurst. He awards
the 'Best Turned-out on Parade' prize to Dauntless Dave – obviously fully
recovered from his stitching-up and so pleased and proud that he slips his
batman a fiver in gratitude.

His smile broadens still further when a few days later, he flies off on
his own. Doggedly, he's made it through a car crash, weeks in hospital,
and a change of instructor and has joined the ranks of the Jet Jockeys.
'At last – we're getting somewhere,' is his low-key remark at his
First Solo party.

***

On Wednesday 15th March, the navigator group is off to London – to
the Planetarium. It's billed as 'background study to position-finding
astronomical exercises'. The travelling party numbers four, the two 81 Entry
originals, plus Anthony and another from 80 Entry, Johnny the Nav, who,
having fallen behind in his course, joined the group at the mid-term break.
Vernon stays in the College, for some one-to-one tuition.

Neither of the new joiners has missed much airborne practice – since
that map-reading exercise in the Varsity a month ago, there have been just
the two three-hour trips, now in the Valetta. Jim for one is concerned about
the gap between them, remarking, 'Not surprisingly, getting up to speed
with what's going on at the start of each flight has taken a fair bit of time,
limiting the training value. Still, it's early days.'

***

Now that they're in sole occupation of Barkston, the 'C' and 'D' pilots have
gained permission to decorate their crew rooms. At weekends, teams of

Flight Cadets can be observed motoring round the Lincs hinterland begging contributions of bamboo poles from carpet shops – the aim being to create a trendy coffee-bar ambiance.

There are changes of instructor. Postings continue, including that of Chris's Red Sankey back to Coastal Command – he is replaced by a Flying Officer from a Meteor squadron in Germany. There are other reasons. Bill, for example, had a first instructor for whom giving praise seemed to be anathema. Bill has survived but now, as the man had started saying, 'I don't think you're going to make it', Bill, as is his right, has asked for a change, and he's got it. 'The new chap's accentuating the positive and it's all going better already.'

Although perfectly happy with Kipper Kemball, Mark's having some difficulty remaining fully conscious during aerobatics.

'You're a tall chap, and when pulling 'G', your heart doesn't quite manage to pump enough blood all the way from heart to head. That's when you black out.'

Mark knows that's serious. Blacking out is something a jet pilot just should not do.

Kipper has obviously sought advice and as a result, Mark's allocated a trip with Master Pilot Good who proceeds to show him a few tricks that a tall lad can use to minimise the effects of centrifugal force.

'Let's show you a loop. We go into the dive, building up speed. Just before we pull up, tense those stomach muscles. That's it! Pulling up…

'If that's not enough, tighten your jaw muscles. As a last resort, crouch forward to reduce head-to-heart distance – if you like, scream through clenched teeth. Well done!

'Round the top and down the other side – keep it going. Pulling through at the bottom – that worked. Let's do another one.'

Into a loop. (*RAF College Journal*)

From now on, Kipper and the other instructors know that when they say to Mark, 'Right, show me your aero sequence', they're to expect in the left-hand seat, a bloke who crouches, grunts and screams. He's not raving mad, just keeping the black-outs at bay.

***

Instrument flying gets properly underway. The trick with that seems to be to concentrate all the senses onto the instrument panel and what you are trying to do, which is to keep the aeroplane on the intended course, at the right speed and at the selected height, without reference to outside horizon. Mark finds that that drives all other distractions from the mind.

That doesn't mean, however, that from time to time there won't be an attack of the dreaded 'leans' – a conscious feeling of turning upside down or sideways. Then, sticking to the instruments is even more the thing to do.

Ability with and experience of I/F are must-haves for flying solo away from base. As the end of term approaches, most have acquired all other necessary ticks in the right boxes.

Spinning: a stall that turns into a stalled corkscrew. Recovery: stick forward, ailerons neutral, full opposite rudder (counter-intuitively, against the spin), then stick fully forward until the spin stops. Centralise controls, recover from the ensuing dive, before powered climb away, checking instruments inside and clearances outside.

Forced landing after engine failure: if no fire, search for a runway for a 'dead-stick' landing – final resort, eject.

Low flying: only in low-flying area, not below 250 feet when dual, navigate with reference to canals and Boston Stump's truncated church steeple – and, it's suggested, if this isn't found to be an absolute buzz, it's time to look for another profession.

On Thursday 23rd March, a 'C' Squadron man does just that. A cultured sort of fellow, from Cranbrook School, hands in his flying and other kit, before leaving the College at his own request. The original 'C' Squadron entry is down from eighteen to fourteen, albeit one of the leavers has gone to 'D' Squadron.

***

The days roll by, with the usual mix of activities. In the workshops, the 'A' Stream's radios are completed, and to the surprise of many, they work. There's a spate of War Studies seminars – students presenting in teams of three. There's a (voluntary) evening debate – attended by just twenty out of 300 Flight Cadets and hence not very inspiring.

Other evening activities range from essay writing to squash. The BBC Northern Orchestra arrives to give a concert – and certain tone-deaf Flight Cadets sneak out at the interval and go down the pub.

Cadets are put on charges and cadets do Strikers, with the inconvenience of uniformed roll-calls morning, noon and night.

Right out of the blue, many in the College fall ill with food poisoning but it doesn't stop the visit of sportsmen from Sandhurst on 17th/18th March, when the post-Guest Night dinner high-jinks turn almost suicidal. Air Force versus Army – all's fair in that war.

***

Two weeks before the end of term, the tension rises at the airfields. It's known that this is 'flak alley' for the flying chop. For those safely through first solo, every other trip is solo, mostly forty-five minutes in the circuit, following a fifteen-minute dual check. But there are increasing amounts of dual I/F, plus map-reading pilot navigation, first dual and then solo. The route most often flown is triangular – Boston Stump, Spalding, and back over the RAF bomber station at Cottesmore, which gives the tyros practice in radio work with an operational Control Tower.

From time to time during March, congestion at Cranwell (where as well as 81 Entry, 79 and 80 are still operating) necessitates 'A' and 'B' Squadron tyros joining the 'Barkston Flyers'. John makes two trips from there the subject of a letter home:

> I've been allowed to go off by myself around the local area. 'Be back in forty-five minutes,' they say. Great fun. I went to Newark, Nottingham, Leicester and back. Later in the day I went east, to Boston and Spalding but the afternoon haze drove me back early.
>
> I flew west until I hit the A1 and turned right. At altitude, I could soon see Barkston's runways but when I'd spiralled down to circuit-joining height, 2,400 feet, the airfield had disappeared in the murk. Tried twice more, no luck. So I press the transmit button on Barkston's frequency and call, 'Bravo Mike – Request steer.'
>
> Back comes, 'Bravo Mike - Steer 020', so I do. Sure enough, pretty soon there's the airfield in front of me. Good circuit and, if I say so myself, the best landing I've done yet.

For the majority then, it's so far, so good – but it's well-known that 'A' Squadron's Pete is having trouble with landings. Others have had that and pulled through – perhaps he'll hack it.

Into the mix is thrown a demanding couple of days in the ceremonial area. The Assistant Commandant's Parade on Saturday 25th is in preparation for a visit on Monday from the Secretary of State for Air in Harold Macmillan's Tory government, the Right Hon. Julian Amery. There's a full Queen's Colour parade, with Vampire formation fly-past, followed by lunch – the latter, with speeches, lasting two long hours.

The Minister's comprehensive address includes much food for thought – it certainly makes Mark consider his position vis-à-vis the V-Force. The Secretary of State asserts, and he of all people should know, 'There can be no adequate defence, in the sense of stopping the enemy getting through, against the hydrogen bomb.' He goes on to say, 'You can only deter nuclear attack if you have the power not to stop it but to hit back, and to deal unacceptable devastation on the aggressor.'

He insists that its few hundred V-bomber aircrews are the elite of the RAF, standing between this country and the threat of nuclear war. He supposes there can be no finer mission for any young man in the country than to be part of that force.

The luncheon over, the Minister tours the station before planting a tree. Mark carefully considers what he's going to say Sally when next he meets her and her CND chums.

***

The very next day, flying flak alley claims the final victims of Term Five. First is the ex-navigator James, who ends up on the runway at Barkston with the undercarriage retracted. This proves a complicated situation. There's very little obvious damage to the aircraft, there was a QFI on board and the talk is that there are technical concerns with JP undercarriages. James is to remain in a state of limbo for a few days but is back in the Navigation Section before the end of March. There's a warm welcome from the staff on his return.

The chop from flying of 'Mitzi' (an inevitable nickname as his surname's Gaynor) is a shock for all. He's doing well in all other departments and has just earned his colours on the College shooting team. He's a Lancastrian, from the Royal Grammar School, and must have scored heavily in the 'potential' box at Daedalus House. But he's another of those who, even after thirty hours of trying, just cannot consistently establish where the ground is. He too, joins the navigators.

***

Friday 31st March is Good Friday. There's no flying – 82 Entry get a lecture from Wingco Green on the new flying syllabus they'll be starting next term, while the 'A' Stream of 81 are busy revising for a three-hour Mathematics exam on Tuesday.

Saturday sees morning drill in the drizzle. Then in the afternoon, in the inter-squadron athletics, Chris is cheered on to a new College record time in the 120 yards Hurdles – his 15.5 seconds beating the previous one by 0.2 of a second.

It is too wet for the planned Easter Sunday ceremonial parade and in the afternoon, a car rally is also much bedevilled by the rain. At least one car is reported crashed and many others find themselves lost.

On Easter Monday, flying resumes, with a holiday programme of dual spinning (starting from 18,000 feet), stalls, steep turns and aerobatics. Later, in the Longcroft Room there's the first of two evening performances of the *Pirates of Penzance*. The Journal reporter acclaims it as 'spirited' and enjoys the gusto brought to the role of Pirate King by Jim the Nav, in long black wig and kinky boots.

Black flag weather dogs the remainder of the week and the student pilots at Barkston put the finishing touches to their coffee bars. Danny invents a special brew in which coffee powder and evaporated milk (the only kind available), together with sugar to taste, is mixed vigorously with a spoon – 'Ockle, ockle, ockle' to the ear. The adding of hot water generates froth to rival any high-street Espresso bar. Henceforth, this speciality is advertised on the 'C' Squadron crew room wall as 'Froffee Coffee – 6d a cup'. It's much in demand among students and instructors alike and is a feature of the crew room parties which round off the term.

On the bus back to College, the back seat group have something to say about progress to date. They are conscious of the fact that all previous entries, have completed their airborne tuition at the College, and graduated fully qualified before going on to an Operational Conversion Unit (OCU) for training on first-tour squadron aircraft.

That won't apply to them. By their graduation, they'll have spent many more hours on the drill square and in academics than in the air, and they'll not have reached the advanced stage. Nine whole terms, and they'll still not know whether they can cope with advanced flying.

All this to fit in with an experiment in academics. But they're through the first term of basic flying, and that's good.

***

The three tyro navigators who started the term together also have mixed feelings about their first months of airborne training.

Jim reports, 'We've flown just seven sorties, all some three hours or more. The routes span much of the UK and the North Sea – one's been map-reading, two general plotting and four which concentrated on using GEE. We've alternated between first and second nav – when first nav, up front with the instructor, we navigate the aircraft while the other two monitor progress with the aid of GEE. It's a start.'

Anthony adds, 'Our pilots, a couple of whom are Polish, are very experienced at flying the set routes and know where they're going. They can be relied upon for the odd helpful hint if so inclined.'

There's a shock for the group on the day before the end of term. Jim's fellow nav from the start is chopped for 'Lack of Officer Qualities' (OQs).

That leaves the navigating group five-strong – two with only three months under their belts and three chopped pilots on a crash-course to catch them up. 'That,' reckons Jim, 'must be a real facer for the training staff.'

The mix leads to an unequal allotment of first nav slots in an effort to bring the newcomers up to speed – he and Anthony have no choice but to grit their teeth and bear it.

***

The 'A' Stream Maths exam results are published – not bad at all. There's just the one who didn't reach the pass mark and he plans to do better next time.

The day is completed with a wet-weather rehearsal for the Commandant's Parade on the morrow, and a final burst of ceremonial – presentation of squadron Prizes in the Lecture Hall, and photographs on the College steps, before a final Guest Night. Chris notes in his diary: 'Good guest night. I leave after jousting, at midnight, but the car racing round the Orange goes on long after.'

On Friday 7th April, the rain relents for a full-ceremonial Commandant's Parade, and at midday, the Flight Cadets go their ways, rejoicing.

***

Mark takes the train down south with Ross, from 81 'A' Squadron. He's a 'C' Streamer from Cornwall and Mark's getting to know him well from the

French set and the hockey team. He turns the conversation to the state of play for the entry.

'We're well past the halfway point now – four terms to go. All through first solo and well set for a summer of flying. Could we dare to think that it might be all downhill from here?'

Ross's reply is thoughtful. 'I've a feeling we'll be lucky if it is. It's this clash between academics and flying that's the problem. Flying instructors and tutors vying for our attention. I'm sure that's what's behind Vernon's change to navigator.'

'You could be right,' says Mark. 'And how about these long breaks between flights? It'll be May before we get back into a JP. Wouldn't happen at an FTS.'

Ross gets to his feet. 'Let's go down to the restaurant car for char and a smoke.'

Before they reach King's Cross, they've taken a week or two off their lives, seeing off too many of Ross's full-strength gaspers – unfiltered *Gitanes*.

Easter Leave 1961

It's to be a busy vacation. Adventurous Flight Cadets are to enjoy College Society-sponsored expeditions to both the heat of Africa and the arctic chill of Norway.

81 Entry's Danny and Peter are straight off with four cadets from 82 Entry plus two escorting officers to spend four weeks on Operation 'Noah's Ark', aimed at saving wildlife from floods created by the Kariba Dam project.

Ten days into the leave, Phil, Kiwi, Mac and Jock take off with a couple of College Land Rovers to the scenes of Jock's boyhood in Kenya, for a 'photographic expedition'.

There's no international jolly for the Geography students of 'C' Stream, unless a storm-tossed flight in a Pig over the Irish Sea to RAF Jurby on the Isle of Man counts as overseas. Their BA syllabus requires Vernon, Brawn, Robert and Ross, to spend the first week of leave on a Field Trip to the Isle of Man. Mac elects to miss out, having been persuaded to join Kiwi in Kenya.

Brawn then joins Mitzi in a party of six for a week's mountaineering on the Isle of Skye while Sid, Nigel, Hugh, Anthony and Blind Bill, led by Flight

Lieutenant Phil Oakley, take another College Land Rover on a demanding jaunt to Tynset. Deep into the heart of the Norwegian mountains, the journey involves two nights on the MV *Braemar*, from Newcastle to Oslo, before a four-hour drive to Lillehammer and a further six hours to Tynset. After two weeks in the local area, mountaineering and practising arctic survival techniques, they plan to reverse the journey to arrive back just in time for the Summer Term.

In the final week, the Russian students are to report to RAF Tangmere in Sussex for oral practice while the remaining chaps still in the UK, together with Flight Commanders, are scheduled for either four days at the Joint Anti-Submarine School (JASS) at the border town of Londonderry, on the shores of Lough Foyle, or for a visit to the Royal Navy, at Portsmouth Command.

***

Mark spends a fair amount of the Easter leave in earnest conversation with Sally and her London chums, discussing matters of moment on the world's stage.

Jack Kennedy, elected President of the United States on January 20th, in just his third month in office authorises a CIA-managed incursion of the new USSR-sponsored Cuban Republic. Launched on 17th April at the Bay of Pigs on the south coast of the island, the intended invasion sees some 1,400 paramilitaries (mostly expatriate Cuban counter-revolutionaries trained by the CIA) overwhelmed within three days by the Cuban Army (personally led by the Cuban President, Fidel Castro). It is an unmitigated disaster which achieves nothing except a strengthening of Cuban ties with the Soviet Union and a weakening of President Kennedy's authority.

Mark, as a War Studies man and trainee Air Force cold-war warrior, is expected to have answers to all the questions posed by Sally's pacifist pals, as well as acting as counsel for the defence of Britain's nuclear stance. He remembers Mr Amery's convincing words but not helping matters is the loss in air-crashes in the States of not just one, but two USAF B-52 Stratofortress bombers in this year so far, both with a pair of nuclear weapons on board. The counsel for the defence has a tough time of it and is pleased to be taking the Grantham Express northwards on Monday 24th April, to join the group bound for Northern Ireland.

***

The following day, a two-hour flight in the Navigation Pigs delivers the College party, seventeen-strong, to RAF Ballykelly, three-quarters of an hour by bus along the seashore road to Londonderry, where the JASS is situated on the Naval Base. A wet afternoon and evening is spent in town, where the visitors find a few friendly pubs but not much more.

Wednesday is spent under instruction at JASS in the complicated arts of submarine hunting before Thursday offers lifelike demos of simulated action. Memorable for some is the Northern Irish-accented repetition by the presenter of a particular line of attack, on a bearing of 'tew, tew, tew degrees trew'. There's also an interesting film, giving an introduction to the new, noisy and reportedly dangerous beasts on the flight-line – helicopters.

There's a dance that evening – an invitation from the charming nurses at a local hospital and a highly entertaining occasion for all.

Friday 28th brings a ninety-minute flight in the Coastal Command Shackletons, on sub-hunting exercise. Four noisy piston engines, low-level flying – it's everything any Biggles fan could wish for. Chris, who drops a dummy depth-charge bang on target, is one who finds the idea of a tour in Coastal Command quite appealing and Mark's another.

The Saturday dawns foggy – a chance to be stuck here for a weekend with the nurses? No such luck. By the afternoon, the fog lifts enough for the Pigs to transport everyone back to the wastes of Lincolnshire. Also back

Shackleton of RAF Coastal Command. (*CGW*)

Bang on target. (*FM*)

at Cranwell are the seafarers, reporting that with the Navy in Portsmouth they not only learnt about plans for atomic defence but also visited Nelson's *Victory* and spent a day at sea on a state-of-the-art destroyer.

Back in his College room, Mark settles down in peace and quiet with his Pilot's Notes. No flying in April at all – he hopes he'll remember what it's all about.

Chapter 9

The Pace Quickens

Term 6: 3rd May-1st Aug 1961

On Monday 1st May, all 81 Entry trainee pilots duly squeeze into the Officers' Mess for another of those epic breakfasts and then take the bus down to Barkston for a couple of extra days' flying before the start of Term Six. In this, they are joined by 82 Entry, whose airborne part of the training now starts.

The talk on the back seat is about Easter Vacation adventures – in Norway and by the Zambezi. Robert tells of a bonus thrill on the Isle of Man. At night, in a hired Mini on the switchback Tourist Trophy circuit, approaching a bridge on a sharp bend, all the car's lights failed at once. Brawn, who was at the wheel, says, 'From the memory of a brief glimpse, I managed to navigate the turn at speed and brake to a standstill – up the hill on the other side of the stream. Astonishment and relief all round!'

***

Mark has an hour dual, with Master Pilot Good – evidently Kipper Kemball's fallen foul of the 'flu. It turns out that's just as well – he has every need of Mister Good's anti-black-out drills and understanding.

To get his pupil back into the feel of flying, as well as carrying out the compulsory pre-solo checks, the instructor's planned the sortie around steep turns and spinning, with a couple of loops thrown in for good measure. The 'crouch' approach works fine on the loops but incipient nausea signals are felt and on the pull-out from the first spin, other forces take over and Mark's Officers' Mess breakfast is in the bag.

Mister Good is a wise and experienced man. He gets his pupil straight back onto the horse. 'You have control. On instruments, call up Approach Control for a Controlled Descent Through Cloud.'

He recalls doing one of these CDTCs a month ago. Now, how did it go?

The UHF radio is set to Barkston Approach so he thumbs the Press to Transmit button on the end of the throttle grip. 'Romeo Alpha, request steer for base and QDH.' He's remembered the Q-code for a CDTC because he's written it, with others, on his flying-suit's Chinagraph knee-pad.

There's no radar at Barkston but his call comes up as a spike on the Tower's cathode-ray tube, giving bearing and distance from base. Using the reciprocal, with an allowance for known winds, the Controller comes back with a compass heading to steer for base, at a stated height and speed. Once overhead, he's given a course to steer outbound at thirty degrees from the runway reciprocal, descending, at specified RPM and 170 knots with airbrakes out, into a known safe area. He's next instructed to make a Rate-1 turn onto a given compass bearing for return to the airfield. Repeated calls allow the controller to pass advisory altitudes at the distances flown. Once below cloud, and with airfield in sight, he switches the UHF to Barkston Local and carries out a circling approach to line up with the runway in use.

Mister Good's pleased, as is Mark. Back in the old routine and, with his mind tightly focused on the job, stomach all in order.

***

In the afternoon, the fickle May weather deteriorates into hailstorms and the chaps spend time planning for navigation flights scheduled for tomorrow.

At day's end, it turns out that Mark's not the only one to have had difficulty getting back into flying after the lay-off. Andy's forgotten to put his wheels down before landing. He's got away with it – the alert corporal in the runway caravan fired off a red light and he initiated the overshoot. Again, it's been a long time since he last flew. 'That's the trouble with these long, university-like vacations,' he says. 'Wouldn't happen at an FTS!'

Chris is lucky with the weather the next day and gets in a dual navigation trip, to Newmarket and return via Boston, followed by two solo sorties of forty minutes each, specifically for aeros and spinning – no queasiness for this chap!

Mark has to wait until the following week before he gets in the air again. The day after term starts he finds himself appointed deputy to the Escorting Officer on a day-trip back to London for 'C' Stream members. There's an afternoon lecture to be given at the London School of Economics (the notoriously bolshie LSE) on 'Allied-American Co-operation in World War II', and the train timetables allow the College party to make it there and back fairly comfortably.

Airborne again, he finds that a similar mix of circuits, spinning and (slightly crouching) aeros, seems to work – no mists, no nausea. He's with Kipper this time and has a full half-hour of I/F thrown in, ten minutes of it in actual cloud. He's reassured – an end-of-hols lapse, that's all.

The very next day, the weather's good enough for two sorties, both hour-long cross-countries, the first dual and the second solo.

This is the real biz! Taking a jet plane all by himself, finding his way down to Cambridge, and back again via Boston, at 5,000 feet. Leaving the Cranwell Air Traffic Control Area, staging through a couple of RAF stations' approach frequencies and with plenty of swivelling to make sure he doesn't get fixated on the map. On the final leg, he even has a go at one of the Aussie Flight Louie's mental formulas, and it works!

For this, Mark will make sure he gets on top of the black-outs.

***

This is the term when 81 is the entry responsible for organising the Graduation Ball of the chaps two above them in the pecking order, No. 79. To get things going, on the first Friday evening of term, the Chairman (OC 'B' Squadron) calls the eight Flight Cadet members of the Ball Committee to a meeting.

John is appointed Secretary, David and Jock have the key area of decoration and Mark is allocated Food and Wine. It becomes obvious that the Ball-organising job has been done many, many times before. Lighting, interior and exterior both, will be in the capable hands of the College and Station electricians. Invitation cards are standard, as are the arrangements for accommodating partners overnight in the Junior Mess – with a 'matron' in attendance. The chairman has this already in hand as he has the matter of the bands. The College Band in the main Dining Hall will be supplemented by a smaller 'informal band, of the Ray Ellington type' in an extended anteroom. The Chairman has already written to one agency and is awaiting a reply.

It seems that the main responsibility of the committee members is to split the entry into hit squads for the various artisan duties, mainly the décor, along with the grunt work of clearing rooms beforehand. Mark gets an important action assigned – to enquire whether oysters are in season in August. 'Hugh will know,' he says.

He gets a chance to speak to Hugh the next day, when Danny's buying drinks in the FGS – his beloved Tottenham Hotspur having done the Football Association League and Cup Double for the first time this century.

The answer is that oysters are not in season until September. Other shellfish however, are safe and the Food and Wine Member reckons he might be able to win the committee over to the newly-fashionable prawn cocktail.

***

The following Monday, there's a piece of really good news – with immediate effect, and for the whole of the RAF, there's to be no more stamping at drill.

It seems that the Air Ministry medics have discovered that the physical impact of the Army-style way of coming to a halt, making turns and marking time is doing the RAF's bones no good at all. In a non-physical combat Service, why do it? Drill Sergeants, even dyed-in-the-wool stampers like Bogbrush, are required to instruct in the new method, which involves sliding the raised foot alongside the grounded one with a smart scrape. Well, well – who ever would have thought it?

The weather remains fair and there's a good run of sorties for all, with increasing amounts of I/F and the added buzz of practice forced landings. For those, the drills for a jet aircraft are quite different from those required for a propeller-driven one. There is not the same positive control of speed and angle of descent that comes from the prop. With the latter, there's instant throttle response and that, combined with the drag effect of a windmilling circular disc up front, give a pilot a chance to bring off a 'dead-stick' landing at a pre-decided point in a chosen field. Many have known the thrill of side-slipping a Tiger Moth down onto the grass, straightening up and sliding her in on three points.

There's none of that with a Jet Provost. There's a lag between throttle movement and engine response – a turbine has far more inertia than a prop. The safest thing for the pilot to do if he loses his engine at low level is not to look for a field but point the aeroplane at an uninhabited area and eject. It is, after all, doing at least a hundred knots or so – try sliding that safely into the turnips!

The Jet Provost is not the worst of gliders. From 20,000 feet, at 120 knots she'll cover twenty-five nautical miles before passing 4,000 feet, circuit-joining height. So if you lost your engine over the North Sea coast, you could make it back to Barkston or Cranwell – your choice. But doing all that is a big slice of a training sortie, so what's taught is a throttled-back practice landing on the airfield in use.

From 4,000 feet over the landing area, you aim to arrive on the down-wind leg opposite the runway threshold. From there, it's undercarriage down, and use flaps – in extremis, airbrakes – to get in. It requires a cool head and good judgment of distance, rate-of-descent and above all, height.

It may be demanding, but fun too – and a triumph when those main wheels kiss the tarmac in approximately the right place.

***

Two weeks into the term, the Knocker Cup is won by 'A' Squadron. Three weeks in, there's a Guest Night and to entertain the diners after the port, the Nordic adventurers have put together an enthralling slideshow of the grandeur of the *fjells* and *fjords*.

Phil, Jock and their fellow safari chums follow that with a ciné film of Land Rovers speeding over hot and dusty Kenyan bush to the rolling soundtrack of Sibelius's *Karelia Suite*. They go on to show how their photographic expedition turned into a mission to rescue rhinoceros from poachers in the Tsavo National Park.

Afterwards, in the anteroom, Jock entertains with an account of his twenty-first birthday celebrations back in the country of his birth, while Danny and Peter regale their colleagues with colourful exploits at the Kariba Lake. The Geography students, grinding their teeth in silent rage, tell of the discomforts of RAF Jurby and their hard labour in the peatbogs of the Isle of Man.

***

Pete soon has the expected meeting with the OC Flying Wing, who tells him, 'We might be able to teach you to fly to the standard required, but certainly not in the time that we've got left.'

The Navigation Staff agree to accept him but on condition that he leaves the 'C' Stream for the 'A', to free his mind for navigator training. Back goes the Anglo-Saxon primer to the Library and Pete transfers to the Navigator Branch before the month's end – with a good deal of catching up to do.

Instrument-flying proves something of a challenge for many. Michael, for instance, finds he has difficulty in working out which way is up, whether in cloud or under the blind-flying hood (a canvas affair that sits on the bone-dome and restricts the student's view to just the instrument panel). At the Guest Night, he confides in John:

> It's a worry. Flying's the make or break factor at this place and just this one bit of difficulty, disorientation, could deal me out of the game. I reckon it could be down to lack of sleep – all this 'C' Stream business of late-night cramming of Anglo-Saxon irregular verbs.
>
> I'm going to make my own luck here. I'll get myself reallocated, like Pete. A flying career beats the hell out of getting a tin-pot general degree. I'll see about it first thing tomorrow.

193

This he does and with his usual low-key determination, gets his way. He joins Pete in the 'A' Stream and works on getting both Jet Provost and his career back on the straight and level.

***

The fear of the dreaded 'flying chop' is thus in the air again. For some, there's the buzz of a Wednesday two-hour bus ride down the A1 for cricket, tennis and rowing against Henlow Technical College to take their minds off the subject but with everyone coming up to the forty-hour mark and a Flight Commander's check due, it's a sweaty couple of weeks.

As he walks out for the check flight on the morning of Friday 26th May with Flight Lieutenant I'Anson (now appointed OC 'D' Flight) Mark tries to tell himself that he couldn't care one way or the other if he passes – after all, he's still young enough for university. But it doesn't work. He'd be failing himself if he got the chop. And what would he say to his mum, not to mention Sally and all the cricketing chums back in the Thames Valley?

Chunky must surely know about his problem with G? It has to be in the instructors' reports. Best to be open about it. All goes smoothly with start-up, taxiing and take-off, and he responds correctly to the simulated engine failure after take-off – above ninety knots, eject! He then faultlessly takes the JP (with plenty of swivelling) above 10,000 feet, where he hears, 'OK Mark, show me your aeros'.

'Roger, Sir,' and he does just that.

It's HASELL checks, before into the dive, into the crouch, stick back, pulling G, up into a loop – no problem. Over the top and down the other side, back into crouch, pull through to straight and level. Hitting own dirty air – good loop.

Still in crouch, pull up to vertical. Out of crouch, speed dropping off, stick central, full left boot – stall-turn. Going back down the way we came in. Not bad.

Pointing at ground, stick forward, gaining speed in the dive, into crouch, full throttle, pulling up into another loop. One-and-a-half slow rolls off the top, now right way up. Barrel roll to finish.

Climb with full power in slow turn back to 10,000 feet, checking sky clear and no warning lights in cockpit.

'That's all good, now show me a spin to starboard.'

'Roger, Sir.'

Climb further, to 18,000 feet, minimum for spinning the JP. HASELL check – no cloud or aircraft below. Close throttle while maintaining altitude and keeping straight. Stick coming progressively back all the way. Judder of stick, point of stall, full right rudder and hold stick fully back. Over she goes, and down she spirals. Altimeter unwinds. Rudder-pedals judder. Two turns – three thousand feet lost.

'Recover!'

'Roger, Sir!'

Full left rudder – two second pause – stick central and eased firmly half-forward – spin stops. Rudder central – into the crouch and pull thankfully out of dive. Six-thousand feet lost in all.

'Well done – take us home.'

'Roger – Sir!'

Mark offers a mental vote of thanks to Mister Good.

***

By the end of May, there have been no further flying chops and everyone's gone solo. The first week of June sees the start of a concentrated programme of I/F, which the academically-released Michael successfully negotiates, along with his colleagues. Consequently, the Guest Night of the eighth is relaxed, if somewhat raucous, with after-dinner mess rugby in the 81 Entry anteroom more than usually robust.

The next day, however, the chaps are in for a mood-changing surprise.

His friends have known throughout the first four terms that the RAF career of one of the 'toffs' has hung by a thread. They can see that he's not from the same mould as the average Flight Cadet of these times but they know from the history of the place that chaps like him have been more than welcome in previous eras. He may be the butt of Drill Sergeants' humour but he's popular among his colleagues and they stand by him. And he's gone solo with the best of them, so he seems to be doing all right with the flying in this fifth term.

So it comes as a mighty shock for all when he's called to Pete Gilliatt's office for some bad news. The Flight Commander's been handed the sad job of informing him that he's to be withdrawn from 81 Entry – the reason, 'Lack of OQs'. There is no procedure of appeal. Finn's to pack his bags, collect his car and return to civilian life.

For a particular chum of his, the Group Captain's son, who has made it quite clear that he'd rather be in Oxfordshire than Lincolnshire any time, this is the breaking-point. He's immediately knocking on Flight Lieutenant Gilliatt's door before packing his bags too, and leaving the course, 'At his Own Request'.

The twelve remaining Flight Cadets of 81 'C', together with many other friends, are down by the Main Gates as the pair of them drive in a defiant Lap of Honour around the Orange. The late-afternoon sun casts photogenic shadows among the lime trees and the greensward's in mid-season form, as the two liberated fellows, grinning from ear-to-ear in the ruby-red Riley regain their freedom. One's on his way back to a kinder environment and the other's off to Uni. Not a bad outcome at all. Those departing grins appear to have been completely genuine.

Everyone feels better.

Over the weekend of 9th to 11th June, it's a relief to cheer on Kiwi, Peter and other pentathletes at the Services UK Championships being held at Cranwell – as well as entertaining friends from Sandhurst and Dartmouth taking part. For those not satisfied, the overlapping two days of the RAF Athletics Championships (with eighteen Stations on show) present more sporting action to watch.

That's followed by a week of I/F, together with nervous-making standardisation checks (with the aptly-named 'Trappers' of CFS) before the mid-term break from 16th to 19th June.

*****

Over the break, Mark manages a Sunday game of cricket. It's for the Stock Exchange team, for whom, he's told, a crate of champers is usually provided in the dressing room. It promises to be enjoyably sociable and Sally accepts his invitation to join him.

To entertain her, he has brought along extracts from 'Notes for the Guidance of Flight Cadets' – not the whole book (that's marked 'Restricted' and 'Not to be taken off the Station') but just the bits that have been underlined by the Authorities as being of particular importance:

> A gentleman is someone who always puts other people at their ease.
>
> The Air Council have stated that they strongly disapprove of officers wearing their service raincoats with plain clothes.
>
> Although dinner need not be an unduly solemn occasion, horseplay is inexcusable.
>
> Do not rest your knife and fork handles on the table.
>
> Always dance with your hostess as soon as you can, then dance with each lady in turn.
>
> In letters, Pilot Officers and Flying Officers (and incidentally, Flight Cadets) are always to be addressed as 'Mister'.

'Next time I write, I'll remember that,' says Sally.

***

THE PACE QUICKENS

Back at Cranwell, the Bachelor of Arts syllabus has reached the decades that 81 Entry chaps have themselves lived through, the Hot and Cold Wars of the 1940s and 1950s.

In an uncertain post-war environment, the reopening of the College was a stuttering affair. The first fifteen cadets reported in October 1946 – all of them having served in the RAF and most having completed a university short course. Joined by fourteen members of the Senior Course at No. 19 FTS, the entry became known as No. 45. Their first two terms were spent in a barrack block on East Camp, in unsavoury conditions and with the status of airmen. In April 1947, they moved into the College building for what was to be another six terms, with the status of Flight Cadets.

Flying training started in the third term, on Tiger Moths for basic and Harvards for advanced. There was also a Navigation Flight with Ansons, and an Equipment and Secretarial Wing at RAF Digby, while through 1947 and '48 the engineering establishment moved to the new RAF Technical Cadet College at Henlow.

Despite shortages of equipment and suitable teaching accommodation, the College settled into a sequence of eight-term entries, lasting just over two-and-a-half years, with graduations in April, July and December.

In the wider world, British forces, in particular the RAF, were from 24th June 1948 involved in one of the first major post-war international crises. In response to the Western Allies introducing the new-issue Deutschemark to West Berlin, the Soviets blocked all rail, road, and canal access to the sectors of Berlin under Western control. This forced the Allies to organize an airlift of vital supplies, during which the Air Forces of the USA, Britain, France, Canada, Australia, New Zealand and South Africa flew over 200,000 flights in all, delivering close on 9,000 tons of fuel and food to the West Berliners each day. The Soviets did not disrupt the airlift for fear this might lead to open conflict and on 12th May 1949, they lifted the blockade. The Berlin Blockade was a highlight of the fast-developing Cold War.

To most, it was not a question of whether WWIII would start but when. The Cold War became hot with the beginning of the Korean War in 1950, where China with the Soviet Union sponsored the north, and the United States the south of what became

> *an ideologically-split peninsula. Similarly, in the Malayan Emergency of the 1950s, the Chinese Government incited Communist Guerrillas against the Colonial British.*
> *But the nuclear stand-off precariously kept the global peace.*

This was the world facing the Flight Cadets of RAF College Entry No. 54, in residence at Cranwell from April 1949 to December 1951. One of their number, then Flight Cadet Sergeant Fred Hoskins, wrote:

> For the first eight months, we lived in barrack rooms, each housing twenty cadets, the senior of the two junior entries on one side of the room and us new boys on the other. We wore the uniform of ordinary airmen, complete with eagle shoulder flashes. After two terms, on reaching the status of Flight Cadets, the eagles were removed and the airman-style cap badges were replaced by those issued to Warrant Officers.
>
> Unlike pre-war cadets who had to pay to be at Cranwell, we were paid.

The barrack-room experiences and curriculum, as well as the disciplines, for the two terms of Junior Entries would in most respects be recognised by the lads of 81 Entry, a decade later, but it was not before moving up to the College Mess in Term 3 that No. 54 received the services of a batman. They certainly had it much harder physically – they endured the first-term boxing, and the crowing received from their seniors on their first Guest Night in the College Mess bordered on the terrifying.

Again Fred writes:

> The old hands were ranged on furniture piled high in one of the anterooms and the novitiates were brought in to perform. One might sing, a small group might perform a sketch. One young man placed a dustbin lid on the floor, a lighted thunder-flash on that, a steel helmet on the thunder-flash and then stood on the steel helmet and blew himself up. He passed, but those who failed to please might find themselves riding bicycles around the Orange with fire-hoses playing on them, or crawling under the carpet in the front hall.

In their time at the College, No. 54 Entry paraded for both MRAF Lord Trenchard and HRH Princess Elizabeth, before graduating in December 1951. Within a year, Fred Hoskins was flying ground-attack Hornets in the Malayan Emergency.

***

George Aylett arrived at Cranwell in January 1954, to join No. 68 Entry – all pilots (including one from Ceylon) plus a few from the Equipment and Secretarial Branches.

The course was still two years, eight months long but the first two terms as Junior Entry were spent in the South Brick Lines, where there were still no batmen. As with Fred's experience, there was no bullying from the entry above, but as George recalls, 'As a relief from the bull, drill and basic academics, we young lads indulged in much mayhem. This consisted mainly of harassing members of the other squadron entries who had in some way displeased us – water down stove chimneys, lashing of their beds to the roof and that sort of thing.'

George remembers, 'We romped through the academics, which were of no more than sixth form difficulty.' The first-term navigation trips in Ansons were used for 'sleeping off the exertions of Junior Cadet life – there was no formal navigation instruction'.

In the third term, the cadets moved into the barrack blocks, each with a room of his own. Basic flying instruction commenced, in Piston Provosts on the North Airfield.

In the fourth term, 68 Entry moved up to the College and the next stage of Flying Training began, on the Balliol at Barkston Heath. The remainder of the training advanced on the Vampire on the South Airfield.

Final academic exams were taken at the end of Term 7, leaving the final term clear for flying. George logged 245 hours at Cranwell, including five hours at night on the Provost.

In Term 8 and Senior Entry, he was an Under Officer. He acquired his first car, a 1935 drophead Austin and in celebration drove a squad of his colleagues around the forbidden Orange. This was just five weeks before graduation – he got two weeks of Duty Under Officer for his sins, but graduated nonetheless, with Wings.

George doesn't especially recall a Survival Camp but in every leave period there was something like that and he remembers an E&E Exercise in Germany. He played cricket at Cranwell, and rugby, at scrum-half, which led to trips to L'Ecole de l'Air, RMA Sandhurst, BRNC Dartmouth and Greenwich.

On the whole, he found his time at Cranwell much the same as that at public school. It took until 20th August 1957 for him to have his first sortie on a squadron, in a Vampire.

***

After a mid-term break, fine June weather allows 81 Entry's flying to get going right away. The air around Sleaford is full of jet planes – Flying Wing's strength now runs at forty-four JPs, twenty-eight Vampires, and three Meteors. Add in the three Valettas and six Varsities of the Navigation Flight (now housed in one of the South Airfield hangars) as well as the ten Chipmunks on the North Airfield and the local populace must be grateful that the College adopts university-style vacations.

Those long breaks do nothing for the continuity of the flying-training programme, which is poor. Andy's done the sums. 'Between January and now, my average is running at under ten hours a month, which is half of that expected at a Direct Entry FTS. Having only three flying periods each week doesn't help. But despite that, it's all great fun and the real reason I've joined the Service!'

The syllabus arrives at an introduction to the Ground Controlled Approach (GCA), which involves an aircraft and its pilot being talked down to the tarmac under radar control. This exercise has to be carried out at Cranwell's South Airfield, which has equipment capable of giving glide path information.

At his first go, Mark spends fifty long minutes under the blind-flying hood. His instructor keeps the lookout throughout and does the take-off and landing but for the rest of the trip, Mark's at the controls, obeying first the instructions of Kipper: 'Turn 180 degrees starboard onto zero-seven-zero, climbing to 5,000 feet and level out,' and then, when straight and level, 'Call Cranwell Approach and request QDH.'

A check on the knee-pad. QDH – yes, that's Controlled Descent Below Cloud.

He then follows the instructions from the Cranwell Tower. When lined up on the extended centre-line at 1,500 feet, he's handed over to the GCA Controller.

This chap sits in the radar room in the Tower with the JP's radar trace on his screen and talks him down the ideal glide path with left, right, up and down directions. Quite restful, really – nothing to do but keep speed constant and follow instructions.

The tension racks right up for the next one, when Kipper has Mark handling all the controls and doing all the checks, including the vital

'Undercarriage Down'. All goes well and on 8th June, he is signed off for his Elementary Instrument-Flying Grading.

Two days later, the Queen's Birthday Parade shows that the new way of drilling takes none of the gloss off the ceremonial. It's on show again at the end of the month, when all flying stops for the Ferris drill competition. The event, again adjudged by Sandhurst, is scheduled for Friday 30th and takes up the morning but getting the clobber ready and the rehearsals eat up much of the two days before. Yet again, Flight Sergeant Holt's 'C' Squadron are the victors.

Ferris Drill June 1961. Under inspection… (*RAF College Journal*)

...at the Present... (*RAF College Journal*)

...and marching past. (*RAF College Journal*)

Continuing good weather means that continuity in the Flying Syllabus picks up somewhat in July, with most of the 81 Entry pilot trainees fitting in at least half-a-dozen lengthy sorties, close on ten hours in total, in the ten working days before the end of the month.

***

Immediately after the Ferris, the sports teams set off for Berkshire for the summer matches against Sandhurst. The timings are pretty tight. The College bus drives off at 1230 hours for the 1313 departure from Grantham, arriving King's Cross 1510. Military transport then takes the travelling party (eight officers with forty-seven cadets) across London for the 1554 from Waterloo (no time for a swift one in the Captain's Cabin) which pulls in at Camberley Station just before 1700. Coaches then deposit the travellers at the Academy Clock Tower at 1715. Just enough time to unpack, brush up the shoes and de-crease the uniforms before being on parade at the 'sippers' gathering before the Guest Night dinner. In preparation, it's a considerable administrative task and in execution, getting close to the effort involved in herding cats.

As Deputy to the Escorting Officer in that LSE trip at the beginning of term, Mark's had some exposure to the Administrative Order and understands how much detail is required to organize the multitude of activities undertaken by the RAF College for its 300-odd Flight Cadets. He now realises that Cranwell, indeed the whole Air Force epitomises that well-known image of the swan – all above water serene and magnificent, all below vigorous and continuous action.

The tennis, swimming, golf (Andy's now the Captain) and sailing are finished in time for the early evening train to London but there's the added twist that this summer's cricket fixture at Sandhurst is to be a two-innings-a-side affair, played over two days. This means that visitors' as well as hosts' management have to keep twenty-four players and two scorers on track for an eleven o'clock start on the Sunday. After Saturday's play, when honours are fairly even, the lure of the metropolis and the Captain's Cabin prove overwhelming. The Cranwell XI manages the Sunday start but fails to make the RMA bat for a second time.

***

Ceremonial Parades, Ferris, sports and Guest Nights – there have been three already this term and two yet to come – are putting pressure on the increasingly-demanding flying training programme, and vice-versa.

Solo sorties, now up to an hour in length and including long periods on instruments, alongside pilot navigation and aerobatics, all need high levels of self-discipline and application.

College Flight Commanders still look for a proper commitment to Societies, as well as to inter-squadron swimming, gymnastic and sports competitions. As if to emphasise that, an Order is issued on July 5th instructing all Flight Cadets to acquire a new College tracksuit, 'to be paid for by a deduction from pay of 5/- a month'.

Michael does himself no harm by winning the Inter-Squadron Sculling Trophy on the River Trent at Newark – that'll count in the final balance. Low-profile Tony is another who finds rowing an acceptable leisure outlet and, ignoring a warning from the authorities that it's 'not a team sport', wins his half-colours in the coxed four.

In that pressurized environment, 81 Entry is becoming divided between those who spend evenings relaxing, or training for sports, or following a hobby, and those who perforce need to work on additional studies and essays. It also doesn't help that the Flight Cadets themselves are taking some of the flak coming from Flying and Academic Wings. There are limits to how the time available can be efficiently split between ground and air training.

They are keenly aware that they are the pioneers in this experiment, being closely watched not only by the College and Air Ministry establishments but also by the three entries now coming up on the same syllabus behind them.

There's something of a split of opinion, however. The non-degree-level chaps are asking, 'Without the need for all that extra academic programme, we would be graduating as fully trained pilots and navigators next spring. Was this half-baked approach what we came to Cranwell for?' Some degree-level men are wondering, 'Will it be worth it? Will it make us better officers?'

'This,' reckons Mark, 'ain't half a challenge. But there you are. They tell us we're the elite of the Air Force, in the top ten per cent for ability of the country's youth. So let's show 'em what we're made of.'

Some still find time for an outing. One evening a few of the 'A' Stream chaps are in the saloon bar of their favourite pub in Caythorpe. They linger right up to closing time, when there's a sudden loud roar. 'Time, Gentlemen – Please!' and from around the corner materializes none other than Flight Sergeant Holt.

The drinkers swiftly down the last of their pints and make a rapid exit. Eyes everywhere, this Bogbrush.

***

On the eve of Ferris, yet another 81 'C' man has packed it all in. He's been a good companion for close on two years. A gifted artist, he's been the one to go to for a good black gloss on the bayonet scabbard (automobile paint courtesy of Blind Bill's dad) and the leading architect of 'C' Squadron's crew room bar at Barkston, as well as a vital member of the Ball Committee. Nevertheless, he's another leaving the College at his own request, in his case to pursue his vocation in the Church. He'll be missed.

81 'C' is now down to eleven – and counting?

***

The final week of flying before the graduation ceremonies of 79 Entry, sees the trainee pilots of 81 introduced to the experience of taking an aircraft away from its home base to land at another airfield. After making a report in the airfield's log, they're to return the machine to its home base. On the Tuesday, Kipper and Mark are routed in the afternoon to the RAF Advanced Flying Training School (AFTS) at Oakington, a few miles west of Cambridge.

That same morning, they complete close on two hours out of the circuit in low flying, forced landing practice and aerobatics. Char and a wad for lunch and he's into the Ops Room and filing a flight plan for the Oakington trip. In a straight line, it's just a seventy-mile jaunt, but Kipper's thrown in some more low-flying and pilot navigation on the way. Also, he's arranged for his student to do a roller landing at RAF Cottesmore to get practice on the radio as well as seeing the layout of another airfield and circuit.

All goes well. It's a glorious summer day and you can see for ever. Mark's coming up to eighty hours on type, twenty of them solo, and considers himself at home in a JP cockpit. But he remembers Wing Commander Green's words. He's past the fifty hours of being terrified – he must be on his guard against any thought that he's anywhere near knowing it all.

Oakington's an interesting base to visit. It hosts the Vampires, Meteors and Varsities on which Direct-Entry pilots fly their advanced training. It's where 81 Entry graduates from Cranwell will go in a year's time to fly the Varsity, should they not be selected for the jet course. Mark reckons he's a racing certainty for the Super-Pig.

The joining procedures, circuit and landing are standard but, taxiing into dispersal, Mark can't help but recall that the 80 Entry Jet Jockeys rather look down on the Jet Provost, as a kid's aeroplane. However, with Kipper in the Ops Room, signing the 'visitors' book', there's a warm welcome, followed by a professional chat over a cup of tea. Thirty minutes after take-off from Oakington, Kipper's on his way to sign back in at Barkston – job done.

Today, they've spent three hours twenty minutes together in the air, in four sorties – only the second time Mark will have had four trips in a day on this much-interrupted course and he's enjoyed every minute. He's heard it often said that 'the more you fly the more you want to fly'. They can say that again.

***

That short experience of continuity doesn't last. Wednesday 26th July sees a group of 81 Entry (Number One Dress with white belts) on parade in the Victoria Embankment Gardens, London. Some are bearing laurel wreaths to hand over to the dignitaries (including Prime Minister Harold Macmillan) at the unveiling of a statue in memory of the late Viscount Trenchard, MRAF.

Lodgings are arranged at RAF Uxbridge (at the very end of the Central Line and distressingly far from the Captain's Cabin) so it's three days later that the chaps are back in the air. Mark spends close on two hours on a solo navex that includes a landing away, at Cranwell, where he leaves the aircraft. Highly enjoyable, real responsibility for both aircraft and his own skin, good sense of progress – but then, that's it for the term. Four days of frantic work on the Graduation Ball, in between delivering a couple of overdue essays, and preparing the ceremonial clobber for 79 Entry's parade, and it'll be leave for six weeks. No more flying until halfway through September. There's a thought.

On the last flying day this term, there's a reminder that jet-pilot training, in spite of the excellent safety record of the Jet Provost, is not without risk. At the South Airfield, there are three bird-strikes. In one of them, Jock is involved, as is a flock of peewits, one of them denting the nose cone of his JP on the approach. The Flight Cadet flies calmly on to land safely – the bird's a goner.

With that incident in the decompression chamber, that's two of Jock's lives accounted for. How many more does he have in his locker?

***

The trainee navigators are making steady progress through their syllabus, 'Although,' says Jim, 'at one sortie a week, it's still not good in the continuity department.'

Anthony reports, 'Most of our airborne work's now in the Varsity, where we sit facing aft at a navigator's desk with access to a full range of instruments. As well as the GIVB magnetic compass we've moved on to the use of a radio compass for bearings and the GEE display has been enhanced with Rebecca/Eureka, also of last war vintage, to provide us with a radar range and bearing.

Jim adds, 'At the same time, we've been introduced to the Mark Nine Bubble Sextant – a heavy affair which is designed to hang from the astrodome. That's to give us sightings on sun and stars to obtain position-lines and calculate fixes.

'Trouble is, being hooked to the airframe, the sextant jumps about when the aircraft does. So we spend a lot of time supporting the thing on the shoulder. What with that and hauling it and our astrological books around, we're candidates for early onset of what they call navigator's stoop.'

Jim also spends a lot of time with the optical drift sight. He's tickled pink by how easy it is to get an accurate wind velocity well out of sight of land. 'You ask the pilot to turn one way through sixty degrees and take a drift reading over one minute. Then turn the other way through 120 degrees and take a second one-minute reading. Turn back onto the original heading, and thus back onto track, for a third drift reading. Put those into the Dalton and you get a small cocked hat where the three lines cross, together with a nice, accurate wind velocity. Simple, and elegant.'

Sufficient aircraft are used to give each student an equal share of first-nav time. The chaps are now working to a regular navigator's cycle, which consists of obtaining a regular position 'fix', or for second best a 'most probable position', with the frequency of fix depending on the work involved. GEE fixes, at some three minutes are more easily obtained than pure astro, which can take up to half-an-hour. Sorties now comprise a number of missions – ranging from using a variety of aids at medium level, including day/night astro, to hours of low-level and 'lumpy wave-hopping over the North Sea' with coastal techniques.

'Only thing is,' says Jim, 'it seems as if what should be a seven-month course in the basics of navigation, is being expanded to three years. And everything else that's going on is there just to fill the time available.'

***

Meanwhile, War Studies comes to the late 1950s – turbulent times for Britain and British aviation.

November 1956 saw the humiliation of Britain, France and Israel in what became known as the Suez Crisis. A military attempt, unsupported by the USA and the UN, to regain control of the Suez Canal, nationalized by the Egyptian leader Colonel Nasser, had lasted just one week and two days.

However, the debacle led to the resignation of Prime Minister Eden and signalled the end of Britain's role as a super-power. That, together with economic restrictions and political expedience, gave impetus to what became known as the 'Retreat from Empire in Asia'.

India was in its tenth year of independence, while after a decade of struggle against Chinese Communist guerrillas, Malaya was granted the same status in 1957, followed by Cyprus in 1959. In these and other struggles, the RAF saw much action but its worldwide footprint was bound to contract.

In April 1957, Defence Minister Duncan Sandys published a White Paper on the future of Britain's Military and its Aircraft Industry. This launched the idea that, as well as the need for the fragmented industry's consolidation, the RAF's manned aircraft might in large part be replaced by guided missiles. In the event, the latter suggestion did not materialize, albeit fighter production was cut back.

No. 76 Entry arrived at the College in January 1957, just weeks after Suez. On the entry was Flight Cadet Michael Graydon, who had grown up during the glory days of British aviation, when heroic test pilots demonstrated a stream of new and exciting world-leading machines before a spellbound public at Farnborough. As far as Michael, an RAF Scholarship boy, remembers:

> The White Paper made its presence felt at Cranwell cadet level hardly at all. We were too busy with pressing College matters to read papers.
>
> Our intake, seventy-strong, half-and-half public and grammar, had a high drop-out rate – thirty-six were suspended or re-brigaded to 77 Entry over the three-year course. This for the prospective pilots, was largely down to the challenge, particularly for a tyro student, of handling the high torque of the tail-wheeled Piston Provost. In those days, instructors, many of whom had seen action in Korea, Suez and Malaya, were tough on slow learners – it was very much, cope or you were out.

On the same entry was Flight Cadet Dick Johns, who remembers that they were the first to exchange the forage cap for a beret, and the first to visit Colorado Springs. He also recalls:

> We were the first to start a three-year, nine-term course, with the intent – not achieved – of raising the academic standards of the College. The hope was to attract boys who might otherwise go up to university. Nevertheless, major academic exams ended at the end of the second year – in the third, there were just two or three periods a week. However, Flight Cadets had to write a thesis – for me the subject was 'Theory and Practice of Blitzkrieg'.
>
> I vividly remember violent crowing and 'larks'. In our second term we dined at a Guest Night in the College for the first time. Afterwards we had to entertain our seniors. Failure to provide sufficient entertainment earned a forfeit. One chap was dropped off on the outskirts of Lincoln in pyjamas having been given a single earring to pair up with the other one in a girl's possession. He was at least given an address and he succeeded in his mission. Others returning to the South Brick Lines found notes on their beds saying, 'Your drill boots are in the hangar at Barkston'. They had to be retrieved in time for morning drill.
>
> Survival Camp, in Germany's Hartz Mountains was a testing examination of fitness before an escape and evasion exercise lasting for several days. Strikers were well populated, one cadet managing eighty days in a row. However, flying training on Piston Provosts from Term Three helped us grow up. For me, advanced flying training on the Meteor in the third year was an enjoyable conclusion to my time at Cranwell. With Wings and Graduation in sight, the final term was great fun.
>
> The three years at Cranwell were intended to train us for the permanent officer cadre of the Service and certainly by the end we had learned self-discipline and developed determination to succeed, as well as forming strong and enduring friendships.

On graduation, in December 1959, the majority of 76 Entry wanted to join Javelin and Hunter fighter squadrons and there was still plenty of opportunity for that, operating out of bases stretching from Hong Kong to Germany and the UK.

***

In preparing the Graduation Ball décor for 79 Entry in the summer of 1961, the 81 Entry Committee members are really missing their departed artist. How do they even start on the transformation of these grand anterooms, having agreed on a Mediterranean theme? Weekend miles are put in, begging everything from fishermen's nets and lobster pots in King's Lynn to Italianate wall-hangings from country houses in Woodhall Spa. Blind Bill follows up with his brand-new Ford Thames van (a present from his parents on his recent twenty-first birthday) ready to do the heavy lifting.

A wealth of Graduation Ball kit is found in the College Society storeroom. So what, if they can't produce an entirely authentic job? After a slap-up dinner and wine by the gallon, no one's going to notice. The College Band, which has done it all many times before, knows the score and the smoking-room quartet will play plenty of stuff to smooch to. The Mess Manager and his staff will make the Dining Hall glitzy enough to rival anything in the West End, the gents will be in best bib and tucker and girlfriends, as well as officers' wives will look marvellous in their glamorous gowns. All will be well.

***

A splendid Passing Out Parade for No. 79 Entry's thirty-six Flight Cadets takes place on Tuesday 1st August. Sovereign's Squadron for the parade is 'C', following a competition which, in the somewhat labyrinthine words of the *Journal*, has been 'the closest ever recorded':

> 'A' Squadron won the Knocker Trophy; 'C' Squadron won the Ferris. The result of the competition depended upon placings from the Chimay Cup. The issue was decided only in the last rowing race. The result was a tie between 'A' and 'D' Squadrons for the Chimay Cup; but, with second place in the Knocker, 'C' Squadron took over as Sovereign's Squadron.

Fourteen Vampires fly overhead in formation. They are now in a minority, with twenty-three on strength against the now forty-five JPs. From next term, it will be just 80 Entry flying them.

For the Graduating Entry, they fly in a Cross of Lorraine formation, in honour of the Reviewing Officer, General Paul Stehlin, Chief of the French Air Staff. The General presents no fewer than seven of the major awards, including the Sword of Honour, to SUO N.R. Hayward (a feat not even closely matched previously) before making an engaging address, urging solidarity between nations.

The weather turns out fine, the old marching tunes come up fresh as always and *Auld Lang Syne* again tugs at the heart strings.

At their first Graduation Ball, the 81 Entry chaps find the banquet magnificent, the wine plentiful and the music loud and eminently danceable. The newly-commissioned Pilot Officers are pleased with the décor. The fisherman's nets and lobster pots add a distinctly salty tang to the atmosphere, but everyone's far too polite to mention it.

Mark and Robert in his Riley deliver their partners to the luxuries of the Woodhall Spa Hotel, enjoying the thought that if all goes well it'll be their turn to enjoy the pomp and circumstance of an RAF College graduation – in just three terms' time.

Summer Leave 1961

But first, there's a second, and last summer vacation to enjoy – all six weeks of it. For most, it's straight off to the home base, for renewing ties with families and friends, but before long, adventure calls.

By Sunday 3rd September, ten days before the start of the Autumn Term, the whole entry have got themselves back at the College, ready for an official visit to the British Army of the Rhine, BAOR, in Germany. The anterooms are full of tales of derring-do in the vacation so far.

Two pairs truly bitten by the flying bug have really pushed the boundaries. With his aunt again making the Hornet Moth available, John and Michael summoned up the courage and resourcefulness to fly the twenty-eight-year-old biplane across the Channel to France and Italy. They borrowed two sleeping bags and a bivouac from the College's Survival Stores and set off from Thruxton in Hampshire on August 5th, clearing customs at Lympne before heading straight across the Channel.

At Berck, on the French north coast, they slept in the sand dunes before taking off for the south. Two days later – forced by the weather down to 400 feet before skimming over the Provençal hills – they were sunbathing on the beaches and impressing *les demoiselles* of Cannes. After four delightful days of that, they coaxed the trusty Moth along the Riviera before turning southwards again, all the way to Rome.

Their route then took them to Venice, and over the Alps through the Brenner Pass. Michael remarks, 'Flying through the Brenner in a biplane was a magnificent experience – it would require a poet, and a good one, to do it true justice.' After a stop in Innsbruck, the intrepid aviators enjoyed a two-day final fling in 'gay Paree' before, after three weeks away, delivering the faithful Moth, unscathed, back to Aunt Marion.

Michael adds, 'Aerial touring, especially without radio or aids of any sort, is a free and un-cramped style of flying. What the flight safety pundits would say about our jaunt I couldn't say but for us, it was fun, and we live to tell the tale.'

The second pair with a Continental string-bag adventure to relate are Boy and Chris, who tells the story:

Tiger Moth and Turbulent. (*RAF College Journal*)

Wave-skimming Turbulents. (*Aeronautics*)

One Saturday morning last term, using my JP flying hours and a Chipmunk dual check, I qualified for a PPL. I later had a dual check in the Club's Tiger Moth to enable me to fly the single-seat Turbulent. This meant that come August, we were able to take a Turbulent each on a two-week trip with four members of the Tiger Club of Redhill. There were four of us in Turbulents, and two in a Jodel, taking a circular route across France and into North Spain, returning via other flying club airfields.

He explains that, apart from Montpelier which had a hard runway, all take-offs and landings were on grass. At Montpelier there was a tricky crosswind and without brakes it was challenging landing on tarmac – no friction on the tail-skid to help keep straight. Boy left the runway during his landing run and damaged the underside of the fuselage on a hidden runway light. A carpenter made repairs and after the glue had dried, Boy was able to catch up a few days later.

In hindsight, Chris admits that taking light aircraft, with a single engine – and that from a VW Beetle – across the English Channel without life jackets or radios was probably not wise! And he admits that some of them 'flew under bridges along the Loire valley – once in Vic-formation'. But they survived, flying back from Berck to the Tiger Club base at Redhill in a mixed formation of various aircraft that had flown over to join them. 'We finished with a seventeen-machine fly-past over Redhill for the local TV.'

No less risky has been a Basic Parachuting Course at RAF Abingdon, where twenty-five Flight Cadets, led by Jim the Nav and including Kraut and Robert, have survived a series of jumps from a balloon, and one from a Beverley transport. 'My logbook,' reports Jim, 'now records one more take-off than landing. And if that ain't good enough, I've got the bruises to prove it!'

***

The College Cadets' Activities Organisation has sponsored several other vacation adventures. Anthony's just arrived back from driving a multi-entry party (with the help of ferries) for a fishing week in County Clare while Kiwi has tales to tell of an expedition to retrace Hannibal's route across the Alps from Valence. They gave it their best shot, but bad weather and wrenched ankles brought them up short of Hannibal's descent into Turin.

Peter has been to Jersey with the Sub-Aqua Section while Robin has expanded his experience with a spot of sailing out of Hamble. Sid has spent three rewarding August weeks climbing in the Atlas Mountains of

Kiwi (left wing, with bottle) and chums in Alps. (*RAF College Journal*)

Morocco – this after a rather disappointing private trip to Paris with Mark and David. 'The idea was to take our girlfriends but one dad vetoed the idea.' The trio went in any event but it took the excitement level down a peg or two. Among much quaffing of coffee in the cafés of the Latin Quarter a highlight was meeting up with a group of Sandhurst blokes. 'Couldn't miss them among the crowds – Parisians don't wear cavalry twills.'

There have been no overseas jaunts for Robert and his colleagues in the degree studies Geography stream. With Vernon amongst them (despite the move to Nav, he's remained in the 'C' Stream) they have just spent a fortnight toiling on a London University Field Study of the heather moors of Malham Tarn in the Yorkshire Dales. Good for mind and body both, and plenty of opportunity 'to put people at their ease' – to quote Notes for Guidance.

Back from Paris, Mark's been earning cash on the building sites. 'Responsible stuff – knocking holes in walls for drainpipes to go through, getting the brickies' muck just right in the concrete-mixer. That sort of thing. Plenty of opportunity for putting people at their ease there – I was detailed to brew tea for the Irish trench-digging squad.'

***

The week's trip to the BAOR beginning on 4th September is a formal part of the officer training syllabus, aimed at 'fostering Inter-Service comradeship, while gaining practical experience of the organisational tasks, training and equipment of the Army'. For the seven Sections of seven cadets each, educational it certainly turns out to be.

Nigel tells the story of his Section's adventures:

> We were assigned to 45 Regiment Royal Artillery at Iserlohn, south-east of Dortmund in the scenic Sauerland forests. After several days of action in Centurion tanks, we were entertained in the base Officers' Mess.
>
> After a slap-up dinner, we got involved in a schooner race. It became so fierce and intense that in trying to pinch the last round, Martin swallowed his false teeth – the front ones he got after Sam rearranged the originals in that Term One roustabout in Hut 149. The Gunners shipped him off to Iserlohn military hospital, where the medics tried to establish where his teeth had got to. No sign. Didn't show up on the X-Ray.

With 45 Regiment Royal Artillery. (*NGB*)

Nigel appears to mean it when he says, 'We're going to ask Wing Commander Green to take Martin up for some seriously violent aerobatics – see if the teeth might be shaken down the system a bit.

'Apart from that, it was a great trip – charging around the countryside in a Centurion's good for the Imperial soul.'

Sid and Mark recount how they were consigned to the tender mercies of the 2nd Battalion, Grenadier Guards, in Hubbelrath, outside Dusseldorf.

They've spent most of their time with the recce platoon, sliding around what woods are left in the Ruhr Valley in Champs – armoured Land Rovers with snorkles – and having to be hauled out of mountain streams by armoured car.

Mark's amazed at the standard of the Guards' hospitality. 'On arrival, we find a small bottle of Vat 69 whisky by each bed-space. Then, on exercise, at every night-stop, down comes the tail-gate on the 3-Tonner and out comes a table, with cloth and Mess Silver, so that all officers can dine in a manner to which they are no doubt accustomed.'

One night, he and Sid are confined in a hut overlooking a steep-sided valley, with a tarmac road down below. Their job is to watch that road like hawks and to report on the radio any troop movements they see. At 0200, Sid hands over to a semi-conscious Mark, who drops off again. While he's asleep, a whole enemy battalion passes through but to his great good fortune, this is the hour when the entire exercise is abandoned because of heavy rain and flooding.

On the final day, the Grenadiers' Education Officer takes his 'C' Squadron charges for an alcoholic cruise on the Rhine, which leads to their arriving back at the Hubbelrath HQ late for the formal dinner being given in their honour. 'The Guards were very polite about it,' reports Bill.

Some of the 'D' Squadron Flight Cadets are with the Yorks and Lancs Regiment at their barracks near Munster before deploying into the field at Vogelsang for a few very wet days with Conqueror tanks. In the Officers Mess at Münster, they are surprised to see one or two Army officers wearing their service hats at breakfast. They're told it's a regimental custom, indicating that during the meal, they do not wish to engage in conversation.

Chapter 10

The Pressure Builds

***Term 7**: 13th Sep-21st Dec 1961*

Preparing for the start of the Autumn Term the Flight Cadets of 81 Entry can now call themselves the 'Button Boys' – for their final year, they sport a single gold button on their gorget patches.

Gathered in the FGS, the balance of opinion appears to be that, despite the *longueurs* of Term Four, fast fading in the memory, it's basically all right, being a Flight Cadet.

The social divisions apparent on arrival in 1959 are being ironed out. Accents are settling down into what appears to be the understated received pronunciation of professionals. And now, after two years of it, the chaps take the discipline for granted. Not just on the Parade Square, but in their day-to-day lives. The Notes for Guidance are becoming their Bible. It could be working, this osmosis process – they seem to be turning into officers.

***

With the start of the syllabus for Term 7, the pressure's back on, and building. The run-up to next summer's internal and external ground and air examinations is already under way, and there have been some unhelpful changes in tutorial personnel.

On the Humanities side, Wing Commander Watts, the Latin wizard who's had the challenging task of launching and directing the revolutionary London BA initiative, has left at the end of a noteworthy tour – posted to HQ Fighter Command at historic Bentley Priory.

At the same time, Squadron Leader Nabarro has, with his family and dog, flown off to RAF Akrotiri, in Cyprus. Under his five-year editorship, the *Journal* has come to show a balance between the official line of the College and the occasionally reactionary opinions of contributors.

Mark feels that not to pass the degree exams, after all the effort put in, would be nothing short of disastrous. He knows that not all his 'C' Stream colleagues feel that way, but there's a good proportion who want to do themselves proud down in London next May. A change of the main helmsmen on the tutorial side at this stage does not help, but such is the wheel of fortune spun by the RAF Air Secretary's Branch.

On the air side, flying gets under way on the second day of term. The back seat boys on the Barkston bus count out the days since their last flights in the Jet Provost. From 28th July to today, that's seven weeks. Would that ever be allowed to happen at an FTS? How is the College's university-style vacation going to affect their flying today? Will they remember how it's done?

Both the Cranwell and Barkston squadrons find themselves the victims of postings-led changes. Mark's profitable relationship with Kipper Kemball is cut off in its prime – the latter moving off to join the staff at CFS.

Jock also finds himself with a new instructor, 'an ex-Hunter man whose idea of low flying turns out to be pretty hairy – even by my standards!'

Tim's another with a new mentor, a man who comes to show a keen interest in matters archaeological. 'Whenever we look down on likely-looking fields where differences in vegetation suggest buried ancient dwellings, our sorties are liable to end with seriously low-level orbits.'

***

The navigators too are concerned lest they've forgotten what they were doing pre-leave. Jim sees that his name's on the airborne roster for the second week of term, which will mean sixty-six days since his last trip. 'I'm down for four hours as first nav – half of that'll be just getting back on the blooming horse.'

***

Mark checks the 3 Squadron Chinagraph board – he's written up for an hour at 1100 with a Flight Lieutenant Gale, a man he's not flown with before, and it's to be all the testing pre-solo exercises, stalling and spinning checks before aerobatics and practice forced landings.

After three hours of nervous waiting, there's a running changeover – instructor remains in situ while for the students it's one out, one in – so there's no briefing, no getting to know each other. An hour or so later, Mark's confiding in Sid, 'In at the deep end or what? Suffice it to say, we don't make the final ten minutes of forced landings. I manage to hold it all in for forty-five minutes – then out with the paper-bag, the morning's nutty makes a reappearance and the Flight Louie brings me home.'

The following day, Mark has a different instructor, and different, less stressful exercises – take-off and climb, approach and landing, followed by low-flying. 'All fine until the bumpy bits over the Lincolnshire Edge – then, out with the flippin' bag again. This is getting worrying.'

***

There's a Guest Night in the first week, with CCF Officers as guests. On the 'C' Squadron sprig, Mark and Danny discover from a Flight Commander that the start of the Autumn Term has been mucked around a bit by the Air Show at Farnborough. RAF officers, NCOs and airmen, including those on College staff, were much in demand for that.

Danny observes, 'Must happen every two years. Of course, we would scarcely have noticed that back in September 'fifty-nine, incarcerated in the South Brick Lines. Now, it's knocked a few days off this vital, final year. That's bar billiards, I suppose.'

The Battle of Britain weekend, with its Sunday Parade, has everyone fully occupied before a Monday of academics keeps the 'C' and 'D' flyers away from Barkston until Tuesday 19th September. Mark's then introduced to his new instructor. Flight Lieutenant Holbourn is a family man with a reassuringly human manner, which puts his student at ease. He's clearly read his Notes for Guidance.

The sortie they're down for this time is well-chosen – I/F, with a radar-assisted approach and landing. Something to concentrate on throughout. After landing back at Barkston, the trip has lasted fifty minutes, forty-five of those logged as being on instruments. No aeros, no nausea, no problem. That's all right then. 'Same time, same place on Thursday, Sir?'

The next session sees a return to the pre-solo checks. In one hour and five minutes of stalls, spins and aeros there's nothing too violent, the crouch approach is accepted and there's no nausea. Mark's sent off for another hour to repeat the whole lot on his own, and gets through unscathed. He's fully back in the saddle, and a much-relieved student pilot.

His euphoria evaporates when the 'C' Squadron Chief Whip, Flight Sergeant Holt, herds them all up for a Knocker Cup training run. This term the competition's cross-country and it's tomorrow. Around the North Airfield they go – urged on by that legendary bark. But on the day, it's 'A' Squadron's turn to be the winners.

***

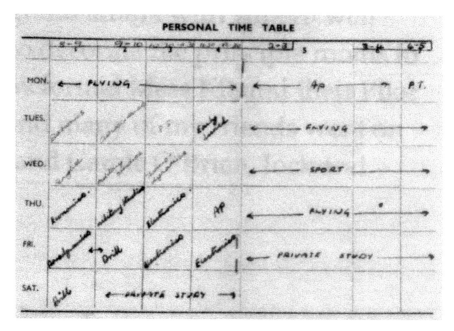

'A' Stream Personal Timetable, Year 3. (*RAFW*)

For 81 'C' and 'D' this term, the sessions at Barkston are marked down for the mornings of Tuesday and Thursday, together with Friday afternoons. Take out Wednesday afternoon for the sacrosanct sports, and that leaves two dozen one-hour periods for other studies.

Everyone's down for an hour on Monday afternoons for lectures on Meteorology from Cu-nim Jim. There's also an hour allocated for Officer Training on Saturday mornings but on five occasions that's to be a ceremonial parade. On top of that, the Ferris Drill looms – the trophy will be decided on 4th November.

That crowded programme limits academic studies, for all streams, to just a dozen face-to-face sessions with tutors in the week. Five hours of Private Study is the buffer, but one of those is in the dead slot of Saturday morning, at 1000 hours – a real test of will-power. At an entry meeting, Dave speaks for the majority of the 'B' Streamers:

> This final year is going to be tough – coping with the mix
> of advanced Aerodynamics, Meteorology, and Electronics,
> as well as the flying training. As time goes on and the Term
> Nine ground and air exams get ever closer, we're really going

to be up against it. Let's hope for help and understanding from both the Academic and Flying Wings – we're going to need it.

Sid has a point to add:

> For the whole of this year, when we're not flying, we'll be attending lectures most of the day – every day during the working week. That's not to mention researching and writing essays in what little time we can spare. It's going to make it difficult to make the most of College Society activities, and sure won't do our sporting chances much good. A clear run, then, for an 'A' Streamer at the Sword of Honour.

Robert puts a degree studies point of view:

> With the Military Studies, there's a clear link with Officer Training – Principles of War, Air Power Studies, communication and presentation techniques and all that. But French, Geography, History and Economics, how much are they going to contribute to our careers? I'm sure that we're going to continue 'buggering on', but personally, the moment I reckon any of it's endangering my flying, I'll think again.

Andy speaks up for the 'A' Streamers:

> My overriding view point is that the course is proving at least a term too long. The flying could and should have started twelve weeks earlier.
>
> I can see that for the few with the right A-levels, a degree or an AFRAeS qualification will be a great prize but for us in the 'A' Stream, how much of the academics is going to serve us well in our careers? Economics of course – we're going to miss Squadron Leader Nabarro there, he made it all come alive – and Military History, all right. But all that soldering-iron stuff!
>
> It seems that on the academics side, we've been filling in time, waiting for the other two streams to catch up and start flying.

But we are where we are, and thank goodness it's the beginning of the final year, at last. Flying, College Society, a couple of exams, sports – and flying again. Those are this 'A' Streamer's priorities now.

The situation is getting to the staff as well. Flying Wing demands from the academic staff sufficient recognition of their time needs, and the academic staff require the same of Flying Wing. There's a third element involved, the Squadron and Flight Commanders, not forgetting the Drill Sergeants, of the College staff. The Flight Cadets are caught in the middle. Management of priorities is sometimes a rocky affair but all sides of the argument set out to make it through to Christmas, again.

***

Unfortunately for the pilot trainees, October 1961 sees a sharp deterioration in the weather. 81 Entry's 'B' Stream make the most of a murky day by making a trip to a Derby Royal Aeronautical Society lecture. Sid, Zak, Terry, Dave, Danny, Tony and Peter are, with varying degrees of grace, grinding through the AFRAeS syllabus, staying the course.

The visibility's below requirements for JP flying for more than a dozen days in the month, with only a third of those being within the limits for solo. When flying is possible, there's many an hour of I/F logged – on one memorable day, a slight miscalculation by Cu-nim Jim leads to a dozen students being talked down through 20,000 feet of cloud for forty long minutes. At least that helps them to keep on track to achieving their Basic Instrument-Flying Grade by the mid-term break.

The flying interruptions give 'B' and 'C' Streamers an opportunity to make essay deadlines but the elation Mark felt at conquering his air-sickness drains away, as he spends hours in the crew room bent over his books. His state of mind does not improve when he reads in one of those a wise observation from a Great War RFC commander, Major Charles Burke:

> Waiting about on an airfield has spoilt more pilots than everything else put together.

***

From conversations at a Guest Night on the twelfth of the month (the guests being twenty-one headmasters from candidate-rich schools) it's clear that staff on both sides of the flying/academic divide are equally aware that the clock is ticking down for their students. Both are seeking discreetly to discourage over-participation in extra-curricular activities.

Nevertheless, it's not only 'A' Streamers who are well into rehearsals for a Noel Coward play, *Nude With Violin*, to be staged in a month's time in the Longcroft Room. The Director and leading man is Sid, while, much to his Economics tutor's frustration, letting his hair down as an American reporter is Mark.

At the same time, casting is in progress for an April production of *HMS Pinafore*, where the Stage Director's again Sid and the Musical Director Jim the Nav, with Welshman Frank standing tall as Captain Corcoran. Helping the search for willing actors, dancers and singers is the news that both shows are to be much enhanced by the participation of WRAF officers from Spitalgate.

On the other hand, it's now just 'A' Streamers who feature on the staff of the College *Journal* – Kiwi and Jim the Nav are Cadet Editors and Nigel the Sub-Editor, Sports. Nigel is also Secretary of the College Music Society. 'It's run by two generous officers who take several of us in their cars to classical concerts at the De Montfort Hall in Leicester and also to the Albert Hall in Nottingham. From time to time, halfway home, they stand us impoverished cadets supper at a pub.'

Mountaineering and caving continue, as well as sports, mostly indoors on account of bad weather. A social highlight is Danny's memorable twenty-first birthday party in the Houblon Arms. It's a bacchanalia, with *haka*, near-the-knuckle stories and songs, but it's the celebrant himself who really ties one on. His tipple is rum and orange and he's going for the record. But his mates hit on the ruse of plying him with endless glasses of just plain orange. It makes no difference – he becomes increasingly, and hilariously for his mates, inebriated.

Danny's party sends all 81 'C' home for the mid-term break on Friday 27th October in good spirits. Mark meets Sally at King's Cross station, when they update on the Cold War. The Polaris submarines have arrived in Holy Loch and Russian and American tanks are facing off at Berlin's 'Check-Point Charlie'. The 'Space Race' too, is hotting up. The Russians sent first a dog and now Yuri Gagarin into orbit and the Americans have followed up with Alan Shepard riding Freedom 7 above the atmosphere. The USSR is just ahead but President Kennedy has pledged to have NASA's Apollo Programme landing a man on the moon by the end of the decade and Congress has allocated $531 million for that.

Although it's clear how much their lives are drifting apart, Mark invites Sally to 80 Entry's Graduation Ball in December and, somewhat to his surprise, she accepts.

To celebrate, he buys a copy of the first edition of *Private Eye* and enjoys reading its satirical and iconoclastic content on the train. He reckons it's probably best to keep it under cover at Cranwell,

As they go about their business in College and Station, Flight Cadets and Staff cannot miss the bold building programme underway around them. A new and palatial Academics block, to be known as 'Whittle Hall' is taking shape at a short remove from the West Wing of the Senior Mess. The decision has also been made that the RAF Technical Cadet College at Henlow will be merged with the Cranwell GD Officers' College (this in part, reportedly, to forestall a mooted Government proposal to centralise all military technical training at Shrivenham) and work has started on the foundations of a Technical Engineering Hall, sited to the east of East Camp. On top of that, work is in hand for a purpose-built Anglican church and the restoration of the Roman Catholic chapel, together with a new pool and gymnasium.

Whittle Hall under construction. (*RAF College Journal*)

Back at College in the late evening of Monday 30th October, the 81 Entry navigators have been joined by three more retread pilot trainees, all of whom have already spent seven and a half terms at Cranwell, with 80 Entry.

George, Noel and Johnny all had the misfortune to be chopped as pilots even after reaching a respectable total of hours – in at least one case 100 – on the Piston Provost. Understandably, they have found it difficult to catch up with the navigators in their original entry and are now joining 81 with the aim of gaining the necessary hours and experience over two further terms.

George, of 'A' Squadron, is an ex-Halton Apprentice, so he will have completed over six and a half years of RAF cadetship by the scheduled graduation date of the end of July next year. He has his colours in the College athletics team, as has Johnny, of 'B' Squadron, who is also captain of cross-country. Noel, of 'D' is a leading light in the world of caving as well as having been mentor to 81 Entry lads in their South Brick Lines days. None of the three is thus in any way a stranger to their new colleagues.

Only one of the current Navigation group has been a volunteer member of the trade from the start, Jim the Nav. Anthony is a re-branded Secretarial Branch man and the remaining seven are ex-pilot trainees at various stages in the navigation syllabus. Despite the phasing problems that brings for the staff, the bookwork, as well as the navigation sorties, keep doggedly on course.

**

The Flight Cadets are grateful for a spell of clear weather but the blue skies allow early-morning Ferris rehearsals to spoil their breakfasts.

David insists, 'It's all good officer training – teaches us to cope in extremis.' At 0600 on the Parade Square, his mates don't find it so easy to buy into that.

For the first days of November, the anticyclonic blue skies continue – the Lincolnshire air is full of solo cadets practising their 'general handling', while engaging in clandestine tail-chases. The men of the Senior Entry, No. 80, probably scarcely notice the weather – they've started three days of final exams. For the student pilots of 81 'A' and 'B' Squadrons, flying from Cranwell, there's an introduction to night flying.

On the fourteenth, John writes home:

> Right away, I must say thank you for the party at half-term. It was enjoyed by all. I hope you didn't mind the invasion – the chaps are threatening to repeat it again next term.
>
> We are night flying for the second time tonight and I should be off solo. I could write pages about it.
>
> I had been a little apprehensive. I'd been told that all you could see of a Jet Provost ahead of you at night was a winking white tail-light – I thought, that must be very difficult to see against the increasing number of lights in the Grantham area. But so far, it has turned out that no more than three aircraft are airborne at any one time so the danger is greatly lessened.
>
> Top of my worry parade is the last few feet of the night landing. One thinks that the runway is about two feet lower than

Night-flying instrument panel. (*AJG*)

JP in the gloaming. (*AJG*)

it is. Each time, I level out earlier than the time before but still we land a split second before I expect. Comes as quite a jolt.

The saving grace is that everyone so far is finding the same problem. We'll get it sorted.

As yet, there's only sporadic night flying at Barkston. Again, it's down to delays in the ground-works contract. The cold-weather problems with the dispersal have led to knock-on delays in installing the runway lights. An attempt is made to solve the problem with a single row of 'gooseneck' flares (watering-can-like containers with a wick protruding from the spout) on the south side of the main runway. When lit, these would rarely blow out.

But the problem is, being placed on just one side of the runway, there's no perspective for judging approach and round-out. One student gets himself on the wrong side of the lights and would have landed on the grass – but for an observant corporal in the caravan with a red Very light.

So Barkston's night flying is put off until at least January, in the hope that by then, the full set of standard electric lighting should be installed.

***

For degree and AFRAeS students, fitting everything into the time available is becoming a real headache and a group has decided to petition the authorities for a change of plan. For a start, selected students keep a daily journal. Peter, in the 'B' (Science) Stream, in response to a specific request from the Assistant Commandant, writes:

The norm would be breakfast at 0700 hours before academics from 0800-1145 followed by a quick early lunch and a dash to catch the bus to Barkston Heath at 1215. There, an afternoon's flying would (if there were time) be followed by a belated tea break back at the College.

I would then change and, at 1745 run down to the gym for fencing or modern pentathlon before finishing up with a swim of forty lengths or so. Back at the College I would just catch the end of supper at around 1945 before retiring to my room and getting my books out. I'd start on a few maths exercises before after half-an-hour, exhaustion would set in and I'd fall asleep for an hour or so.

I'd then start work again before possibly fitting in a short coffee break at 2300 – and maybe a chat with other 'B' Stream members in my squadron.

Another hour's work and I would eventually get into bed sometime after midnight, when my brain was so active that it would take me an hour to drop off.

Peter reckons that he's averaging less than six hours' sleep a night. The group reports similarly and assert that the constant burning of the midnight oil is adversely affecting academic and flying progress both.

They resolve to take their case forward in the New Year.

***

There's much excitement at the South Airfield on Saturday 2nd December, a Jet Provost Mark 4 is flown in, the first of an expected fourteen. Following an Assistant Commandant's early-morning parade, many a Flight Cadet finds his way down to take a look. There's not actually anything to see – basically, it's identical to the Mark 3. The secret lies in the engine.

The Viper 102 in the Mark 3 develops a maximum of 1,750 lb of static thrust at sea level, enough to climb to 30,000 feet in half an hour. The Viper 202 in the Mark 4 delivers 2,500 lb of thrust and makes the same altitude in half that time. Top speed increases from 350 to 400 knots. Pilot trainees can now truly claim to be flying a machine that can match the performance of the Spitfire. They cannot wait to get their hands on one.

However, most of them have to wait. The Lincs winter climate again gains the upper hand and flying days become a scarce commodity – but the few hours flown are much enlivened by the introduction to the syllabus of formation sorties.

Again, John writes:

> We go up in pairs, each with an instructor. One of us flies straight and level while the other chap comes up to try and keep into position, behind and just below the wingtip. Doing that, both of us jump around a bit at first.
>
> The instructor tells me to forget all about the Hornet Moth and Chipmunk – there, you have the propeller, instantly ready to respond to the throttle and pull you forward or back. With a jet aircraft, there's a lag, and you're tempted to overcorrect. The trick is, small movements – edge her up into position.
>
> Difficult to describe – but it's OK once you've got the knack of it.

228

Right: Jet Provost Mk 4. (*RAF College Journal*)

Below: JPs in formation. (*RAF College Journal*)

Mark also writes, to Sally:

> This formation flying's what it's all about. Concentration – in spades. Blimey, you're wallowing around like great silver fish in a bowl – just a few feet from each other – trying to keep far enough away. But not too far – don't want to fall out of the echelon.
>
> You forget about everything else. No worries about where we are or whether we're up, down or sideways – just keep position. Best not to wonder what course the leader's steering – if he flew into a mountain you'd still have to follow him.
>
> I think of those fighter boys in the Battle of Britain. Must have taken iron will to stay in formation with all that mayhem going on all round.
>
> I've had just the three hours so far – can't wait for more.

By 10th of December, John's again writing:

> I've just had my fourth formation flight, the second one with three planes in a Vic. Each of us spends twenty minutes in each position.
>
> Number three, on the left of the Vic is the most difficult. You have to look across the cockpit, right past the instructor's helmet, but clear of the edge of the sliding hood. Apart from that, it's the same trick – nudge her into position and forget everything else.
>
> The weather was awful during the trip but it didn't matter. Turns out formatting in cloud is somehow easier – not distracted by the horizon – suspended in space and time, as it were, and never mind the snow.
>
> The snow got so bad that we had to call for a radar steer to the airfield. We went into line-astern – twelve feet back and the same distance down – following every movement of the fellow in front. I was mesmerised – forgot the snow and cloud. Came to when the instructor suddenly said, 'I have control'. Looked up and there we were on the approach.
>
> 'Undercarriage down, John.' 'Roger, Sir. Undercarriage down. Three greens.'

The instructors, determined to keep their students' interest going, wherever possible ginger things up with tail-chases and simulated dogfights. Another diversion, if it's possible to climb above the cloud and into the clear by 20,000 feet, is to fly a high-level familiarisation sortie to 30,000.

THE PRESSURE BUILDS

Flight Lieutenant Holbourn takes his student up there one December day for the first time and Mark finds it so surreal that he's compelled to write to Sally again:

> Imagine it. Think of getting into your Ford convertible with me alongside you, closing the roof and driving for thirty minutes up a steep road to about a thousand feet higher than Everest. No pressurisation, so ears a-popping all the way up. Heating yes – but about halfway up you can start to feel the chill in your boots. If you've got a face mask connected to an oxygen cylinder you'll be all right, but keep an eye on it – it's your lifesaver.
>
> Up here it's very, very lonely. You can see that our planet is indeed round, but be careful to watch out. Trouble is, your eyes focus on the distant horizon – they lose sight of closer things, say another Ford, before it's on top of you and it's too late to do anything about it.
>
> You're not exactly bothered when I suggest it's time to go home. You haven't got much left in the tank so you turn round, and it's full-tilt back down through the clouds, going faster than the fastest train and getting down to sea-level, ears a-throbbing, in just over six minutes.
>
> Then you realise – you'll have covered 120 miles on the ground getting up there. Better call base for a steer, quick.

***

The new blood in the Navigation group seems to have lifted spirits somewhat. Noel in particular has a refreshing approach:

> At Clifton College, as well as 'A' level Maths, Physics and Chemistry, I passed the Civil Service Admission Exam and applied for Cranwell. It took a year to get here, during which I enjoyed myself caving, with a summer job as guide at Wookey Hole – that financed a uniquely terrible Austin Seven.
>
> But I wasn't a piloting fanatic. Perhaps that's why I was eventually chopped at my 100-hour check – for 'slow progress' in the Piston Provost. That, despite my managing to survive the bottom two cylinders blowing off the Alvis Leonides engine at 7,000 feet –and a dead-stick and flapless landing downwind back at Barkston – all on my third solo.

231

In any event, I'm not too disappointed. I'd come to Cranwell with the aim of being a navigator and was surprised to discover that I was ever considered as a potential pilot. Air navigation's important – why? Simply because all aircraft fly in winds, which bugger up our planned tracks and groundspeeds.

In December, adverse weather has once again held the navigators back – robust as they may be, Pigs are not the best at coping with airframe icing. The last airborne exercises take place in the first week of the month.

The disappointing beat-rate of roughly one sortie per week is continuing and Jim confesses to Jock that he's not the happiest of bunnies.

'I am, quite honestly loathing this final year. I'm seriously contemplating a transfer to a Direct Entry course. I'll have a word with Annie Oakley and we'll see.'

**

The second weekend of December sees the hard-pressed Geographers of the 'C' Streams of 81, 83 and 85 Entries carrying out chilly field studies in the fenlands of East Anglia. Then, on two evenings of the following week, Sid and Mark and their WRAF Officer friends from Spitalgate tread the boards with their *Nude With Violin*, to muted applause.

There's a good house but it seems that the title of the piece has given many of the playgoers the wrong idea – of artist's models and stringed instruments there's not a sign. Sid is commended for his production work and Mark gets a tick in the box marked 'sustained American accent'. It's been fun and made a change, so that's all good.

The weather relents enough for Mark to fly a Progress Check on the Friday – one hour with Master Pilot Jackson, running through the lot. It's his first trip with Dave's favourite instructor and he's most impressed – he most certainly puts him at his ease. All goes well – stall turns, rolls off the top, and it's beginning to come naturally.

That's it for both flying and academics for the term and from now on, it's going to be all about 80 Entry's graduation, right through to the Ball on Tuesday.

After the Saturday morning rehearsal for the Graduation Parade, a motorcade leaves the Cadets' Garage on a thirty-six hour pass. Among the cars is Jock's Mini, with passengers Tony and Adrian, hell-bent on getting down south to London as soon as they can.

At full tilt, on the single-carriageway A1 trunk-road at Alconbury Weston, Adrian, from his seat in the back, looks up and sees, filling the windscreen, the radiator and lights of a heavy lorry, heading north on the wrong side of the road. It flashes across his mind, 'We're going to hit that.'

He comes round next day in Huntingdon Hospital, severely concussed. Jock, in the same ward, doesn't properly wake up for three-and-a-half days. Tony is injured in the right eye by a swinging rally-lamp. The Mini's a complete write-off.

The police say that the lives of those in the front seats had been saved by the recently fitted seat belts, some of the first they'd seen. Adrian, unbelted in the back seat, had been hit by the unsecured TV set stowed beside him as well as head-butting the car's roof.

Everyone agrees that, where cars and aircraft are concerned, you never know what's round the corner.

How many lives does Jock have left?

***

The Yuletide celebrations arrive, with the traditional Festival of Nine Lessons and Carols pulling in the crowds at St Michael's. There's a Graduation Parade wet-weather rehearsal in the hangar, but in the event the weather relents and the main parade takes place on Tuesday 19th December on the College Parade Ground. For the first time ever, the Sword of Honour goes to a navigator, SUO Conran-Smith.

The graduating cadets of 80 Entry have a further distinction. They are the last to complete Advanced Flying Training at the College and progress directly to an Operational Conversion Unit. With them, go the Vampires and Meteors.

Following the parade, 81 Entry hand in their rifles – they'll not need those on parade in their final two terms. Then, at the Graduation Ball that evening, effectively now the Senior Entry, they proudly wear their newly-issued, made-to-measure Number Fives Mess Kit. A dozen of them stand perhaps more proudly than the rest – they're the ones promoted to Under Officer status for the entry's next, and last two terms. Senior Under Officers are to be Hugh, Mac, Boy and Kiwi – no surprises there. In January the final race to the Sword will start.

Blind Bill has kindly offered to transport Terry and Mark, together with all three of their partners from a B&B in Grantham to the Ball and back. After the event, when Bill finally manages to herd his passengers back into the van it's well into the small hours. So, on arrival at their lodgings, they find themselves locked out and unable to rouse the landlady.

As a result, three members of the future elite of the RAF's officer class, together with their long-suffering girls, find themselves dossing down in the depths of winter for what shut-eye they can get in a Ford Thames van – in the middle of the Ace Café car park.

When their landlady eventually opens her door, it's a noticeably subdued group that sits down for post-party bacon and eggs.

Mid-Winter Leave 1961/62

Over the mid-winter leave, no fewer than three parties of Flight Cadets go abroad for College Society-sponsored trips involving the increasingly popular sport of skiing: to Zermatt (where the intrepid Robin enjoys his baptism of the *pistes*) to Norway (by overnight boat and led by the indefatigable Kiwi) and to Saint Moritz, for the newly-inaugurated British Services Colleges Ski Championships. In the latter, results are shaded towards Dartmouth and Sandhurst but one of the Cranwell team saves the College's honour by winning the Giant Slalom.

Meanwhile, Mark's debate over matters nuclear with Sally's chums continues. On 30th October, the USSR had massively raised the stakes in the nuclear poker game. Over a remote island in the Russian far and frozen north, the Soviets had detonated a 30-megaton hydrogen bomb – far bigger than anything before it, or in the western powers' arsenals.

The mushroom cloud stretched seven times the height of Mount Everest. The heat from the explosion could have caused third-degree burns to people as far away as sixty-two miles from ground zero and the shockwave broke windows 560 miles away. Sensors continued to identify the shockwaves after their third trip around the globe. World leaders rushed to condemn the Russians' escalation of the Arms Race – as do Sally's chums. Mark is for once speechless – the enormity of the whole affair is beyond his comprehension.

Then there's the whole question of the escalating stand-off between the United States and the North Vietnamese. As 1962 arrives, the Americans have positioned 18,000 so-called 'Military Advisers' in South Vietnam, together with a fleet of helicopters assigned to transport the Advisers and 400 Regular Military personnel. Here, the one question on most lips is, 'Can Harold Macmillan and his Tory Cabinet keep us out of it?'

Against this belligerent and stressful background, Mark is amused when for a Christmas present, Sally gives him a copy of Joseph Heller's newly-published military satire, *Catch 22*. Yossarian's travails in the face of military absurdities ring a good few bells with him but he deems it sensible to leave that one on the bookshelves at home.

Chapter 11

Top of the Tree

Term 8: *10th Jan-10th Apr 1962*

At the start of the Spring Term, Mark finds opinions on the nuclear question among his colleagues are split. Some are convinced that without the Brits and Americans having nuclear weapons in the 1940s, Stalin would have invaded Western Europe and NATO cannot afford to lose ground in the nuclear stakes now. Others say that without their own nuclear arsenals, politicians would be weakened in any international negotiations. A few keep their thoughts to themselves but the whole business of the arms race and the threat of nuclear war cannot be ignored and won't go away.

Unsurprisingly, even among the most gung-ho of the entry, no one seems keen to join the American allies in their Indo-Chinese adventure anytime soon.

All most certainly agree that these are tense times and they're aware that in seven short months' time, they'll be away from the College and plunging into the maelstrom.

***

Despite all possible pitfalls, forty-one survivors of the original fifty-five members of 81 Entry have arrived back at College as the Senior Entry. In addition to the dozen who have not stayed the course, four have been re-mustered to 82 Entry while six have been retreaded from 80 Entry. The net result is that the new Senior Entry numbers forty-seven souls, sitting atop the College pyramid which comprises 290 Flight Cadets. Of these, 243 are pilots, twenty-six are navigators and twenty Equipment and Secretarial, and for the very first time, there's representation from the RAF Regiment – one all on his own in 86, the Junior Entry.

Jock and Adrian are back. Following the car-crash before Christmas, Jock has been diagnosed with a degree of brain damage but has been

235

deemed fit to fly and so returns to the course with everyone else. Adrian however, is grounded with a suspected paralysed eye muscle which gives him intermittent double-vision and poor depth perception. Pending further developments, he is continuing academic and ground studies with the rest.

***

Batmen have effected the necessary changes in uniform. Senior Under Officers need an inverted chevron of Flying Officer braid on each sleeve and Under Officers the same, but of thinner Pilot Officer braid. All members of the entry have their brass-buttoned gorgets enhanced with pilot officer gold braid.

Among the long-standing privileges afforded to the Senior Entry – use of the Senior Mess front door, access to the Atrium carpet and surrounds and immunity from Strikers – the most immediately useful is a fleet of RAF-blue bicycles, stowed at both east and west wings. The chaps now have more mobility, coupled with freedom from marching in squads wherever they go. On top of that, SUOs and UOs move into modest flats – within the existing cadet wings of the building but provided with private bathroom and more study space.

The Senior Flight Cadets get a taste of duty by taking their turn as Adjutant, one for each of the four squadrons. The tasks include typing up and publishing the cadet duty list for each week – Orderly Cadet and so forth – as well as preparing the Flight Commander's office for charge hearings, and publicising anything that the Flight Sergeant or the Flight Commander might have in mind.

At least that job keeps a man off the roster for Orderly Cadet, which among other administrative duties requires being out on the Parade Ground early in the morning taking the 0600 hours Strikers parade before saluting the College Flag as it's raised at 0800 and reversing the procedure at the 1630 sunset ceremony. It is noted that the Instructions for Orderly Cadets insist that no matter what the weather, 'Orderly Cadets are not to wear raincoats on this parade'.

'A' Squadron excelled themselves in the Autumn Term, winning both the Knocker and the Ferris competition and thus are Sovereign's Squadron for this penultimate term. They'll have the centre sprig at Guest Nights and one of their UOs (Nigel or Jim) will be carrying the Colour on ceremonial parades.

***

236

The degree-level studies group waste no time in putting their proposals for change forward. These basically involve a complete cessation of flying for the specialist streams for a period of four weeks before their final external exams, the loss of flying hours to be regained when they're completed.

Flight and Squadron Commanders accept this proposal in the spirit in which it is offered and take the matter up the command chain.

***

Flying gets underway on Friday, 12th January. The usual passengers on the Barkston bus find themselves sharing Fangio and his driving team with their colleagues from 83 Entry, now resident in the Senior Mess and starting their Jet Provost training this term.

From these new boys, the relatively old lags of 81 Entry hear that the Chipmunk programme has been considerably gingered up since their day. To fly the ten Chippies on strength, sufficient QFIs and training hours were made available last term to send twenty-six of 83 Entry's trainees solo.

Mark is still aware of the possibility of the chop. His first two sorties are with Bill's old instructor, the hard man on the QFI team. He decides to treat them as check-rides and apparently does the business. Early the following week he enjoys two hours' General Handling with Flight Lieutenant Holbourn before being sent off for two solo sorties, for one of which he's cleared for solo spins. Exciting? You betcha!

Later, relaxing in the FGS, and clear of all fear of the flying chop, he compares notes (utilising plentiful hand gestures in time-honoured pilot fashion) with Tim, who's also spun solo and observes:

> It takes an element of bravado to put yourself into a spin. I sure had to psych myself up for it. But up I go, carry out the HASELL checks, close the throttle and kick the JP over into a left-hand spin. After no more than two turns, I put a stop to it with full right rudder, stick forward and ease out of the dive, applying power in the approved manner. No sweat.
>
> I'm sorely tempted not to risk my neck again, but I know that I really should have a go the other way. So I do – to the right, with three turns this time. Then – a further spin to the left, and four turns. After this I reckon I shouldn't push my luck – and fly home.
>
> Of course, back in the crew room I just have to tell everyone what I've done. Know what? They're amazed. 'Did you really

do all this? None of *us* actually did any solo spinning – it seems a crazy sort of thing to do on your own.'

Do you know, at the time I actually believed they meant it.

No matter what, all spin-merchants agree that they're pleased to have done it. They now know that if necessary they could recognise and recover from a spin, and will feel much more confident in taking on aero sequences that include stall turns.

***

Before the week is out, there's their first Guest Night as Senior Entry, and a chance to enjoy their new status at the head of the sprigs, alongside, on this occasion, senior Commonwealth Dignitaries over for a conference.

There's amusement when Mister Vice seeks to respond to the President's toast – so much so that Mac is moved to write home about it:

> The boys have enjoyed their dinner, drink and chatter and the call from the top table's a toast to 'the Heads of State of Nations here represented'.
>
> Mister Vice, who's the youngest of 83 Entry and bewildered by his first experience of a Senior Mess function, tries his very best to repeat. But there's a veritable train-crash of failures. Too many close sibilants by far to be anywhere near accurate.
>
> 'Gentlemen, the toast is the nations of heads…' Tries again, 'the state of nations…' Poor lad.
>
> But then, of course the diners have, *en masse*, the impossible task of repeating whatever it is that Mister Vice has finally managed to get out. Choose your own version! All now in state of complete collapse. Simply repeating what the President had originally said is now beyond the wit of man.
>
> The gavel and a call to the horn player for his world-famous Post Horn Gallop allows all the respite of a seated recovery. Now of course, we're all waiting for what happens when the poor chap who's down to be the next Mister Vice replays the whole glorious scenario.

In the mess games following the port, cigars and speeches, the new Senior Entry just cannot resist the call of 'Bicycles, Bicycles, Bicycles!' from the more junior men. Honour is at stake.

So it is that two bikes are fetched in from their racks outside East and West doors while brave volunteers draw lots for the inaugural joust. At the same time, mops and dustbin lids are sought from behind the kitchens and bone-domes are brought down from their wardrobe-top perches.

Two of the elected squadron pairs then make their ways separately to the two first corners in the main corridor, some hundred yards apart. There, the bike is positioned centrally, pointing back at the Founders' Gallery under the Rotunda and the burliest of the couple, by now bone-domed, clambers aboard and firmly grasps the handlebars. Then, the lighter of the pair, also bone-domed, with the help of supporters scrambles up to sit astride the shoulders of his 'horse', feet secured under his steed's armpits. The 'rider', is then handed a mop (the lance) and a dustbin-lid (the shield). All set!

On the call from the umpire (the Sovereign's Squadron SUO), 'Ride!' pedals are pushed, lift-off speed is reached and the two wobbly crews hurtle down the corridor, lances cocked, shields up. The rule of the road here is keep to the left.

With the most enormous clatter, the two outfits meet in the middle just about alongside the portrait of Her Majesty. Lances are knocked askew by shields that more often than not fall to the floor, lances meet chests and on occasion, about one in ten, one outfit falls over and the other is victorious.

Still upright! (*NGB*)

But nine times out of ten, bicycles, mops, dustbin-lids, horses and riders end up in a tangled heap on the floor. Bone-domes, as well as the amount of alcohol taken on board by all concerned, miraculously keep injuries to everything and everyone – including spectators – down to the minor variety.

Guests, if they haven't already retired, are astounded – as are the new boys of 83 Entry. When the final race, usually of four, has run its course, the cadets then start to build human pyramids to see which squadron can get a man up onto the gallery and back down the stairs again to HMQ's picture in the shortest time.

Anything for a challenge – they say it's all part of the training.

***

Also part of the training is the Knocker Cup. This term, again it's swimming – in an unheated pool in the middle of a Lincolnshire winter. It's uncomfortable but safer than the jousting – just in case, there's a medic standing by. This time, 'C' Squadron win.

With that behind them, the start of night flying for 81 Entry seems almost a joyride. For Mark, it really is. He writes home:

> I had two sorties yesterday – close on two hours' worth, dual, with Flight Lieutenant Holbourn. The whole thing was a complete eye-opener and highly enjoyable.
>
> The first thing was setting off to work in the evening (after a specially laid-on high tea) down to Barkston Heath in the bus. At the airfield, we all troop in for a Night Ops briefing. We're told there's night-flying at Cranwell too but normal air-traffic procedures will make sure we keep apart. The Met-man says the clear skies are forecast to last until a few hours before dawn. So that's okay.
>
> Walking out to the aircraft, under starry skies is the stuff of so many flying stories it's almost hackneyed, but I tell you Mum, it ain't half something.
>
> The next thing is – the lights. Inside the cockpit, all softly glowing at night-time settings, and outside, all amber (to starboard) and blue (to port) alongside the taxiways to help you find your way – and then as you soar up, pinpoints to help you orientate to the ground below. If you're lucky, there's a distinct horizon too – stars above, dark with the odd village

streetlamp below. Then, you can fly head-up but need to keep a regular eye on the instruments for monitoring speeds, heights and engine settings.

It's odd, but I don't find it at all scary. Safe as houses in a warm cocoon. But then comes the landing.

Barkston has a new set of runway lights, so lining up to land is a doddle. Then, you have to use the altimeter as well as your instincts to judge the descent to the runway. The instructor did the first couple with me following him on the controls. It strikes me on the second go that with the nose-up attitude in the last hundred feet, letting the aircraft sink to the ground is rather like letting yourself down into a bath! I kept that to myself but by golly, it worked!

No trouble at all. Flt Lt Holbourn says I should go solo next time.

To cap all that, when we got back to College, there was a fry-up supper waiting for us. What's not to like about night-flying?

***

A couple of days later, on the Barkston bus, the stories are going around about the night's events. Across the two airfields, one of the JPs had a flame-out as the instructor was attempting some forbidden night aeros – the aircraft suffered damage in the subsequent heavy dead-stick landing. The tail-pipe of another had struck the ground on landing and yet another ran off the taxiway. None of these incidents resulted in bodily harm but the establishment of serviceable JPs is down to thirty-seven.

Also on the grapevine is the news that another from 'C' Squadron, a King's School Grantham man, has left the College – for medical reasons associated with sinuses. This brings the original 81 Entry 'C' Squadron contingent down to ten.

***

Meanwhile, the navigators have got back in the air. Noel has a take, for any pilot who wants to hear it, on what that means in terms of work:

Our charts for UK flights are large scale – one to a million – Mercator maps with virtually no topographic information on them at all, just airfields printed on otherwise blank maps.

We have to lay the map onto an illuminated glass cabinet and trace in all the airways and restricted areas from a master copy underneath. Then we plot in all the beacons that might come in useful. Next we draw the route, and across it, all the magnetic variation lines. This is all against the clock – we're not allowed to prepare anything in advance.

I guess it's all part of putting pressure on the flight planning process – in any event, it's a regal pain in the arse. It's not until that's done that we do the flight planning – calculating heading, distance and time for each leg.

Then comes the flight and navigating the Pig around the nation for three sweaty hours of discomfort.

It takes Jim until the nineteenth of the month to fly his first mission of the term – fifty-three days since his last. By now, he's had his conversation with Flight Lieutenant Oakley, initiated as it happens by the instructor himself.

Again, Jim confides in Jock:

I'd decided to plod on, mostly through fear of being thrown out of the RAF on my ear. But now, our nice Phil Oakley has taken me on one side and explained that – very much to his own amazement – I've been boarded for suspension from the College!

I've had little routine feedback but as far as I know, there's no reason why I shouldn't be reckoned a 'fully-rounded' cadet. They've made me an Under Officer for heaven's sake. From what Phil says, I reckon that it's my Economics and Military Studies results that are the problem. I've been shafted by tutors!

Phil's a friend anyhow – he'll fight my corner.

So, well into his sixth year as an RAF Cadet, Jim does plod on.

He's not the only Under Officer in the group of 81 Entry navigators. 'B' Squadron has Vernon and John the Nav, and 'D' has Anthony (alongside pilot Andy). 'C' Squadron alone has a trio of pilots at the top, Sid and Robert joining SUO Kiwi.

***

The good weather continues and on the first day of February, following an hour dual, Mark satisfactorily completes ACR7 radar approaches at

Cranwell (you never know when you might need one of those at night) and is qualified to go solo. The 'bath let-down' approach works a treat and he finds the whole experience hugely satisfying – so much so that he writes in his logbook '45 mins solo', in red.

There's also the thrill of landing and taking off from two further satellite airstrips – the one a couple of miles west of the College at Fulbeck and the other over to the west of Grantham at Bottesford. A big part of that thrill is that the strips are marked out with gooseneck flares. Biggles, eat your heart out.

There's more excitement the very next day, when he flies another milestone sortie – his first in a JP4. His instructor takes him up in the new and powerful machine for further High Level Familiarisation. The climb to 30,000 feet in fifteen minutes is exhilarating when compared with the Mark 3's half-an-hour, and there's time for more upper-air work.

On the descent, there's still time for a few aeros and Mark's impressed. Like many of the entry, he joins the club that seeks to get their hands on a Mark 4 whenever possible.

This is the day when, for the first time at Cranwell, he logs five sorties in a day's flying, and three of those are at night. After fifteen minutes dual in the circuit, he's sent off for twenty-five minutes, followed by another forty, of circuits and landings, all designed to set him up for cross-country exercises next week.

With academics to be fitted in, it's good that it's Friday, and there's nothing but private study tomorrow. It's another first when Mark sleeps in and misses breakfast. He's not the only one.

While the cadets enjoy a few hours of relative quiet, far above their level of consciousness, asleep or awake, there are continued machinations over the Cranwell syllabus – indeed about the very make-up of the College.

The measures taken in the 1950s to attract a greater percentage of grammar and technical schoolboys have had an unexpected result. They've certainly reduced the number of Flight Cadets entering the College from Headmasters' Conference Schools – that's fallen from 50 per cent for 80 Entry in January 1959 to 22 per cent for 85 in September 1961. But now, the College is not attracting sufficient numbers of the top brains – it seems that most of those are now going on to University. What's to be done?

Under consideration at the Air Ministry is the option of awarding publicly-funded scholarships to suitable candidates who would join the Service after graduation. Thus, Graduate Entry is on the agenda – those who had already obtained degrees, supported by an RAF Scholarship, and trained in basic flying at an RAF UAS, would arrive at Cranwell for professional and advanced flying-training only.

The newly-appointed AOC-in-C Flying Training Command, Air Marshal Augustus (Gus) Walker, enters the fray. In attending a series of summer 1961 meetings in the Commandant's office, the Air Marshal has noted the main causes of concern at the College. First, the overall GD wastage rate (those who leave the College prematurely) from 1955 to 61 averaged a disappointing 33% (although from 81 Entry and onwards, the Jet Provost era, the rate is much reduced).

The AOC accepts that the current syllabus puts pressure on flying training but the investment in the Chipmunk stage is paying dividends by achieving the target of forty-nine basic flying hours per cadet.

He acknowledges that the intensity of flying is too low, particularly at the critical early and final stages of training. To fix this, he proposes an increase in Jet Provost hours by sixteen per cadet and asks that the additional aircraft be made available as soon as possible.

He recognizes the increased load on 'B' and 'C' streams of exams when, as Senior Entry, they have additional responsibilities. However, as 81 Entry has yet to complete the first experience of the new syllabus, it is premature to pass judgement. He also sees the imbalance caused by there being no London University exams in December, leaving the even-numbered entries no opportunity to try for an external BA and asks for a full investigation of options.

He also asks for an early review of the effects on the curriculum of the coming Henlow merger, as well as recommending a strong publicity and recruiting campaign be mounted with the aim of attracting high quality cadets for Cranwell. In conclusion the paper recommends the 'Cranwell syllabus be stabilized until the end of 1964, on the basis of these proposals'.

With the full support of the Commandant, the AOC, (since the New Year's Honours, Air Chief Marshal Sir Augustus Walker, KCB) delivers his findings to the CAS, on 5th February 1962. The recommendations are accepted and implementation undertaken, but debate continues. Meanwhile, at the forefront of Staff minds are the practicalities of handling the merger with Henlow, which is to see an extra 100 cadets, together with 250 student officers, descend on the station by 1965. Seen as a critical path is moving equipment eighty miles while keeping the training running at both ends. A second Air Ministry Working Party is set up.

Of greater concern in the wider world, are mounting tensions in Cuba. On February 7th, a U.S. embargo ordered by President Kennedy goes into effect on all imports from Cuba, including tobacco, seafood, fruits and vegetables. What will be the Soviet reaction?

The roll-call for the night programme has included Jock, who has miraculously resumed flying training. His I/F is not as good as it could be but everything else is remarkably serviceable.

Adrian, however, is to do no more flying at Cranwell. The eye muscle has remained paralyzed and the prognosis is that it will remain so for life. He will be completing the ground-based syllabus with the entry and, with success in the final examinations will graduate and be commissioned with his colleagues. He remains a champion shot and his officer qualities are not in doubt.

***

Advanced I/F Grades are awarded before the next session of night-flying in the second week of February. The AIFG qualifies the trainee pilots to carry out radar-guided approaches to the runway, and this in turn clears them to fly the challenging Night Navigation exercises scheduled the same week. The second of these will be solo. On the hour-long first sortie with Flight Lieutenant Holbourn, Mark finds that lights on the ground do not necessarily correspond precisely with towns marked on the maps – he's much confused by the lights of Corby's steelworks being so much more extensive than suggested by the chart. But the electronic Distance Measuring Equipment (DME) comes to his aid and all's well – as it is on the solo trip. The route's the same, but the wind's capricious and the sense of achievement on landing is considerable.

That same evening, on Tim's first solo night cross-country, things are not quite so straightforward:

> I find my way around with no difficulty and perform an immaculate re-join to the Barkston circuit only to wonder as I turn onto finals why there are now so many unexpected lights on the ground to my right, where only fields should be.
>
> Then, it dawns. I've aligned myself with the active runway at Cranwell, not Barkston.
>
> I sheepishly increase power, raise the wheels and flaps and sneak off to my home airfield – from which the Air Traffic Controller's now saying he can't see me. I confirm that I'm on 'long finals', lower the flaps and wheels once again, and gratefully land back at home.
>
> Nobody's said anything – so far.

On the Barkston bus for night flying the following week, the story on the grapevine is that somebody, who shall remain nameless, lined up for final approach on the lights of Ancaster High Street. Fortunately he did not let down into someone's bath.

***

Two weeks into February, there's a further Guest Night. The word gets around from 83 Entry that they're in the process of installing oil-fired central heating in the South Brick Lines and that henceforth they're to be known as First Term Cadet Accommodation.

Apart from that, the night's a fairly subdued affair – many of the leading roisterers are taking an early-morning bus the next day for the annual soccer, squash, basketball and cross-country contests at Henlow. Others are taking seriously next Monday's start, in London, of further Civil Service Linguist and Interpreter oral and written French tests. UO Anthony takes a party of seven for Linguist tests and the success rate is high. SUO Hugh and SFC Mark are entered for the Interpreter exam – Hugh (raised in Cannes) passes, Mark (raised in Surrey) doesn't. He drowns his disappointment in the Captain's Cabin before meeting up with Sally and her theatrical chums in her flat in the Finchley Road.

The final week of February sees two more sorties of night cross-country before the College shuts down for a four-day mid-term break.

***

246

The rugby and soccer teams fly off in the Navigation Flight's aircraft to spend the weekend testing their endurance on sports field and in bar with the tough men of RAF Gütersloh in Germany, formerly a Luftwaffe airfield much loved by Hermann Göring.

Nine other brave young men, led by the pioneering Mike, return to the Cairngorms – this time to test the burgeoning skiing facilities and the warmth of the welcome at the Alt-na-Craig Hotel, Aviemore. They are not disappointed – snow and snifters are in good supply.

***

Back at College, flying is underway in the first week of March and Mark has a truly memorable experience – two trips to 30,000 feet in a JP4.

The first is in the form of a checkride, again with the QFI who got Bill's goat months before and who's now the Flight Commander. No holds are barred. Steep turns at altitude, high-level aeros and max-rate descent follow one another in a potentially bewildering stream. To his great relief, sinuses, eardrums, blood and guts meet all requirements and he's cleared to do the whole thing again within the hour – this time solo. He finds the experience more than usually testing.

As always, he shares his thoughts with Sid.

'It's bloody strange, sitting up there all on your tod in an unpressurized aluminium cigar tube, with nothing between the seat of your pants and terra firma than a bang-seat. Eerily quiet, no weather outside and the universe above. Surreal.

'And I'll tell you what – the JP4's a great piece of kit but she needs a lot more more attention at the limits. Quite a challenge – but the right sort of training for a combat pilot. What do you reckon?'

Sid sucks on his pipe and wisely keeps his counsel. 'Come on, the bus is waiting.'

***

A favourable response to the Studies group's proposal comes back from the powers-that-be, but while the details are being sorted out between the Flying and College Wings, flying in March whistles along.

Weather and continuity are good. In the second week, there are more formation exercises, both dual and solo. Mark flies on his own as Number 2 in Blue Formation for a whole exciting hour – before falling asleep in front of his Economics tutor in the afternoon.

The night-flying programme is completed the following week. On the first evening, it's two one-and-a-half-hour night cross-countries in the JP4, again the first dual and the second solo, and both concluding with radar-guided approaches.

Blue Formation closing up. (*RAF College Journal*)

Everyone gets a tick in the box for the exercise and there's general agreement that it's been fun – taking a high-performance aircraft and navigating around the skies of Middle England at night, by definition makes a man feel a cut above the rest.

The following night, dual practices for the Final Night Test begin. Mark flies for close on two hours before passing the test two days later in a seventy-five-minute sortie with the Squadron Commander. A major milestone towards Wings and a test in which all succeed.

Mark's up again the very next day, for an hour's solo in a JP4 soaring up to 30,000 feet and back again, with all the business in between, and after one cup of ockled coffee, flying for a further hour's dual as Blue 3 in echelon-starboard.

'A' Stream men are delighted. 'Wow! Six sorties in four days. That's the sort of continuity they get at an FTS – that's more like it.'

But the 'B' and 'C' Stream students see the flip-side – those essays and papers just have to be done. Midnight oil is in great demand.

Dave speaks for them all. 'The AFRAeS and BA exams are coming up in a dozen short weeks' time and require non-stop work. This month so far, I've been flying night solos until two-thirty in the morning, before study next morning and more flying in the afternoon.

'The revision has to wait until the evenings – and on into the small hours. I'm setting two alarm clocks to wake me up in morning.

'They wouldn't allow that at an FTS, would they?'

Eyes down, cramming. (*FM*)

'A' Stream extra-curricular instruction at 'Sleaford Tech'. (*AJG*)

As well as the flying and academics, the other pressures on revision time continue. March has two Guest Nights scheduled in its first two weeks, the second in honour of visitors from the RAF Staff College at Bracknell, and 81 Entry, all three streams, are detailed to act as personal guides for that – no arguments.

There's further bulling and practice for the Ferris drill competition. The show put on for the Sandhurst judges on the tenth of the month is immaculate, with a debut in the competition for 84 Entry. But it's eaten up further potential revision hours. The winners? Flight Sergeant Holt's 'C' Squadron, naturally.

Sport, of course, continues on its merry way. The earlier hockey match against Dartmouth having been postponed (down to an outbreak of particularly virulent measles) potential BAs Mark and Ross find themselves with the team on an early-morning Valetta for a ninety-minute flight down to Exeter. They play the match (a draw) have a cup of tea and then return to Cranwell by train, arriving Grantham late evening. More study-time missed.

Then, on Thursday March 22nd, a party from L'Ecole de l'Air visits for rugby and fencing matches. Twenty-seven of what they call *Aspirants* steal the show, at both the College and in the local area.

L'Ecole de l'Air victorious. (*RAF College Journal*)

On the rugby field, they beat the College, captained by Mac, for the first time since the war, and in the pubs and clubs they make further conquests. Jock, one of the French-speaking hosts remarks, 'We had a bit of trouble with the local lads at a dance at Navenby village hall, when they took exception to the smooth French chaps in their uniforms moving in on the local lasses!'

***

The good flying weather continues throughout March and into the first week of April. By the end of term, as well as the Final Night Test, the pilots of 81 Entry have completed a dual and solo low-level cross-country (round the Boston Stump), as well as, for some, a solo formation landing-away trip to RAF Cottesmore, to assist in the celebrations of its reopening as an operational station.

The dual sortie entails that great show-stopper, a formation run-in and break. This is where the leader takes the formation in at low level and high speed in echelon across the threshold of the duty runway before calling, 'Break', the signal for a steep climbing turn, one by one to downwind and circuit height, before a stream approach and landing. 'The real bee's knees,' reckons Mark, 'especially in a JP4 with that extra poke.'

On the final Friday of the month, Flight Lieutenant Holbourn takes him on a land-away cross-country to RAF Aldergrove, in Northern Ireland. With twenty-five minutes actual instrument minutes and an airway crossing on the way out, the trip is his longest so far, at one hour forty-five minutes, and he finds it a highly rewarding experience. On arrival back at Barkston, he shakes his instructor's hand with heartfelt thanks for the last seven months together.

***

Jim the Nav has heard nothing more of the possible suspension proceedings – 'I put that down to Phil Oakley's efforts' – and something has at last been done about the continuity problem.

The beat-rate is still one mission a week (although to compensate for the mid-term break, there are two lengthy sorties on each of three days in March) but the first nav/second nav changeover has come at mid-term. The students have four goes in a row as the route-finder followed by four more on the sextant. Continuity at a stroke.

***

The penultimate week of term is a particularly busy one, in the air and on the ground.

Monday 2nd April is the first night of two colourful offerings of Gilbert and Sullivan's comic operetta *HMS Pinafore*. Despite the AFRAeS situation, UO Sid has found the time and motivation to take on the role of long-suffering Producer and 'A' Streamer UO Jim works his magic as Musical Director. As usual, the whole crew thanks their lucky stars for the presence of Spitalgate WRAFs and Cranwell's wives and daughters and the evening's a great antidote to the tensions of Flight Cadet life.

Captain Corcoran on deck...   ...admired by Buttercup and ladies of the
(*RAF College Journal*)   chorus. (*RAF College Journal*)

Three days later, one of those cadets has a truly frightening experience. An 82 Entry man, solo in cloud, sees lightning strike his starboard tip tank. When the tank begins to break up in the slipstream, and directional control is lost, he has no option but to resort to his Martin-Baker ejector seat and lands safely. The Jet Provost crashes into the fields one mile south of Rauceby Hospital.

***

The 81 Entry pilot trainees have now completed some 150 hours of the flying syllabus – just thirty to go to the end of the course. Dates for the BA and AFRAeS exams are now known – for the former, the first papers (for War Studies), are to be sat on 29th and 30th May. The dates of the AFRAeS exam, to be sat under the local control of the science tutors, have been set to coincide with the last of the London papers. In line with the plan agreed between the Wings, by soon after the beginning of next term, which will be on 2nd May, there will be no more flying for the 'B' and 'C' Stream pilots – for five weeks until after their exams.

Post-exams, there will then be just six weeks to conclude the Jet Provost hours. 'Eight hours a week – could be done,' reckon the examinees. 'And of course, for the first month of next term the General Streamers will have aircraft and instructors at their beck and call and we should have their full attention thereafter.'

'But what a performance it all is,' say some.

***

So the pressure's on to log the necessary exercises in this final week of flying.

Danny and Mark are among the many detailed for solo land-away high-level cross-countries, all the way up to RAF Leuchars, a fighter base north of St Andrews on the North Sea coast. On the trip, Mark has a problem with ice:

> I'd got past the Humber crossing and was coming up to York when I found I couldn't move the elevator trimmers. I reckoned that was probably ice that would melt away on the descent but what if it was something more serious? I could press on, but I was only a third of the way to Leuchars and I didn't fancy flying up there with frozen controls.
>
> So, I put out a PAN call on the emergency frequency and get diverted to the Number One FTS base at Linton-on-Ouse.
>
> The icing problem melts away as I lose height but the die is cast, as it were, and I land, parking in a line of Jet Provosts, feeling rather conspicuous with the Cranwell Cranes gleaming in the sunshine. I'm made very welcome and taken to lunch in the Mess - where I'm conscious I'm the only one in a flying suit.
>
> I then file a flight plan for Barkston, start up and fly home. The Flight Commander says I've fulfilled all the requirements of a land-away sortie and gained experience of a live PAN call into the bargain. He gives me a tick in the box for it.
>
> I just feel a bit sheepish about the whole thing.

In contrast, Danny's full of his trip – the experience of his flying life so far. He tells his story to the back seat boys:

> I've done the flight plan – it's to be one hour fifty minutes, at altitude. All the way up the East Coast, past Edinburgh and on.
>
> All goes well – lovely day – just a question of keeping the sea to starboard really. So, arrived at my destination, and

in a JP4, I decide to spice things up a bit by showing these Javelin jocks how a run and break is done!

High speed down the dead side, close the throttle, pull hard up and round whilst deploying airbrakes – but airbrakes iced in so disappear back up into the stratosphere!

I keep my head down in the flight hut.

Blind Bill lands just behind me. He has a problem with his aircraft that involves an engine ground-run. Unfortunately the jet efflux is pointing straight at the Wingco Ops office window. To say the least, he is not impressed.

Bill's aircraft is still u/s so how does he get back to Cranwell? With me of course! Over the phone from BH, the Flight Commander – one senses almost on his knees in supplication – says he will authorise us to return together but we must, must, *must* behave ourselves.

We do – and Bill becomes the first passenger I've ever flown.

Dave is another who makes it to Leuchars in a memorable way:

I climb to 25,000 feet en route and feeling exultant, I dive the whole way down over the final fifty miles for run-in and break into the circuit. It's something I'd practised dual but the Leuchars staff evidently don't appreciate it.

Hand smack on return from the Flight Commander.

***

After a Guest Night in the penultimate week, the bicycle jousting goes sadly awry. A priceless glass globe is smashed to smithereens and bikes are banned from the corridor, indefinitely.

The final business of the term can now be concluded. There are to be four additional Under Officers for the Summer Term – Pete ('A' Squadron) is one, John ('B'), Mark ('C'), and Phil ('D') are the others.

Following a count up of points from the competitions, 'C' are the Sovereign's Squadron for 81 Entry's final term and will provide the escort for the Queen's Colour at the Passing Out Parade at the end of July.

The Spring Term ends on Tuesday 10th April, but none of 81 or 82 Entries go home – they're already on board an RAF Transport Command Britannia, bucketing through Atlantic turbulence, en route the United States.

Easter Leave 1962

For the BA and AFRAeS students of 81 Entry, no time is available yet to revise for the exams just a few weeks away. From April 9th to 19th, 81 and 82 Entries, (in a party of twelve officers and ninety-five Flight Cadets, led by the Commandant himself), make a College liaison visit to the USA, visiting among other establishments, the United States Air Force Academy at Colorado Springs and the US Army Academy at West Point, New York.

A comprehensive Administrative Order has been raised for the trip within which the chaps are intrigued to see their SUOs appointed I/C parts of the logistics: Kiwi, 'Admin and Discipline'; Mac, 'Movements'; Hugh, 'Baggage'; Boy, 'In-flight Rations'. The more inventive among the party look forward to some potentially entertaining incidents on all four of those fronts as the tour progresses.

Not among the cadet travellers are navigators George and Noel – they did the USA trip the year before with 80 Entry. They've a jaunt to RAF Khormaksar in Aden instead. The rest have been issued with a pay book. These are for the administration of allowances to be paid daily against incidental expenses – US$10.50 per day in the big cities, US$9.50 elsewhere. They have also been allotted a cash advance and twenty US dollar notes are burning holes in their pockets.

Hundred-knot headwinds ensure eight hours of entrapped discomfort over the ocean and force a refuelling stop at Ernest Harman Air Force Base in Newfoundland. Boy comes under pressure to obtain emergency in-flight rations, for it's estimated that arrival at Bolling Air Force Base in Washington DC will not be before five o'clock local time. So it transpires, and the sandwiches and bottled water he's managed to scrounge save the day.

The welcome party at Bolling is incredulous. 'You crossed the Atlantic in *that*?' It won't be the last time they'll be hearing that kind of thing in the States. In service since 1952, the Britannia's turboprops are already giving the aircraft a dated appearance and performance when compared with the Boeing 707 jets now in service in America and worldwide.

***

Two and a half days are spent in the US capital, the visitors being escorted by officers of the resident Embassy staff. Lodgings however, are at the Air Force Base, where rations are plentiful but where the lavatories give quite a few cadets cause for concern. In this egalitarian USAF, they are designed to bring everyone down to a low squat, on long ranks of pedestals.

Many manage to wait until a visit to the Air and Space Exhibition in the Smithsonian Institute, and its more discreet facilities.

It's cherry-blossom time and the capital is looking its best. Several in the group stroll beside the Tidal Basin while others join the crowds on Pennsylvania Avenue welcoming the visiting Shah of Persia and his radiant Queen Farah, escorted by President Kennedy and First Lady Jackie in open-top Cadillacs.

The Britannia flies four hours, halfway across the continent, for the next stop, Offutt Air Force Base in Nebraska. Boy basks in reflected glory after distributing the most generous in-flight 'meal packages' provided by the USAF. However, that dims somewhat when the first item on the agenda at Offutt is a vast three-course lunch – with a whole chicken between three. It's not to be the last test of the capacity of chaps brought up on the restricted British diet of the 1940s and 50s.

Constructed at the Offutt base were the planes that in 1945 dropped 'Fat Man' and 'Little Boy' over Hiroshima and Nagasaki. It is now the home of the US Strategic Air Command HQ, where the US ground and aerial Nuclear War Command Centers are housed in a multi-floor bunker. Deep in the ground, the Cranwell party are given a privileged view as to how Armageddon might start.

Jim the Nav, making notes for the *Journal*, writes:

> Two hours later, a visibly shaken group emerges from the abyss into the bright Nebraskan sunshine having seen the heart of the most powerful force ever created by man. An impression of incredible efficiency and organisation – nothing left to chance, everybody doing their job calmly and confidently.

There's not much talking in the Britannia (food for stomach and thought both in over-supply) as she eats up another four hours of fuel flying westward to the Rockies and Colorado Springs.

The views on the approach to Peterson Air Force Base are awe-inspiring – towering, craggy mountains bathed in sunshine and capped with snow. They become even more impressive as Air Force buses carry the Cranwell visitors up to the campus itself. The futuristic chapel in the foreground stands starkly against the mountain peaks.

Met in a stunning sunset by a full Air Force band and the strains of *The Lincolnshire Poacher* played in swing-time, the party is soon enjoying a most memorable weekend.

Transport Command Britannia, among nuclear bombers. (*PJA*)

At drill with USAF Cadets at Colorado Springs. (*PJA*)

Jim the Reporter again makes notes:

> Perfect summer weather – assortment of very fast cars
> show much of Colorado and Rockies – gigantic dinner and
> dance night with 'blind date' with 200 participants – several
> Colorado steers being killed to provide dinner-plate size
> steaks – Cranwell win rugby and draw soccer but lose the
> soft-ball – day's skiing in the Rockies – friendships for
> life made.

The discipline is something else again. First-year rookies are required to raise their forks to their mouths at right angles and a draconian 'honour code' is in place for all. This puts the blight on Mark's Sunday when his host turns himself in for collecting a speeding ticket while treating his guest to a cruise down the Colorado Springs strip in his Chevrolet drophead Impala. This leads to his being 'gated' for the duration, together with his hapless guest. Instead of going skiing with his beautiful blonde partner of the Saturday evening, Mark finds himself in a lonely barrack block watching American Football on the television.

Bill finds time to write a postcard home:

> Colorado Springs has provided a strong contrast to Cranwell.
> Magnificent mountain setting but a four-year course with no
> flying at all! And the discipline's soul-destroying. I could never
> live with that. One thing though – it has made Cranwell seem
> just so much better.

***

On Monday, the faithful Britannia embarks the entire party at Peterson base for the trip back to the east. The runway stands at 7,000 feet altitude and it's the hottest day of the year so far.

Jim the Reporter's pen goes into overdrive:

> As we turn onto the runway, the navigator's hanging out of the
> back door! Funny, we think.
>
> All is revealed when the pilot selects REVERSE on the
> props and very carefully edges backwards, with the navigator
> directing, until the main gear is only a few feet from the start
> of the paved surface. Navigator shuts the door – resumes seat

259

up front. Pilot selects GO FORWARD on all four engines –
and performs certainly the longest take-off any of us have ever
experienced.

Not surprisingly there's a deathly hush and holding of
breath in the rear cabin, but I'm here to tell you that we made
it – just.

***

Arrived at Stewart Air Force Base in New York State, the Cranwell party is
taken by bus to West Point, where the lifestyle of a cadet makes the Springs
seem something like a holiday camp.

Jim again is moved to commit his thoughts to paper:

On a bluff over the Hudson River, West Point is only about
sixty miles north of New York but as far as its inhabitants are
concerned, it might as well be on the moon.

An inordinately severe type of discipline keeps the cadets
there almost without a break for four years. Very little
professional training is taught, the cadets seemingly spending
a lot of time making up for their previous lack of education.

Not surprisingly, of the four hundred or so cadets due to
pass out in July this year, one hundred and eighty will celebrate
their marriage ceremonies on their graduation day.

After just one night, it's a relief to be bussed down the banks of the
Hudson to New York, where for the last night of the trip, a fine old time
is had by all.

SUO Hugh has done a splendid job with the luggage and not one
bag's missing as the chaps and their escorting officers check in for an
overnight stay at high-rise downtown hotels. The bedrooms are king-
sized, the views from the windows iconic, but only minimal unpacking is
done before the sights and sounds of the 'Big Apple' draw the cadets out
onto the streets.

Greenwich Village and Fifth Avenue are targeted, as are Times Square
and Central Park. Some make it over to the Statue of Liberty – many
more to the burlesque joints. Many leave those hotel rooms unused
before tucking into ham and eggs 'over easy' in breakfast diners along
the Avenues.

SUO Kiwi, his fellow SUOs and supporting UOs have the thankless task of rounding everyone up and getting them into their Number Ones for the official visit to the United Nations Headquarters. They very nearly succeed but the formal photo on the famous steps shows at least half a dozen notable absentees.

Three of those, UO Andy, together with Jock and Adrian, admit to gorging themselves on gigantic T-bone steaks (Jock manages two) somewhere near Times Square. They have to produce their RAF Forms 1250 to get into bars (much impressing the waitresses) before getting on down at a Miles Davis all-night session in Greenwich Village.

Not a cent of that US$10.50 allowance is left unspent and New York has exhausted them all. It's a satisfied bunch of blokes that spends the next night speeding with the prevailing winds back across the Pond. The Britannia doesn't let them down and they're home in time for Easter.

***

Two days after that trip, a couple of the intrepid stateside party have to get themselves together for the annual Devizes to Westminster canoe race. Senior Flight Cadet Bill, and Flight Cadet Paul (Mark and Sid's erstwhile crow hut-mate) plus four other younger cadets transport three canoes across to Wiltshire for the Good Friday start of the gruelling 125-mile event.

Bill and Paul man the heaviest boat, selflessly letting the younger lads have the lighter craft. The first stage follows the Kennet and Avon Canal for fifty-two miles to Reading and the junction with the River Thames. Then it's on down to Teddington and the final lock – the course will have required the competitors to carry their canoes around seventy-seven of them.

Then, they face the dangers of the Tideway, with its swarms of commercial launches, dredgers, rowing boats, and clamouring seabirds. By this stage, Bill has to report, 'Both crews of young hares had burnt out and the old tortoises just had to struggle on to the finish, for the honour of the College.'

They pull their canoe, and themselves, away from Westminster Pier on Easter Sunday after thirty-four hours of non-stop, back, arm and soul-breaking effort. The College's honour can seldom have been better upheld.

Approaching Marlow Lock. (*RAF College Journal*)

Chapter 12

The Final Hurdles

Term 9 – 2nd May-31st Sep 1962

For 81 Entry, it's time for the final leg. Fully understood are the hurdles they need to clear in just three months. First and foremost comes qualification in their chosen professional skills – without reaching the piloting and navigational standards required by the RAF, then what would these nine terms of toil have been about? The pilots have those thirty hours to complete and the navigators are working up to an overseas trainer to Gibraltar scheduled for June. No problem there for the majority but for those pilots on the degree-level courses, much of their flying is going to have to wait until after the mid-term break, when things could become hectic.

Meanwhile, the remaining six BA students have the dates of their first exams etched in their minds – 29th and 30th May – three papers in War Studies in the University of London Examination Rooms in Bloomsbury Square. The final paper will be on 22nd June. This means Vernon will miss the Gibraltar trip.

The AFRAeS exams, for the eight still there in the 'B' Stream, are to be taken at the College in the wooden huts on the Science Site in the middle two weeks of June.

'A' Stream men are also facing final internal exams. All the professional papers are out of the way – Meteorology, Aerodynamics and Thermodynamics. But awaiting in June are Maths for all, Economics for Andy and Chris, and Russian for the specialists.

On a more humdrum note, Noel takes over from Pete as Adjutant to 'A' Squadron for the final term, admitting to those in the FGS that he's not exactly best pleased. 'Pete has his own typewriter and can type. I have neither attribute and it generally takes me three tries to get a decent duplicator sheet done – lots of pink correcting fluid on the duplicator skin and black ink on mine.'

***

A significant thought for everyone is that in three months' time, the Flight Cadets of 81 Entry will be forcibly ejected from their privileged existence in the College into the yet-to-be-experienced stresses and strains of life as an Air Force officer. After three years climbing the ladder to the top of the College, how will it be, starting again as the most junior of Pilot Officers?

What about the ex-Apprentices? In July they will have been under training, at Halton and Locking, plus Cranwell, for six years. Now, here they go again. Frank remembers his previous Passing Out Parade at Locking. 'It had to be indoors because it was a wet day. I was Flight Commander of our passing out entry, the 84th. Jim was the Parade Commander and the Reviewing Officer was Sir Hubert L. Patch, KCB, CBE, Air Member for Personnel. The date was 28th July 1959.'

Then, there's the whole business of personal relationships. It hasn't been easy keeping a steady girlfriend while cooped up in the wilds of Lincolnshire. Some have managed it – half a dozen are already planning their nuptials for August, straight after graduation. Others will be starting relationships from scratch. It's going to take some serious retuning. The recent trip to America came at just the right time for that. Girls hand-picked for them, fast cars and the easy opportunities of Greenwich Village. But that was all superficial. They'll be in the real world soon.

***

The four entries now flying the JP at Cranwell and Barkston have an establishment of thirty-four Mark 3s and twenty-one Mark 4s at their disposal. They are in the air promptly in the first week of term, taking advantage of the fine weather. There's particular urgency among the students and instructors to get as many exercises as possible in before the examinees reach their lay-off dates – Friday 11th May for the degree candidates and Friday 25th for the AFRAeS men.

This has a knock-on effect – academic staff want their pound of flesh too, as the exams approach.

The Science stream's Dave writes:

> In this final term, things are very busy. During the day, we're talking aircraft stability, stick-fixed and stick-free,

supersonic airflow, and all the equations that go with that, while in the air we're flying back-to-back solo formation and low-level aeros in the JP4. Afterwards, it's revision until the early hours.

I'm keeping going on strong coffee every hour on the hour.

Sid, another AFRAeS candidate, reports:

> In this final stage of our flying training, the strain of keeping up with the air and ground syllabuses is taking its toll. For myself, learning to fly to the very high standards required by the RAF is a taxing business involving both physical and mental effort. Flying two sorties in the morning leaves me with little energy or enthusiasm for classroom study in the afternoon.
>
> It's not unknown for students to fall asleep in the middle of lectures, and on one occasion when this happened we all tiptoed out of the lecture room leaving the sleeping cadet at his desk. Entering into the spirit of the joke, the next class silently entered and took their places, so that the hapless cadet awoke with a new class, new lecturer and an entirely different subject. Much amusement all round and a much-needed spot of comic relief.
>
> It's all led to my deciding to concentrate my efforts on successfully completing flying training, the key to graduating in July. I'm not alone in that. Most of us in the AFRAeS stream have to choose between one and the other.

Danny's ecstatic when on the first weekend of term, Spurs retain the FA Cup for the fourth time, beating Burnley 3-1 but aside from that, it's a working weekend. The Queen's Colour is paraded on the Sunday, when it's handed over from 'A' Squadron to 'C'. Under Officer Robert, the Colour Bearer, is given special dispensation by the RC Padre to take part in the Church of England service for the occasion.

***

In the second week of term, four Valiant V-Bombers of 207 Squadron from Marham fly in to Cranwell South Airfield to stay the week on the dispersals off the east end of the main runway. Why? No one knows.

The whole thing is absolutely Top Secret and not to be discussed, but the sight and sound of a four-Valiant stream take-off is an impressive spectacle.

***

The next week, all flying for 'C' Stream members ceases for five weeks. The scheme to let them concentrate on academics, although well-intentioned, turns out to have its snags.

As with the AFRAeS students, not all the half-dozen BA candidates are fully motivated to bury their heads in books at this stage in the course. Those keen to pass muster, let alone excel in their final twenty-odd hours of flying are not best pleased at the sudden break in continuity.

On top of that, it's not easy concentrating on evening revision when the rest of the entry is keener on making mayhem in the corridors of the Senior Mess than in maintaining a studious calm.

***

The good weather lasts and flying for all others continues apace. Jock's logbook entries are typical. In the month, in addition to regular General Handling exercises, he flies six formation trips, a land-away airway-crossing flight to Valley and back, a further high-level nav trip and four low-level nav exercises, together with the Final Navigation Test.

As ever, sport occupies a large part of College life. The inaugural run of the Henlow-Cranwell Road Relay Race sees swarms of cadets pounding the eighty road miles between the Technical and Flying Colleges.

Nothing is allowed to stand in the way of the traditional inter-college fixtures and on the weekend of 25th to 27th, 81 Entry men are in the party that travels down to sunny Dartmouth for the summer games. The results are fairly evenly split – Cranwell win the tennis and golf and the cricket match is drawn, but in the swimming, water polo and sailing the naval hosts are the victors.

SUO Mac, down there for the water polo, turns out to be the star of the show. Those on the Saturday-morning picket boat trip will never forget it.

The helmsman on one of the boats is giving the RAF 'Crabs' what for. At full speed ahead, he's spinning the wheel and cutting foaming curves in the choppy estuary. Mac, along with everyone else, is hanging on to whatever he can find. In his case, that's the mid-ships side rail. 'Safe enough,' he's saying. 'Hearts of Oak and all that…' when he freezes in mid-sentence.

The beastly rail's come off in his hands and the champion swimmer does a not so elegant back-flop into the treacherous waters of the Dart.

Pandemonium. Klaxons sound, cadets shout and boats swarm to the rescue. Where is he? Nowhere to be seen. Then, like the proverbial cork, up pops a hand, holding high a precious wallet.

The wallet's followed by an arm and a familiar head. A picket boat closes in and Mac's hauled aboard first by a grappling-hook and then willing hands. It's off to the sick-bay for a check-over and a warm bath. He's right as rain for the afternoon match, where he vigorously, but vainly, seeks his revenge.

The wallet's put in a low oven to recover.

***

SUO Mac, along with UOs Robert and Mark, travel back from Dartmouth to take up residence in the RAF Officers' Club in Piccadilly on the Monday night, ready for the Bachelor of Arts Exams starting the following day.

Meeting up at the Club with their colleagues – SFCs Brawn, Ross and UO Vernon – the cadets are impressed by the old-world, clubland atmosphere of what's to be their home-from-home, on and off for the next few weeks. Dress code (jacket and tie) is strictly enforced by a uniformed concierge at all times, the lifts are of the sliding-cage-door vintage and the toilet facilities for the single rooms are down the corridor. They are taken aback to see that ladies, even officers' wives and daughters, are required to enter by the side entrance in gloomy Old Park Lane. But why should the cadets complain? Here they are in Mayfair, the supper's decent and the bill's being picked up by Her Majesty, just across the park.

Nonetheless, the quiet club atmosphere soon has the exam candidates seeking more life outside. They find a trendy coffee-bar around the corner and over a high-price cup of the stuff, they discuss the prospects for the morrow.

SUO Mac, who has been identified in the Admin Order as in command of the party, is more nervous than he's ever been on the rugby field. 'I'm not confident about these exams – I can't believe I've soaked up what's needed to understand the questions we're going to get, let alone answer them.'

UO Robert, who's been appointed to look after the money float and accounts, responds. 'I'd have thought that during all those hours in the classroom, not forgetting the number of essays we've researched and written, we've absorbed just as much as any of the candidates, surely. We've certainly covered the syllabus.'

SFC Brawn cheerfully remarks, 'One thing's for sure. If we don't know enough to do the business, it's too darned late to do anything about it now. Let's go over to Shepherd's Market and see what's going on.'

So, they do.

***

The next day, in their best casual civvies, the six aspiring Bachelors of Art present themselves in Bloomsbury for the first of the three papers on War Studies. The exams are for External Students of the University and candidates appear to be from all walks of life and of varying ages. The Cranwell men stand out from the rest only in the severity of their haircuts.

The first paper requires four questions to be answered in the three hours from 10am to 1pm. Under the general heading of 'History of War to 1914', subjects range from 'Feudal Military Organisation', through 'Development of Naval Artillery in the XVI Century', to the 'Soundness of the Schlieffen Plan'.

After the usual 'bowels to water' feeling of the examination room, the cadets get to writing and whatever knowledge they have absorbed spills out onto the paper.

At the lunch-break, the ice-cream van in Bloomsbury Square does good business and the chaps agree it could have been worse. After a sandwich lunch (not to hammer the float too much) they knuckle down to the three hours of the afternoon paper on 'History of War from 1914'.

That evening, the cadets see what they can afford in the way of London night-life (a ticket to see the showgirls at the Windmill Theatre is the best return on investment) and the next morning the third paper on 'Economic Aspects of War' sucks what's left of military knowledge from their memory banks.

Robert pays off their combined bill at the Club and, following the traditional visit to the Captain's Cabin, the party find their way to King's Cross and Lincolnshire. They agree that if nothing else, the two days in the Metropolis have widened their horizons, as well as seeing the first lot of exams done. 'For better or worse,' reckons Brawn.

***

While the BA hopefuls have been sweating over hot pens in London, 81 Entry's flying has continued at full throttle – but not now for the remaining AFRAeS men. It's their turn to have their wings clipped in order to prepare for exams.

Aerodynamics, Meteorology and Electronics feature largest in their minds but there may also be questions on Thermodynamics and Structures and Strength of Materials. 'You never can tell,' says UO Sid.

To freshen their minds, he leads them early in the first week on a visit to nearby RAF Bloodhound Missile Stations at North Luffenham and Woolfox Lodge, to supplement their Electronics instruction.

Despite that well-intentioned effort, Danny's not sanguine about the Part II prospects of the group. Hearing Mark's upbeat report on the Bloomsbury campaign, he regrets that he doesn't hold out much hope for the results of the AFRAeS adventure.

'I fear we've all been let down by poor instruction, poor planning, little regard for how to balance academics and flying, and for most, our own lack of academic brain power!'

***

The new Anglican church is dedicated on Friday 1st June. The great and the good of the Air Force are there, including Chief of the Air Staff, MRAF Sir Thomas Pike. The Secretary of State for Air is also in attendance. During the inaugural service, the old Queen's Colour is paraded and laid up.

The next day, there's more ceremonial – a full Cadet Wing Parade in honour of the Queen's Official Birthday.

Just two days later, Brawn, Ross and Mark are back on the train tracks for a further two-day jaunt in Mayfair and Bloomsbury, this time for the French papers. For them, that's two subjects wrapped up.

***

The 'A' Streamers now have the 81 Entry flying slots, instructors and aircraft to themselves and make the most of it.

There's one sortie that Tim has particularly enjoyed. He writes:

This morning, the weather was excellent with just a few cotton-wool clouds in the sky and you could see for ever. The instructors stayed on the ground and sent all of us cadets up into the air for 'General Handling'. What a leap of faith that was, not knowing what trouble we might get ourselves into.

A plan was hatched to meet overhead Newton, a diversion airfield not far away and swarm around there. A couple of us had been allocated Mark 4s so we operated as an independent formation pair.

We formed up after take-off and I led us to the skies over Newton where we conducted some Battle of Britain style attacks on our lesser-performing colleagues below. After that we all had great fun weaving in and out of the little clouds before coming back to earth once again.

Great stuff. What a memory!

Just before the mid-term break, a flight of nine Jet Provost 4s take off for a five-day visit to RAF Wildenrath, a Canberra station in Germany. Led by Chunky, the pilots are all available 'A' Streamers, exams and flying mostly completed. They include UO Martin, whose errant teeth are presumed digested and Blind Bill, whose flying skills have blossomed since that earlier change of instructor. The visit is intended to give the chaps experience of an operational station as well as wide-battle formation flying on an overseas mission.

Jock's not made the trip but he's making up for that elsewhere. Roaring through the more advanced exercises he says his instructor is targeting a Final Handling Test before month end.

***

In the second week of June, the navigator trainees are filing their flight plans for a four-day sortie in the Pigs from Cranwell to Gibraltar, via Orange in the south of France for refuelling – and back again. It's one of the more advanced trips in the latter part of nav training and is so arranged that the first and second navs swap positions to do one airways and one oceanic leg each. There will be two days for the thirty-one-strong party (led by the Cranwell Station Commander) to enjoy what the British colony on the Rock can offer.

All goes very well on the first day, Monday 8th. Four aircraft, taking off in the dawn light at fifteen-minute intervals, give the eight trainees ample opportunity for alternate turns as first and second navigator. After a short hop up to RAF Waddington for customs and emigration clearance, the leg to Orange for refuelling is four hours exactly and from there to Gib takes another four hours thirty minutes.

There still seems to be a need for the staff to weight the first-nav slots towards the less accomplished of the group. Jim is disappointed to be allotted the leg over the Mediterranean, thus missing out on the chance to tackle the French airways but he consoles himself with the thought that he must be reckoned experienced enough already.

After three days of sunshine, pale ale and chips among the real Rock apes, the flight of four sets off back to Lincolnshire. But at Orange, the forecast winds are far stronger than plan, with the Mistral roaring down the Rhône valley.

Nevertheless, they decide to give it a try and take off at 1500, only to find that the headwinds at height are even stronger than predicted and that the aircraft cannot make it back to Cranwell in the time allowed. The decision's therefore made to turn back to Orange and try again tomorrow.

It's been a great test for the aspiring navigators and they've coped well, and now they're rewarded by an unexpected night-stop in glorious Orange, the Provençal city which 2,000 years in the past was known as 'a miniature Rome'. That was before the Visigoths rearranged things somewhat in the fourth century.

The next day, the wind eases in time for the Pigs to take off at 1430 and make the trip back to Cranwell (via RAF Waddington for entry clearance) before dark.

***

The navigators are back in the College just in time to welcome a visiting party from the USAF Academy, Colorado Springs, arriving on Thursday 14th for a two-night stay. A company of cadets, 124-strong, is escorted by eight officers.

USAF Cadets at drill at Cranwell... (*RAF College Journal*)

...and admiring JP at Barkston. (*RAF College Journal*)

They enjoy the gentrified traditions of a full Guest Night (entering with spirit into the anterooms games) as well as relishing the atmosphere of Barkston Heath (not surprisingly, they are reminded of Second World War movies). They bravely take on the College at cricket, golf, softball (the Cranwell team captained by Jim the Nav) and .22 rifle-shooting on the indoor range. They particularly appreciate the friendly freedom found in the local pubs – being under twenty-one, at home they're not yet allowed access to alcohol.

Not surprisingly, on departure, they thank their hosts for what's been a 'high old time'.

***

SUO Mac, UOs Robert and Vernon miss out on the fun – they're back down in Bloomsbury Square for the two days of History papers. Friday 15th is the first day of the mid-term break, so after emptying their brainboxes of every last drop of knowledge of Raleigh and Robespierre, they go their own ways for the weekend. But the respite is short, for on Sunday evening they're meeting up again with Brawn and Ross in the RAF Club, ready for their final exam-room stint on the Monday and Tuesday – the Geography papers.

THE FINAL HURDLES

Mark now feels isolated from his fellow cadets. With his Economics papers due, and the AFRAeS Part II examinations underway this week, he and the last persevering members of the 'B' Stream are the only cadets in the entry with their minds still on academics.

The strain begins to tell. Hurtling out of his UO's flat to protest at the row in the corridor, Mark finds himself confronting his good friend Danny, who's celebrating with others, the finish of the Aerodynamics paper.

It's a relief to set off on the Wednesday for the relative peace and quiet of Piccadilly and Bloomsbury. He is pleasantly surprised to have quite a lot to say in answer to 'How far were the changes taking place in the organisation of cotton manufacture between 1780 and 1830 typical of British industry as a whole?' Obviously enough has managed to stick in his brain cells over the months of study, given all the drill, bull and G-pulling that's gone on alongside.

In the soulless wooden huts of the Science Site, some of the AFRAeS men have faced the papers armed with little more than a brave smile. Danny admits to 'remembering little about them and writing even less'. He adds, 'I recall filling in my name at the top and then sitting there for however long exchanging rueful grins and Senior Service smokes with Terry.'

There are however, perhaps three or four among the scientists who, despite it being demanding both mentally and physically, have found the work intriguing and rewarding. They are looking forward to hearing their results, as are the BA hopefuls, before the end of term. Then, to the great joy of all the 'undergrads', the pioneering degree-level experiment will be handed over to entries coming up behind.

***

The 'C' Stream pilots and Vernon the navigator are back in the air and crossing off the training exercises one by one. They are now joined by Mark and their 'B' Stream counterparts. For the remaining month of the term, everyone in the entry pursues a path common to all previous graduates – professional training alongside pomp and circumstance. The important exception is that they will not have done their advanced professional training. That still sticks in most throats.

Jim the Nav confides, 'When I made that parachute exit from a Beverley all those months ago, the captain was a chap I'd been in the Air Cadets with as a teenager. Made me think – there he was, a captain, and there was I, four years of training done and two yet to come, if lucky. Now, when it looks as if I am going to be graduating, I still won't be fully qualified professionally. Makes we wonder – have I taken the right course?'

***

Back on their squadrons, the examinees have found that two aspiring 'A' Stream pilots are missing. One, from 'B' Squadron, has left the College at his own request. The other is the popular Jordanian, Sam. It turns out he's had the misfortune to have sustained damage to his left ear drum, requiring an operation at Nocton Hall. He has consequently missed over a month of flying and at the last moment been re-coursed to 82 Entry.

Every other 'A' Stream pilot has made hay while the others were away, and Chris has as usual been looking to maximize his time in the air:

> With less work to do, I've sometimes stayed behind at Barkston after Wednesday morning flying and flown with the instructors when they were doing Staff Continuation Training. That way, I've been introduced to flying battle formation as well as getting plenty of low-level stuff.
>
> I've flown in the co-pilot's seat in the Varsity, too – droning away over the North Sea while the navs in the back plot away. I've been able to fly the aircraft, as well – mostly straight and level over the North Sea but still valuable cockpit time.

The navs are on track to reach their syllabus target of 167 hours by term end, with two four-hour sorties completed since the Gibraltar trip. There are just two more of the same length to come in the final month.

***

With no academics now scheduled, the pilots can spend all day at the airfields. At Barkston, that means lunch is available at the Officers' Mess, making the chaps feels more part of the station. Introductions are made to the local farmer, who demonstrates up close the two impressive engines they've seen ploughing the fields at Steam Festival time.

***

June 1962 comes to an end with a Ferris Parade, won triumphantly by 'C' Squadron. UOs Robert, Sid and Mark all profess to enjoy the morale-boosting effects of a well-performed parade – the aesthetic of a perfectly-coordinated set of manoeuvres, the rewards to be gained from teamwork and the pleasure of putting on a successful show. It's a fitting climax for Flight Sergeant Holt's relationship with 81 Entry, as well as a timely prize for the Parade Commander, SUO Kiwi, in the run-up to, who knows – the Sword?

The entry's penultimate month ends with an announcement that the RAF Institute of Technology building – under construction in preparation for the confirmed merger with Henlow in 1965 – is to be to be known as Trenchard Hall.

Mark and Sid are down there taking a look (albeit not much to see as yet, just holes in the ground for the foundations) when a shiny new Armstrong-Siddeley Argosy tactical transport leaves after a route-proving visit. The sight of it as it soars into the air, together with the whistling sound of its four Rolls-Royce Dart turboprops, make quite an impression on the shoo-in for the Oakington course. 'Wouldn't mind flying one of those, Sid.'

They hear from a Junior Mess spectator that on the Chipmunk Flight, 85 and 86 Entries have both logged a collective 180 hours in the month. 'If only we could have done that in our day,' growls Sid.

***

With exams over, academics and scientists both can join the generalists to watch the Film Society's offerings in the Longcroft Room. The programme ranges from the post-nuclear fantasy *On the Beach*, through *Nouvelle Vague* stuff in French to Bing, Satchmo and Sinatra strutting their stuff with gorgeous Grace in the lush and lyrical *High Society*. 'This,' reckons Terry, 'is officer training at its very best.'

Mark can even find time to sit in the crew room and read the summer edition of the College *Journal*. He's attracted by a piece from an anonymous contributor who reminisces about his two years as a Flight Cadet thirty years ago. He scans the pages:

> At College, the squadron more important than entry – but it's the fellows in same entry you remember. Training divided into academics, officer training and flying – last being the most important for cadets. First solo, in Avro Tutor, much anticipated but no big deal in the event. Unauthorised formation and dogfights – low-flying a highlight. Best instructors don't shout and swear. One accident – trying to take off with brakes on. With ten hours completed on Hawker Fury chasing cu-nims becomes pure joy – makes flying all that really matters. One chap stands out as best pilot – everyone else thinks themselves next best.

No change there, then, thinks Mark.

> Sport plays very big part in syllabus – first term boxing more dreadful in anticipation than in event. Academic studies more notable for ink pellets and japes than learning, save for War Studies, which hold attention. Much time spent in instructional workshops.
>
> Officer and leadership training characterised mostly by drill, deportment and dress – the latter the domain of batmen. Guest and Dining-in Nights providing opportunities for more larks – as well as in anterooms afterwards.

No change there, either, apart from the boxing and academics. The piece continues with what the writer admits to remembering best – off-duty activities:

> Motor cars in the forefront, and what you can do in them. Saturday night trips to the clubs and girls of Nottingham, races down the Leadenham straight and crawls around the many and various hostelries of the College hinterland are clearly recalled.
>
> For posting, graduates have the choice of army co-operation, light bombers or fighters. Most opt for the last – most are disappointed.
>
> The Graduation Parade, in those days taking place the morning after the Graduation Ball, much to the detriment of the drill, gives further opportunities for a lark. At one, the Commandant turns up on a horse, dressed in mess kit trousers (him, not the horse).

Overall, it seems to Mark to have been much of a big-boys' toys, public-school orientated party, with flying attached.

The writer must have thought that too, for he concludes:

> The foregoing reminiscences may have given the impression that life at Cranwell, in those days, was all play and very little work. This was not so, of course – we had to work jolly hard.
>
> However, one thing is quite clear. Cadets today have much more to learn and they learn it much better than we did.

> Anyone who says that Cranwell cadets are not what they used to be are quite right – they're a great improvement on their predecessors.

That strikes Mark as a brave conclusion for a man to make, and he hopes 81 Entry will be judged to have maintained that 'great improvement'. At the same time, he wouldn't want to see them out-doing that 1930 entry in one respect – of the thirty souls who graduated with that anonymous writer, no less than half were to be killed in action in the Second World War.

He also picks up on that point about one chap standing out as best pilot. As far as he can see, with the high-altitude training aircraft of the present day, only the instructors can know who really comes top of the class. The cadets of 81 have never flown with each other (except close-up in formation, and the time when Danny gave Bill a lift home) and have only boasts and hearsay to measure themselves against. The one certainty is that all must be meeting the standards required in order to have got this far.

***

Danny has another of his stories for the back seat boys in the Barkston bus:

> Today, I've come the closest yet to dying in an aeroplane.
>
> I'm on my airways-crossing navex, solo, and getting close to Airway Blue One. I'm terrified of going in without clearance, so I'm struggling to find a UHF frequency to contact the controller.
>
> Forgetting all the rules, I'm head down in the cockpit, no lookout at all – fingers all thumbs on the UHF switches.
>
> For some reason, I look up – to see a bloody great Gloster Meteor whistling across the windscreen, right in front of me. So close, I burble through his wake!
>
> He's never deviated from his course so he's not seen me either. Heavens to Betsy! Close or not?
>
> Needless to say I've not mentioned this to my instructor!

***

In the first weekend of July, Sandhurst cadets visit Cranwell for Guest Night and Games, but both SUO Hugh and UO Mark, together with three Flight Cadets, have another engagement – a Varsity trip to the South of France to represent the College at l'Ecole de l'Air Graduation Parade. It's an honour and a privilege. The weather's fine and hot, and the hospitality spectacular. Relations, already good, are resolutely reinforced. To the hosts' astonishment, Hugh speaks more formal French than many of their own countrymen.

At the same time, the athletics team with Chris (the captain), UO Martin, Ross, George and David fly in a Varsity to Guernsey for the annual athletics competition against the islanders. A week later, it's Cranwell's turn again to entertain Officer Cadets. This time they're from the Royal Norwegian Air Force Academy, Trondheim, and it's SUO Hugh's job to head up the hosts, armed with stories of trekking through the heart of their glorious country.

And that's it for visits, hosting or guesting, until parents and girlfriends arrive for the final ceremonials for 81 Entry at month's end. There's much to do on the professional front, however, for pilots and navigators both.

***

The assorted bunch of tyro navs, despite continuity and phasing problems have gained the necessary hours, skills and knowledge to satisfy the examiners and are notified they've qualified for Navigator Flying Badges.

All, that is, save one. The assessors judge that more hours will be needed to bring Pete to the required standard for onward posting with his colleagues to Advanced Navigation School at RAF Stradishall, in Suffolk. He's to join 82 Entry for one more term at the College.

After all the individual changes of fortune within the group, there will be eight Navigator Flying Badges awarded at the end of July.

***

Each pilot is on course to log those 180 flying hours, with all exercises finished. The target for the latter is Number 120, the Final Handling Test.

The FHT covers all aspects of training over the course, except for Pilot Navigation and I/F, which are both tested on a separate dual sortie with a Flight Commander from another squadron. For most, the Final Nav Tests have been completed by the end of June, whereas the Instrument Rating Tests and FHT are yet to come – albeit the indefatigable Jock got his FHT out of the way as early as 27th June.

Also to come is the Low-Level Aeros Competition, flown dual and not below 1,500 feet, scheduled for the penultimate week of term. This is to be contested by one pilot from each of the four squadrons, and the selection of those gives a pretty strong indication of who the best pilots are, at least in aerobatics.

Along with that crowded programme, the CFS Trappers are still around and keen to ensure that in the face of all the pressure, there's no fall-off in Flying Training Command's strict standards.

Robin takes his FHT and that evening entertains his mates in the FGS:

> I was a bit nervous about it – Wing Commander Green in the right-hand seat and all that, and Friday the thirteenth as well. Crunch time.
>
> Anyway, it's all going OK but then I fall out of stall turns, twice. I manage to recover from the spins and he doesn't say anything, But in the debrief it's, 'Well, you're a lousy pilot, but I'll say this – you've got guts.'
>
> I've decided to take that as his blunt Canadian way of handing out a compliment but, no matter what – he's passed me for my Wings!

The Wingco does the same for Robert on the eleventh, Danny on the sixteenth and Chris the eighteenth. Dauntless Dave gets the tick from his Squadron Leader on the twelfth and Boy wins the Aeros Competition on the twentieth – so the chaps reckon he's probably in line for the top flying prizes.

***

There are calls to report to College Headquarters when the degree-level exam results come through.

On the Bachelor of Arts front, Robert, Mark and Ross have their degrees, Class 3. Mac is reserved in just one subject, Geography – apparently because he missed that soggy field trip on the Isle of Man at Easter last year. There's talk of an appeal – 'Exigencies of the Service' and all that.

The AFRAeS results show Dave and Tom as having satisfied the examiners and achieved Class II level. Peter is reserved in just one subject.

It's a result. Whether it has justified all the effort and sacrifice of cadets and staff both, and set the College on a brave new course, remains to be seen. But for now at least, the Commandant and the Assistant Commandant, together with the Tutorial Staff are all smiles.

***

As 'C' is the Sovereign's Squadron for the term, SUO Kiwi will be taking the Passing Out Parade, which means that UO Robert will be commanding 'C' in his place. He won't be able to carry the Queen's Colour, so UO Mark's deputized to have that honour in his place.

279

This requires an hour with Flight Sergeant Holt, together with Colour Warrant Officer SFC Peter, and the two 82 Entry Flight Cadet Escorts, refreshing the drills for handling the flagstaff. The Colour must not get entwined with swords and bayonets, nor should it be allowed to fly free in the wind and knock hats off.

JP and newly-qualified pilot at Barkston. (*FM*)

Year		AIRCRAFT		Captain or 1st Pilot	Co-pilot 2nd Pilot Pupil or Crew	DUTY (Including number of day or night landings as 1st Pilot or Dual)	Day Flying		
Month	Date	Type and Mark	No.				Pilot 1)	2nd Pilot (2)	Dual (3)
—	—	—	—	—	—	— Totals brought forward			

Certified that Pilot Officer has completed the course in accordance with the current authorised syllabus and that he is awarded the Flying Badge in accordance with Q.R. and A.C.I., Para 770, with effect from 31st July, 1962.

(C.F. GREEN) Wing Commander, Officer Commanding Flying Wing, Royal Air Force College

Wings Certificate in logbook. (*Air Ministry*)

THE FINAL HURDLES

***

By the end of the final full week, there are no last-minute chops and all thirty-seven trainee pilots qualify for their Wings. All have their 'White Card' Instrument Pilot Rating and some have finished in spectacular fashion. Danny, for instance, finishes off with seven consecutive solo formation trips, and when Sid counts up his July sorties he finds, 'Between the second and the twenty-fourth, I've flown thirty-five times, and been at Barkston Heath almost every day. With that sort of continuity throughout, the entire flying course would have been a breeze!'

The chaps troop into the Longcroft Room for the announcement of prize-winners.

SUO Kiwi has impressed the Commandant and won the Sword of Honour and UO Robert's come top in the Order of Merit and will take the Queen's Medal. SUO Mac, has the Philip Sassoon Memorial Prize – just pipped at the post for the Sword. Next, the R.M. Groves and Kinkead, for the top man in flying, goes as predicted to SUO CJ and SFC Chris comes in as runner-up with the Hicks Memorial Trophy. UO Jim is the popular winner of the two Navigator prizes and the Mathematics and Science awards go to SFC Dave (all those cups of coffee have paid off) while those for War Studies and Humanities are awarded to SFC Ross (kept awake by his *Gitanes*).

SUO Kiwi sweeps up the J.A. Chance Memorial for being, in the judgement of the Squadron Commanders, outstanding in practically everything. SUO CJ takes the Dickson and Hill Prize for Instrument Flying and UO Mark brings up the rear with the award of l'Ecole de l'Air Trophy for French Studies – he reckons it would have gone to SUO Hugh were he not ninety per cent a Frenchman.

It's now time to raise a glass or two in the FGS to Commandant and College Wing staff, Wing Commander Green and all the Flying Wing, not forgetting Director of Studies and Tutorial Staff, for shepherding the entry through the new experimental syllabus, in spite of the obstacles placed in their path. Then, it's off to the Waggon & Horses at Caythorpe for the combined twenty-first birthday party of James and Chris. Kiwi gives his final *haka* and all's right with the world.

***

After Friday evening dinner, the Longcroft Room is packed again, with well-refreshed Senior Mess members and Headquarters and College Wing Staff for the traditional Senior Entry Review.

'WE SEEK THE HIGHEST'

Jim the Nav and pals have produced a flyer, announcing:

IT'S ALL BEEN CHANGED
...or 'The Assistant Commandant Regrets'
............an entertainment by the Senior of Entries

All forty-five graduating cadets take part, under the direction of Jim and Sid, the thespian stars of the entry. The sketches are many and varied, and everyone has a role.

Blind Bill plays the part of a drunken Reviewing Officer who manages to thrust the butt of the flag pole into the tenderer parts of the Colour Bearer, a grimacing Terry. Danny, on bongos, together with his 'too loud' vocalist Jonny, mime to Stan Freberg's hilarious pastiche of Harry Belafonte's 'Banana Boat Song'. It has the audience in fits, the applause reaching a climax when the banished but still eager singer leaps triumphantly back on the scene with, 'I come through the window!'

Back in the FGS bar, the party demands an encore, whereupon the athletic assistant scales a ten-foot wall to 'come through the window' again.

***

Part of the final weekend finishes the chaps' nine-term stay at the College in the manner of its beginning – with bull. There are still those tricky white belts needing tender loving care, as well as boots requiring a final hour or so of polish and elbow-grease while Mister Riley, still plying his trade, trims the hairline.

Those in the entry still without them, have been allocated personal bank accounts – the first half of the alphabet to Lloyds, Cox's and King's Branch and the second to Glyn, Mills & Co – into which have been paid allowances for the purchase of extra items of uniform prescribed for commissioned RAF officers. First, the greatcoat – for which there's been a trip to a small enterprise in Newark that does an affordable line in second-hand kit. Then, brand-new, fitted Number Ones from RE City or Gieves, already delivered and furnished with Pilot Officer rings. They won't be needed for the parade – it's the hard-wearing versions they drew from stores nine terms ago that'll be worn for that – but the graduates will change into them immediately afterwards, in time for luncheon.

So it'll be, 'Wings (or Navigator Flying Badge) on the left breast, please, faithful batman.'

All set.

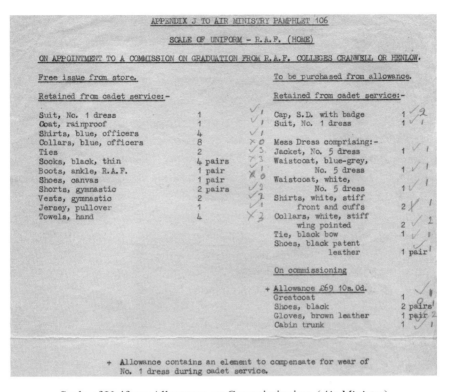

APPENDIX J TO AIR MINISTRY PAMPHLET 106

SCALE OF UNIFORM - R.A.F. (HOME)

ON APPOINTMENT TO A COMMISSION ON GRADUATION FROM R.A.F. COLLEGES CRANWELL OR HENLOW.

Free issue from store.

Retained from cadet service:-

Suit, No. 1 dress	1	
Coat, rainproof	1	
Shirts, blue, officers	4	
Collars, blue, officers	8	
Ties	2	
Socks, black, thin	4 pairs	
Boots, ankle, R.A.F.	1 pair	
Shoes, canvas	1 pair	
Shorts, gymnastic	2 pairs	
Vests, gymnastic	2	
Jersey, pullover	1	
Towels, hand	4	

To be purchased from allowance.

Retained from cadet service:-

Cap, S.D. with badge	1
Suit, No. 1 dress	1
Mess Dress comprising:-	
Jacket, No. 5 dress	1
Waistcoat, blue-grey, No. 5 dress	1
Waistcoat, white, No. 5 dress	1
Shirts, white, stiff front and cuffs	2
Collars, white, stiff wing pointed	2
Tie, black bow	1
Shoes, black patent leather	1 pair

On commissioning

+ Allowance £69 10s. 0d.	
Greatcoat	1
Shoes, black	2 pairs
Gloves, brown leather	1 pair
Cabin trunk	1

+ Allowance contains an element to compensate for wear of No. 1 dress during cadet service.

Scale of Uniform Allowance on Commissioning. (*Air Ministry*)

Glyn Mills & Co.
(*RAF College Journal*)

Lloyds Bank, Cox's & King's Branch.
(*RAF College Journal*)

***

On Sunday 29th, the drilling begins with the church ceremonial and then with a run-through of the wet-weather back-up version of the Passing Out Parade in Hangar 29. The cadets then have a few hours to themselves, many popping off to collect early-arriving guests from railhead and bus stations, for installation in B&Bs, hotels and obliging private houses.

Everyone involved in the Monday events is back in good time. The first is a full run-through of the parade that's filmed by Anglia Television. It's all a bit tricky as there's a full gale blowing across the Parade Ground from the south-west. The odd hat blows off and UO Mark has a fight to keep the Queen's Colour aloft, but an interview with the Commandant goes well and the ensuing transmission is well received.

After lunch, the chaps of 81 Entry assemble in the Longcroft Room to await the Wings and Prizes presentation by Marshal of the Royal Air Force Sir John Slessor, GCB, DSO, MC.

Television recording of 81 Entry's Passing Out Parade. (*RAF College Journal*)

One by one their names are called – Pilot's Wings first, followed by Navigator Flying Badges. Each recipient strides forward to have the badge pinned to his chest, thus achieving that burning ambition – entry to the RAF aircrew community.

Next come the prize-winners, before Sir John presents the Cadet Wing trophies. 'B' Squadron have won the Junior Entries Drill Trophy, 'C' the Ferris, the Trenchard Cup for Service Training and the Majali Cup for Small Arms Training, while 'D' have taken the Knocker, the Royal Swedish Air Force Trophy and the Hennessy Cup for Leadership. That leaves just the Chimay Cup for games for 'A' Squadron, but by the almost impenetrable method of Cadet Wing scoring, that's enough to win the Prince of Wales Trophy and become Sovereign's Squadron for the Autumn Term.

Sir John, a renowned leader and highly respected figure served in both the RFC and the RAF in wartime and was CAS in the early 1950s. He gives a few words of advice to those passing out, saying that as ex-Cranwell officers they'd be expected to 'pull out just that little bit extra' if they wanted to climb the promotion ladder. On the other hand, they were not to work too hard. 'Chaps who do nothing but work are usually frightful bores. Cultivate some interests outside the Service, as well as the habit of looking cheerful.' Looking around his audience, he adds, 'And don't go and get married too young.' At this, there's some squirming in seats by those already with plans in that direction.

***

That evening, there are guests to be looked after and for the prize-winners there's the pleasure of escorting them to a drinks reception at the Commandant's House, 'The Lodge'. For Mark, this turns out to be an especially memorable occasion.

The Commandant, the Assistant Commandant, College Staff Officers and their wives, are skilled at making people welcome and they're able to hit all the right buttons when it comes to offering congratulations on achievement. All three Bachelors of Arts, and the top AFRAeS man have won prizes and so are there, able to see how much their achievement means to their hosts and the College. It's become clear that the knives would have been out for the Cranwell management team had the academics experiment fallen at the first fence.

The Commandant's steward wields a splendid, and seemingly everlasting, jug of iced gin and tonic – Mark's mum's favourite. After a while, she's past noticing that her glass is being regularly refilled. All the old stories come out – the prowess of her son 'country sprancing' round the maypole as a boy and later, his early dates with French au-pair girls.

Kiwi's mother and his Sword-winning brother have flown in from New Zealand. She, for the second time in four years, will see a son of hers win the Sword of Honour and Mark's mother is able to tell her how much Kiwi has enlivened Thames Valley life over these last three years with his risqué songs and dances.

The hosts keep her and everyone else at their ease and it strikes Mark that it's probably the best Officer Training hour he's had so far at 'Cranners'.

***

The following morning at breakfast, the mood of the forty-five soon-to-be graduates is relaxed but expectant. The ease comes from the knowledge that they are, without exception, over all the hurdles. The expectation comes from the knowledge that they are today, Tuesday 31st July 1962, going out to put on their last show as Cranwell cadets – curtain up on the grand finale. There's also the satisfaction of finally being in a uniform bearing flying badges.

There's sympathy for Pete and Adrian, as well as the others re-coursed and going on parade with 82 Entry, but everyone knows about the whims of the fickle finger of Fate.

The march-on is scheduled for 1108 hours, so there's still time to start packing bags, ready for the off tomorrow morning after a few items of admin. For a start, they know that once they're officers, they'll be called upon to sign the Official Secrets Act.

But soon they're giving the ceremonial boots their last polish, dusting off everything brass and brushing down those well-worn Number Ones. On for the final time with pesky white-blancoed belt and white-rimmed cadet's hat. Pick up brown leather gloves, last check in the mirror, QNP – and off we go.

At 1000, the graduating cadets and their guests reassemble for a service at St Michael's where the men of God invite the soon-to-be warrior aircrew to dedicate the years that lie before them to the Almighty.

An hour later, escorted by the lads of 86 Entry over the lush grass of the Orange to their seats, the guests watch the band march smartly on, to take their place on the College steps. At 1108 precisely, they strike up the *RAF College Quick March* and the four squadrons march on from East and West Wings to form up in line of review. The Parade Warrant Officer (the College WO) brings the parade to attention, and the spectators to their feet, ready for the march-on of the Parade Commander (SUO Kiwi), the Graduating Entry and the Queen's Colour.

At the first note of *The Point of War*, SUO Kiwi marches the Graduating Entry through the main College doors in single file to take their places as the fourth rank in front of their squadrons. He peels off to take his place as Parade Commander as does UO Jim the Nav, to the rear of the ranks as the Parade Adjutant.

On command from the Parade Commander, the ranks present arms, the band strikes up *The Lincolnshire Poacher* and UO Mark and the Colour Party launch themselves, flagstaff aloft, through the College main doors and down the steps. As spectators salute or uncover, the Colour is carried around the front ranks before the party halts between the middle squadrons. With a smart about-turn, they're facing the Saluting Base.

At 1128, the entire parade is brought to attention and the Colour is lifted aloft. The Reviewing Officer, no less a personage than Marshal of the Royal Air Force Sir Thomas Pike, GCB, CBE, DFC and Chief of the Air Staff, steps onto the red carpet. As the CAS is escorted by the Commandant and entourage to the Saluting Base, the trumpeters sound a welcoming fanfare, before a formation of twelve Jet Provosts and three Valettas of the Flying Wing roars overhead.

SUO Kiwi then gives the command, 'Parade – General Salute. Pre-e-e-sent – Arms!' The band sounds the RAF General Salute while Parade Commander and Adjutants, together with Squadron Commanders, present swords and the ranks present rifles. The Graduating Entry salutes and the Colour Bearer brings the flagstaff slowly round in a descending arc until the ferrule touches the ground and the Queen's Colour is fully displayed.

On the command, 'Slope – Arms!' rifles are lifted smartly to the shoulder, swords are raised and the Colour gathered in. 'Order – Arms!' brings rifle butts and Colour grounded at the side.

The Parade Commander invites the Reviewing Officer to inspect the parade and the College Band plays quieter numbers from their repertoire as the CAS makes the rounds of the ranks, every cadet's eyes resolutely focused on the distance. Alert again, the parade marches past in slow and quick time, the old tunes coming up fresh, as always. A dramatic Advance in Review Order is followed by a further General Salute and a repeat of the procedure with the Colour.

The Reviewing Officer presents the Sword of Honour to SUO Kiwi (a supreme moment for him, his brother and his mother) and the Queen's Medal to UO Robert (he and his family equally proud of his position at the top of the Order of Merit) before giving his address, first commending the Cadet Wing on the parade:

> I want to congratulate all of you on an excellent parade. Your
> turnout and drill do you credit and I am glad to see you are

Reviewing Officer inspects the ranks. (*RAF College Journal*)

living up to the reputation of our Service – that when the RAF really sets its mind to a job, no one can beat it.

He expresses his confidence that the Graduating Entry will maintain that competence in their careers:

> You start well. You have chosen to be officers because you have displayed qualities of efficiency, energy and resolution. You have been tried and not found wanting. You have had the benefit of a first-class training. But as you leave Cranwell, resolve to put into practice all that you have learned here, and all that you will learn from your seniors.
>
> God Speed and good luck to you all.

It's now time for the big finish. The Parade Commander obtains permission to 'March off the Queen's Colour and the Passing Out Entry', which is granted.

The Cadet Wing presents arms. UO Mark hoists the Colour into its sling before he and the Colour Party proudly lead the march, in single file, of 81 Entry cadets back up the steps and into the College. Tradition has it that as they pass through the doors, that's the moment they become RAF officers.

UO Jim the Nav is the last but one in, and SUO Kiwi the final cadet to come through the symbolic doorway and onto the Atrium carpet. In a further traditional act, the new officers triumphantly fling their cadet hats as high as they can into the air. It's a moment of joyous and utter relief. As their hats go up, away with them goes their cadet status of nine terms. They have the Queen's Commission!

***

While the Reviewing Officer processes with Commandant and Entourage to the Eastern Avenue, to plant the traditional tree, the newly-graduated Pilot Officers rush to their rooms, to change out of their well-worn cadet Number Ones into those with all the right adornments. Hats are passed to batmen, along with a generous tip, for the surgical removal of those white cadet bands.

It's an emotional moment. Most of the batmen have seen it many times before but they've built a bond over the years with their young charges. Pilot Officer Robert reports that he's been bidden farewell with, 'Fly high, Sir, but not too high. Go carefully.'

Then, it's out to the Parade Ground to embrace relations and pose for photographs with all and sundry, before escorting personal guests for luncheon with the CAS in the Dining Hall. Along all the sprigs, it's judged to have been a 'damn good show!'

***

Throughout the afternoon, the College, its grounds and adjoining buildings are open to visitors. Before long, guests begin to depart and partners are collected for the evening's Graduation Ball.

The buffet is superb, 83 Entry have done a splendid job with the decorations and Acker Bilk's clarinet and band are as smooth as ever. It's a wonderful night for the new Pilot Officers, forgiven for strutting just a little with those small golden wings and flying-badges on their lapels, and thin rings on their sleeves.

They've made it.

***

Above: Wining, dining… (*RAF College Journal*)

Left: … and dancing. (*JGL*)

THE FINAL HURDLES

The following day, they're off on leave, bearing in their luggage their official Notification of Commissioning, their copy of the Official Secrets Act just signed, together with notices of posting. For a score of them it's advanced flying training on jets at RAF Valley and a dozen will fly twin-engine Varsities at RAF Oakington. The eight navigators go to RAF Stradishall for their next stage.

Mahmoud is to return to Jordan to serve King Hussein and Kiwi and Phil are to be welcomed back (after six years away) by the Royal New Zealand and Royal Rhodesian Air Force respectively.

They'll all have forged relationships with fellow-cadets, as well as with staff, that will continue for the whole of their Air Force careers and for many of them, for life. They have also been pioneers of all-through jet training and of an academic approach which will lead to great changes for the Cranwell curriculum and future aspiring graduates. Together they've all, in their various ways, 'sought the highest'.

Echoing the CAS, they wish each other well.

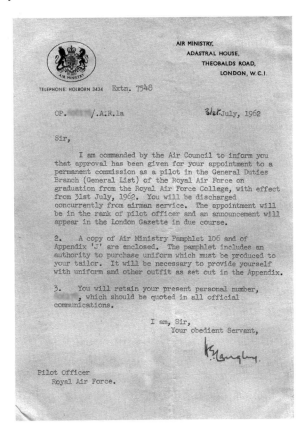

Official Commissioning
Notification.
(*Air Ministry*)

Chapter 13

Into the Promised Land

Aug 1962-Aug 1967

For some of the 81 Entry graduates, the connection with Cranwell was not yet broken, for Society-sponsored activities beckoned. Two days after graduation, Pilot Officers Sid and Mitzi journeyed with the Mountaineering Section for a fortnight in the Taurus Range in Turkey. Soon after, keen as ever to get airborne, Pilot Officer CJ followed them on to the Continent – this time alone, in one of the Flying Club's single-seat Turbulents, aiming for Rome.

Not to be outdone, Pilot Officer John, who managed to fly his fiancée Anne in the Hornet Moth up to the College for the graduation ceremonies, set off with Pilot Officer Michael for another spot of private air-touring – this time in Nordic climes. They reached Trondheim, where they were able to offer joyrides to the Norwegian cadets who had visited Cranwell just a month before.

Pilot Officer John, with betrothed and Hornet Moth, August 1962. (*JGL*)

Meanwhile, the new Senior Entry of cadets was soon on the move. From 14th to 22nd August, they enjoyed the hospitality of NATO formations and units in Europe, as well as that of HQ Allied Forces Central Europe (SHAPE). Travelling in an Argosy of RAF Transport Command, their route took them to Laarbruch, Düsseldorf, Paris and the Château of Fontainebleau. Among their number were Sam (fully-restored) and Adrian (who was scenting success in his campaign to regain his pilot's Medical Category) and Pete the navigator (retaining his Under Officer rank).

***

In the penultimate week of August, those from 81 Entry who had been selected for advanced flying training on jets, arrived at No. 4 FTS at RAF Valley where they heard 'it's all been changed' again. The Folland Gnats they were supposed to be flying hadn't arrived. In fact they were so late, that it was going to be the Vampire T11 for the whole of their six-month, seventy-hour course.

It thus became yet another record for 81 Entry – the first, and last to fly both Jet Provost and Vampire for their 250 hours of flying training.

They were aware of tension arising in the Mess between them and the Acting Pilot Officers (APOs) at the same stage of flying training, 180 hours flown, but without their Wings. Some were keen to take the mickey out of ex-Cranwell types with their 'baby' Wings – most of the chaps turned the other cheek.

They found the Vampire only marginally outdid the Jet Provost 4 in performance (having a maximum speed of 550mph and ceiling of 40,000 feet) but it had a few vices. To help with that, Flight Lieutenant Michael Graydon, graduate of 76 Entry, found himself seconded to Valley from Linton-on-Ouse, where he was a Vampire instructor with the Fleet Air Arm. He was to spend two months with the students introducing them to the vagaries of spinning the aircraft, which over the years had seen some strange recovery techniques. His logbook includes most of the names of the POs who were Junior Entry when he graduated from the College.

***

Those of the new officers selected for multi-engine advanced flying training arrived at RAF Oakington on Wednesday 22nd August. Their course was also scheduled to log seventy flying hours over six months.

The chaps formed a tight unit and soon felt themselves out of step with others on the Varsity squadron. For a start, apart from the sessions relating specifically to the Varsity and piston-engine mechanics and operation, they had already covered the ground school curriculum at Cranwell. At the same time, they sometimes found it necessary to remind any instructor with an overbearing attitude that they were commissioned, not acting, POs. It was reassuring to have confirmation of that when they received Commissioning Scrolls safely in the post, signed 11th September by Her Majesty herself.

As at Valley, there was similar tension with the APOs, but it was usually resolved over a few jars.

***

The six-month Advanced Navigation course on the Varsities at RAF Stradishall for the ex-81 Entry chaps began in September.

Jim the Nav recalls:

> It was in many ways a breath of fresh air. We were there with the sole aim of building on the basic knowledge and skills already learned and practised at Cranwell. No bull, no crowing, no academic syllabus, no compulsory sports or other distractions. So in principle, we should have achieved a seamless progression.
>
> Sadly, it soon became clear to the tutors and staff that we were just not up to speed with basic navigation skills, especially in the air. We weren't just a tad rusty from the long lay-off since our last flights in July, the basics just hadn't taken root. For that, the finger pointed at the lack of continuity arising from the 'experimental' academic syllabus at Cranwell.
>
> In any event, the 'wheels' at Straddie decided we should all be given a six-week refresher course in basic navigation, both in the classroom and in the air. This proved to be exactly what was needed. All of us regained the required basic standard, and we went on to undertake the advanced course.

Anthony adds:

> It was all down to that understandable loss of focus following final term academic exams, pre-graduation preparation and the ceremonial itself, plus that post-graduation long leave. At the same time, with our Navigators' Flying Badges, we stood out from our colleagues straight from South Cerney, and we delivered less than expected of us as 'Cranwell elite'.

Fortunately, the switched-on staff at Stradishall recognised the problem and gave our group special attention. We flew a lot for a month or so, did what we were told and got back up to speed.

The Cranwell group improved sufficiently to cope with the necessary two weeks at RAF Thorney Island on the Meteor 14, as a taster for high speed and high altitude flying.

***

There was a short break for Pilot Officers Robert and Mac, from Valley and Oakington respectively, when they were called to Adastral House in London to meet a panel of senior officers tasked with assessing the effects of the Degree Syllabus on 81 Entry's 'undergrads'. Both spoke from their hearts ('highly disruptive') as well as their heads ('a worthy challenge, nonetheless') and were listened to attentively. There was no feedback.

***

The Old Cranwellian grapevine, and copies of the *Journal* arriving in the Mess, meant that all the new Pilot Officers could also, if they wanted, keep up to speed with happenings back at the College – some good, some bad.

In September, the lads of 87 Entry arrived, with more RAF Regiment Flight Cadets.

There was also the sickening news that on 24th October, an 82 Entry Flight Cadet from the Royal Air Force of Ceylon, perished in a crash on a radar approach to RAF Waddington, at night. Reportedly, he failed to respond to repeated RT calls from the controller. The only other evidence was a big bang, and a hole in the ground. The suspicion arose that as an AFRAeS-studies man in his final term, the poor man had just fallen asleep.

***

Meanwhile, as they took their first faltering steps into the promised land of the RAF, events in their immediate service lives had to compete for attention with potentially devastating developments in the wider world.

The launch of the Telstar satellite, enabling live television pictures to be transmitted across the Atlantic, brought the Cold War onto the screens in Messes throughout the RAF. The Cuban Missile Crisis was taking the world to the brink of possible nuclear war.

From April to October 1962, Cuban and Soviet governments secretly began to build nine missile bases in Cuba for launching medium-range and intermediate-range ballistic missiles, capable of reaching 2,800 miles and covering most of the United States.

On 7th August the US government protested to the Soviet Union who refuted the allegation. Then on October 14th, a United States Air Force U-2 airplane on a photo reconnaissance mission captured photographic proof of Soviet missile bases under construction in Cuba. Two days later, President Kennedy was informed before, on the seventeenth, a further U-2 flight discovered intermediate range (IRBMs) SS-5 nuclear missiles installed in Southern Cuba.

The following day, at a personal meeting with President Kennedy, the Soviet Minister of Foreign Affairs, Andrei Gromyko, gave an assurance that the installations were purely defensive.

On October 21st, further U-2 flights discovered more missile bases in Northern Cuba, together with increasing numbers of Soviet bombers and MIG fighters. The following day, President Kennedy addressed the nation and the world in a televised speech, announcing the presence of offensive missile sites in Cuba. Within the day, US Forces went to a state of DEFCON 3, and US warships sailed to take up position 500 miles offshore to blockade Cuba.

By October 24th, most Soviet shipping had slowed down or turned around except one ship carrying missiles. The same day, US Forces went to DEFCON 2: no fewer than 1,436 B-52 bombers were dispersed on fifteen minutes' notice, 145 intercontinental ballistic missiles stood on ready alert while Air Defense Command deployed 161 interceptors to sixteen dispersal fields, one third of the aircraft on fifteen-minute alert status. The finger of the Americans was truly on the trigger and doubtless the Soviets had the same stance.

Full-scale war was a hair's breadth away and the world held its breath. At least the belligerents were still talking.

On October 25th, discussions focused on the withdrawal of U.S. missiles from Turkey in exchange for the withdrawal of Soviet missiles in Cuba. The following day, the Soviet Premier Nikita Khrushchev proposed removing Soviet missiles if President Kennedy would publicly announce that the U.S. would never again invade Cuba. Two days later, the tension increased as an American U-2 was shot down over Cuba while on reconnaissance, but behind the scenes, the deal had been brokered.

On November 20th, following confirmation missiles had been removed from Cuba the United States blockade was called off. Because the Soviet Union and the United States had come the closest in history to all-out war, a direct communications hot-line was established between Moscow and Washington, DC.

As a follow-up, in December 1962, 1,113 prisoners taken during the attempted invasion of the Bay of Pigs were exchanged for US$53 million in food and medicine.

The Cuban crisis had been brought under control but there was no controlling the weather. On Boxing Day, while students and staff were on Yuletide leave, the temperature plunged across Britain, and it began to snow. It didn't stop and the drifts grew higher.

At Oakington, there were no snow-clearance measures in place so the bosses called on the Vampires to act as ad-hoc snow-blowers. They managed to melt some of the snow – which then became six inches of sheet ice. Every student pilot available was issued with a pick or shovel and the chaps could see a long job ahead of them. The NAAFI van did good business.

Eventually, one half of the runway was cleared sufficiently to get the aircraft flown off to RAF Wyton, an operational station with full snow-clearance facilities. There, the Varsity course stuttered along. There were no frost-free nights until 5th March 1963 and no one logged the full seventy hours. Danny managed just fifty-five, and those over seven months. He finished on 5th April, when he with most of the others, was posted to the Hastings transport OCU at RAF Thorney Island. There was one Shackleton posting available and Hugh's was the lucky name drawn from the hat. Ross took his exotic *Gitanes* off to the even more atmospheric Muscat and Oman, where he was to serve the Sultan on his Chipmunk air arm.

By that time, Pilot Officers Mark, Mike and Brawn were long gone, hauled off the Varsity (after hastily-arranged FHTs) on 11th January, with just forty-five hours or so, to fill co-pilot slots on the Argosy tactical transports of 215 Squadron. The outfit had been re-mustered for service in the Far East, where British Borneo's relations with the Indonesians were worsening by the month.

***

Hours were also below target for the Vampire pilots at Valley. When, just before the Christmas break, the urgent call came from Bomber Command for two co-pilots for the Vulcans, Pilot Officers Bill and Nigel were the ones fingered – they had logged ten hours more than the rest. They reported to the Vulcan OCU on 2nd January and were not best pleased to miss out on the formation and night flying elements at Valley, which cost them in the course Order of Merit. But Nigel accepted his lot and was soon in his stride at RAF Finningley. Bill was however dismayed with the posting, having bad memories of seeing a Vulcan disintegrate at a 1958 Battle of Britain Air display at Syerston.

Jock used up another of his nine lives in experiencing another bird-strike. Just over the rocky shoreline before the Valley threshold, his Vampire took a Canada goose in the port intake. Both bird and engine were chewed up and, too low to eject, Jock just managed to coax the machine onto the grass undershoot. However, he was having trouble with a vital discipline – in his own words, his 'I/F was rubbish'. The result was that he was referred to the Central Medical Establishment which grounded him for medical reasons resulting from his car crash. He did however keep his Wings, and his first contacts with the Provost Branch were encouraging.

**

Despite the weather, at RAF Stradishall the ex-81 Entry navigators managed close on 170 Varsity hours in six months, only slightly less than the total they'd managed over two and a half years at Cranwell. The total of thirty-three flights (half at night) averaged one every four working days, four times the frequency during their time at the College.

'That continuity,' reckoned Pilot Officer Jim, 'was what did the trick, helped by a fifty/fifty mix as first and second navigator. We all passed out – albeit in March 1963, some weeks later than scheduled – and we all had respectable results.'

**

Thus, all 81 Entry graduates, save Jock, were successfully through the advanced stage of their flying training and en-route operational squadrons. Meanwhile, College life continued, with many, including Air Chief Marshal Walker, watching the Flight Cadets' academic progress like a hawk. The next to graduate, 82 Entry, had no General Degree option but the scientists studied for AFRAeS papers Parts I and II, and the humanists for the Civil Service Exam.

In July 1963, 83 Entry graduated, the first after 81 to attempt the External Degree option. One among a seven-strong 'C' Stream was Tom

Eeles, whose subjects, alongside Military Studies, were English and French. Prior to arriving at the College, he'd had an insider view of the curriculum, recalling:

> My father was Commandant at Cranwell in the mid-1950s and I remember him saying, with feeling, that the College was not attracting people of sufficient calibre – those were mostly going to university. He was sure that Cranwell had to do something to make itself more attractive to those undergraduates.
>
> According to the documents at Kew Archives, not all the great and the good at the Air Ministry seemed to agree. The majority view was, 'Why should anyone embarking on a career as an Air Force pilot need a degree? What use is that going to be to anyone?' It all seems to have been a bit of a battle.
>
> On 83 Entry, we were within days divided up into streams according to our A-level results – I had History, English and French and was a certainty for the 'C' Stream. Everything was in place for the degree course and I was soon struggling with Anglo-Saxon texts.
>
> The BA studies overshadowed everything else. They affected all professional training, including coping with Jet Provost flying.
>
> The AFRAeS guys were studying in parallel but we had little contact with them. From what I saw of the 'A' Stream, they did what Cranwell wanted them to do – rather, I imagine, like the Flight Cadets of my father's era. We in the Degree stream, were apart – swotting in our rooms while others caroused in the FGS.

A worry for the 'C' Stream chaps was what would happen if they didn't pass the degree exams. Shortly before going down to London for the first papers, they got their answer. The DoS, still Mr Boyes, told them not to worry – whatever their results, they would graduate on time. As a result, Tom made a decision:

> Having already passed my FHT on the JP, I proceeded to spend a relaxed fortnight in London doing no revision and having a good time during those final exams. I got a Third-Class BA.

Then, when I got to Valley, the step to Gnats was tough. It was an altogether more demanding aircraft than the JP – everything happened at far greater speed. The 'A' Stream men turned out to be the more talented pilots and were handed the Lightning slots. I came somewhere in the middle and went on Canberras, before Buccaneers – first on loan to the Navy and then back in the RAF.

Those at the bottom of the markings went to the V-Force. It turned out later that Bomber Command got fed up with being handed the lowest quality output from Valley – they started taking the top Varsity guys from Oakington.

As for the degree, it really did very little to enhance my subsequent career in the RAF, apart from finding myself being given secondary duties involving writing, such as squadron F540 compiler. Even when I reached senior rank little notice was taken of it, more emphasis being placed on previous experience and performance in role.

Strangely, following retirement from full time and reservist service in 2010, I have found my degree useful in my research and writing activities on aviation matters and as editor of the Honourable Company of Air Pilots' magazine.

Out of the seven of 83 Entry who were launched on the General BA studies, four, including Tom Eeles, obtained a degree.

***

David Cousins was a Flight Cadet on 84 Entry, where the recruits were only some forty per cent from HMC schools – he was one of them.

His father was in the Coldstream Guards, before the oil business took him to Libya. He found his son an HMC boarding school in Malta, run by a Benedictine monk from Downside School. 'With classes of just eight pupils, I had a fantastic education, taking Maths and Physics A-levels, as well as the Civil Service exam in order to get to Cranwell earlier. I became Head of House and played plenty of sport. But at the end, I was left completely at a loss with girls. I was, in effect, being groomed for Cranwell!'

From David's evidence, the crowers were back with a vengeance. 'With my school experience, I expected a certain amount of bullying but the trashing of kit, drenching of beds, keeping us up all night, I found infuriating. On the other hand, it was reportedly much easier than in pre-war times.'

He reckoned there must have been an element of sanctioning by the authorities (it helped them to see how the lads could cope with adversity) but when he became SUO of 'B' Squadron he made sure not only to cut crowing right back but also to be personally helpful and encouraging to the Junior Entries.

It being an autumn exams entry, David was not offered the chance of joining a Degree Studies stream. He found the academics in the General stream to be quite sufficient, and mostly geared to helping understand his chosen profession. The Maths, however, were mainly a rerun of his A-level work.

With no Flying Scholarship, he welcomed the Chipmunk flying in Year One and went solo. Come the JP stage, however, things got tough – the Flying Wing seemed content to chop at an earlier stage than with previous entries. However, David stayed the course and made the grade, graduating in December 1963 with an enormous sense of relief.

84 Entry Passing out Parade and fly-past, December 1963. (*RAF College Journal*)

As a Junior Officer, Pilot Officer Cousins was disappointed to find that no one in a position of responsibility ever said thank you. The challenges and the aggression continued.

At Valley, it occurred to him to wonder why, at Cranwell, there had been those three years of academic studies? It meant that the 180 hours of jet-flying training had been stretched out over a period of two years, which made for poor continuity. At Valley, the Direct-Entry chaps had had the same basic course but over a much shorter period of time. It was they, not the Cranwell graduates, who got the plum Hunter postings.

David was however, posted to Lightnings, and his RAF career took off.

Throughout the 1960s, the RAF was still fighting for its share of the Defence Budget, to ensure the right aircraft and missiles for the job in hand, but an extensive building programme at the RAF College continued to be funded. There were also continuing machinations with the syllabus, all aimed, in the words of the Air Council, 'to provide the best possible all-round training to fit an officer for a full career in the Royal Air Force'.

In September 1962, a new gymnasium and swimming pool had opened for the start of the Autumn Term, the latter sub-Olympic in size but offering a five-metre high diving-board.

Whittle Hall opened its doors for classes in Science and Humanities from the same date, despite not being officially opened until 4th October 1962 by Sir Frank himself. The West Site was demolished.

The foundation stone of Trenchard Hall was laid by the CAS in June 1964 – the planned opening date to be May 1966, catering for the merger with RAF Technical College at Henlow.

Alongside those developments, decisions were being taken on the direction of the RAF College itself and its syllabus. In line with the AOC's recommendation that the syllabus should remain stabilized until the end of 1964, a working party had been set up under his Deputy, Air Vice-Marshal Holder, in November 1962, to review the Degree Studies experiment.

Its report was submitted in August 1963, recommending that in October 1964, with the arrival of 91 Entry, the degree-level studies, as well as the three-year course should end. It was finally decided that degree studies were too much to pack into a cadet's training schedule. In its place would come a reversion to a course of some two and a half years, with each year divided into two terms, hence five terms in all. In what became known as the 'Holder Syllabus', the schedule was to be thus:

Term 1, Officer Training and Academics, plus Chipmunk flying for pilots;

*Terms 2 and 3, mainly academic studies with a continuing
thread of officer training;
Terms 4 and 5, officer training for all, JP (including AFT)
for pilots and specialist training for others.*

*90 Entry, due to arrive in April 1964, were to be the last of the
three-year entries – No. 91, in October the same year, would have the
honour of starting off the new syllabus. An early manifestation of all
that for the Flight Cadets was a drastically reduced drill programme.
With the number of cadets at the College planned to outgrow the
parade ground, the graduation ceremonial for 85 Entry in summer
1964 was much compressed, and now centred on the handing over
of the Queen's Colour to the following term's Sovereign's Squadron.
General Training took a step forward and 90 Entry could look forward
to rock-climbing and canoeing in Germany.*

*Despite the mix of syllabi as the new Holder arrangements were
introduced, the entries would all continue to get together for sport
and the regular confrontations with Sandhurst and Dartmouth would
still take place.*

*In June 1964, an Air Force Board made up its mind that an all-
Graduate Entry approach, with the College providing professional
training, would eventually be the most promising solution for the
RAF both financially and operationally. There had in fact been such
a scheme, albeit short-lived, from 1934 to 1939. Three courses of
graduates came for six months, five of which were dedicated to flying
training. The cadets who passed through served with distinction in
the war and afterwards but it had proved difficult, administratively,
to fit the graduates into the College pattern. Perhaps mindful of that,
thirty years later the College went forward with its proposed bi-polar
syllabus, while planning furiously for the arrival of Henlow.*

In December 1965, it was 88 Entry's turn to march off parade and throw their
hats aloft. Among their number was Mike Dudgeon, an Eton man of RAF
lineage. Coming straight from a brief apprenticeship with English Electric,
Mike made his mark early – he arrived in January 1963 in a wide-brimmed
fedora hat, which he soon re-moulded into pork-pie style.

Mike observes, 'The received wisdom was that the bright ones got their
A-level passes in August and went up to Cranwell in September – it was the

not-so-bright ones who tended to form the January entries.' He went into the General stream where he found that, 'despite its name, we followed testing studies where professional subjects, such as Thermodynamics and Aerodynamics were concerned. Some in the Science and Humanities streams gained degree-level qualifications but at huge personal cost in time and effort'. He managed to 'bumble along' through the twin demands of academics and flying.

Mike, whose father at the time was a senior RAF officer posted to the recently merged Ministry of Defence, has something to add to the debate on Cranwell's future. 'He was involved in efforts to get the Department of Education to allow Cranwell to offer its own degree. They eventually said, "Yes, as long as we control it." That scuppered that.'

He missed the Leadership Camp in Cyprus in the Summer Vacation due to having broken an arm in post-Guest Night jousting (piggy-backed – bicycles still banned) on the shoulders of a fellow Old Etonian. He vividly remembers the visit to Colorado Springs. 'On the joint parade, compared to the rubber-soled American cadets, our steel-reinforced heels made a report that echoed around the surrounding mountain slopes.' He also has fond memories of the night when 88 Entry accepted an invitation to squire the Miss World contestants at the Café de Paris in Regent Street, where one chap remarked, 'I've never had so much bosom against my chest in my life!'

At the Wings and Prizes Ceremony, the graduates received their Wings and their AFTS postings. Mike was slated to go to Valley but at the last moment the Wing Commander Flying was asked to find three men for helicopters – Mike immediately put his hand up for that. He was to be one of the first Cranwell graduates to go rotary.

He explains his decision:

> I had always wanted to fly from kid-hood. However, on a CCF visit I was given a trip in a Meteor. Up through cloud and back again – might just as well have been in an airliner. Boring – why should I want to spend my life doing that?
>
> Immediately after, at Old Sarum, the Joint Helicopter Experimental Unit, I was put in the right-hand seat of a Sycamore and flown at tree-top height up and down the wooded slopes. That, I found thrilling. That convinced me to join the RAF. So when the OC Flying that day in the final term said, 'Think about it carefully and make your decision – now!' I could scarcely believe my luck.

Mike went for rotary training at Tern Hill where, in the Sycamore again, he had no difficulty converting from fixed-wing. He reports that there, he and his fellow 'Cranberries' were at first 'oddities' – career, or even young officers were at the time rare in the rotary world. But they soon blended in with everyone else, save that the staff officers and instructors reckoned the Cranwell graduates stood out for always doing what they were asked to do, promptly and well. Mike reckons that after three years of professionalism, they automatically 'got on with stuff and just did it'.

He remarks that he found the College's 'Expectations of a Flight Cadet', with their demands for 'goody-goody' behaviour, to have been 'a tad sanctimonious in the real world of the RAF'. He also says, 'At Old Sarum, the School of Joint Warfare's excellent lectures on the nitty gritty of Army thinking were the perfect foil to the College's more ethereal War Studies – essential learning for sprog Support Helicopter pilots.'

***

Another on 88 Entry who put his hand up for rotaries was Dick Kingston, a man who says he had a great time at the College. He'd been attracted at school by catchy RAF recruiting tag-lines, one of which was: *Want to fly a Lightning and take your thunder with you?*

Dick decided that that was just what he wanted to do and at Cranwell he did all the right things to work towards that. He made sure he got on the right sports teams – 1st XV Rugby full-back and javelin thrower, where he was on the team that beat Dartmouth and Sandhurst in the 1965 Triangular, for only the second time in history. Dick reckoned he was practically chop-proof.

He professes, 'From the start, I found the whole Cranwell system fantastic – working your way onwards and upwards, through to the heady heights of the Senior Entry. But not the academics, they were an irritation. I was in the A3 Set – no AFRAeS studies for me.'

Dick says that the Whittle Hall instructors, all from the RAF Education Branch, failed to inspire him, and the exams set were no more than tests. 'No one ever seemed to fail any of these – too much time, effort and money was invested in us on the flying training to allow for students to be chopped for academics.'

The flying training started in the second term, in May 1963, in a proper elementary training programme hosted by the North Airfield Chipmunk Flight. Under a thoroughly competent Master Pilot instructor, Dick went solo after eight sorties of one hour and by the time the entry's Chipmunk flying was complete, in June 1964, he'd logged fifty-three sorties and thirty-nine hours in total.

Jet Provost flying started immediately after. 'The Flying Wing atmosphere was real-world – operational. I went solo in seven hours. The JP was a revelation. The kick in the pants on take-off, smooth and silent with the engine behind you, 350 knots – wonderful.'

By the time he got to Senior Entry, and the award of an Under Officer's stripe, together with a corner flat, Dick felt he was 'walking on water'. At graduation, he didn't win any prizes but he'd been to BAOR, l'Ecole de l'Air, Cyprus, Fontainbleau, Hamburg's Reeperbahn, Colorado Springs, El Adem in Libya, the Camargue – and at the Café de Paris he'd partnered Miss Finland. And he'd got through, winning his Wings.

But he didn't get to fly the Lightning. 'Never mind. By then, helicopters were coming to the forefront of the RAF's cutting edge, particularly in the amphibious and colonial policing roles. In 1966, after Tern Hill, I was down for posting to 230 Squadron Whirlwinds based at Labuan but during the final exercise a wire strike and serious head injury put an end to that.'

Nine months later, with medical flying category restored, Dick did make it to the Far East, on 66 Squadron Belvederes at Seletar, in Singapore. By the age of thirty-one he was OC 28 Squadron Wessex in Hong Kong, but hearing loss from that Tern Hill head injury led him to take honourable retirement at age thirty-eight.

***

The final Flight Cadet entry to take on External BA studies was No. 89. When they graduated in the summer of 1964, three had been awarded passes by London University, bringing the grand total for Cranwell's GD, Equipment and Secretarial Flight Cadets to just fifteen. The 'bold experiment' came to its quiet end.

When 91 Entry arrived at the RAF College in the summer of 1964, they were duly handed the Holder Syllabus with its five terms – two of twenty weeks each in the year, over two and a half years – and the merger with Henlow was due in January 1966. Since the graduation of 81 Entry, the lot of the beleaguered Flight Cadets had been a kaleidoscope of syllabi and systems.

306

Chapter 14

A 21st Century Graduation

Fast-forward to the spring of 2016, when 81 Entry's Mark returns to Cranwell, for just one day, as guest of a young relative at her Graduation Parade.

Despite the passage of five-and-a-half decades since his Passing Out, the scene on the Orange seems much the same. The lime trees stand firm in their arrow-straight rows, and they and the lawns are emerald green in the sunshine. The male and female Junior Mess Officer Cadets guiding guests to their seats on the raked stands are noticeably not all straight from school – many have at least a little fair wear and tear in their faces. Mark's heard about all that from his host, an engineer by trade, who at dinner the evening before has given him a run down on her selection for Initial Officer Training – IOT. The RAF College kaleidoscope has evidently shifted to a much altered pattern:

> It was while I was studying for an Engineering degree at Coventry, and a member of the University Air Squadron, that I decided to try for a place at Cranwell. I soon found that following a harsh Spending Review in 2010, the RAF had stopped recruiting.
>
> I went on to Cranfield for a year-long Masters course and then took a job with an aerospace company. By November 2014 the word on the street was that the RAF was to start recruiting following the 2015 Spending Review, so I got on the Internet and applied.
>
> Eventually, in the summer of last year, I was called to the Candidates' Mess at Cranwell for the two-day Officer Selection. On Day One, issued with overalls and a bib with number and letter, the first thing was a fitness test, followed by a day on hangar exercises – individual and group. We were

given the results the next morning. Out of the eighteen in my group, nine were sent home – I stayed.

Day Two was formal interviews of forty-five minutes with two officers – reasons for joining and that sort of thing. The result was that I was invited to report to Cranwell's Officer and Aircrew Training Unit – OACTU – on Sunday 15th October 2015 wearing trousers, or skirt below knee-length and a blouse with collar – for men, it was a lounge suit – to join IOT Course Number 43.

Sitting comfortably in a spectator's seat, reading the beautifully produced, full-colour 32-page brochure handed out to all guests, Mark reads that IOT 43's course was scheduled to be of three terms of ten weeks each, with a week's leave between terms. He has learned however, that two weeks had to be chopped from Term Three. Following the favourable Spending Review, many more platforms were to come into service, requiring many more junior officers. Room had therefore to be made at OACTU for a recruitment surge.

The course intake had been ninety-strong, comprising 30% ex-rankers, 70% direct from school or university, and included two Jamaicans, three Ukranians, and one Tanzanian. Officer Cadets were male and female, some married. Passing out are seventy-eight – a number have been re-coursed but to the international group have been added one Jordanian and one Albanian. They parade as 'Queen's Squadron' as do all IOT Graduating Entries.

They all start the course as Officer Cadets but they pass out with a mixture of ranks, depending on their academic qualifications. The twenty-two engineers, mostly Bachelors and Masters, graduate as Flying Officers, as do the sixteen pilots – elsewhere, there's a fair sprinkling of Pilot Officers. The foreigners are either Lieutenant or 2nd Lieutenant.

There's a stark difference from 81 Entry's graduation in 1962 in the variety of trades on parade. There are sixteen pilots and of Aerospace Battle Managers there are eight. No navigators – that trade's disappeared. The others are four in Intelligence Branch, three in Flight Operations, three Regiment, five in Logistics and three in Personnel Support.

There's a scattering of Merit and Distinction awards, and one of the Engineer Officer Cadets is singled out as Senior Under Officer.

Mark's young relative has told him:

The Senior Under Officer scheme came back two courses before ours. It works like this – in Term Two, the position is advertised, interested Cadets from the three Flights apply and a voting system selects the top two on each. Their names go forward to the Squadron Commander and the one he chooses is SUO for Term Three. On IOT 43, they've extended the system to Junior Under Officers. I suppose it's a reversion to your Flight Cadet system of self-discipline.

She has also told him that Term One was in Number One Mess – two sharing. Staff were multi-service – her Flight Commander was a Naval Lieutenant. The main points of contact for all were the Flight Sergeants, in requirements, tasking, dress and discipline.

Day One was a briefing by Flight Sergeants and Flight Commanders, plus Attestation and Oath in College Hall and administration. Day Two was issuing of kit and on Day Three, the real militarisation started. There was much in all that which Mark recognised from 1959.

For the first month, they worked seven days a week – daily reveille 0600, first inspection 0700. PT every day – drill most days, for forty-five minutes a time, in boots from the very start. Strikers – pretty much the same. What had been Survival Camp, the brochure now calls Force Development – in Wales.

Here's another difference – after four weeks confined to barracks, they're able to leave camp at weekends. Like most of her colleagues, his young host has had the benefit of a car – parked on Number One Mess Parade Square!

'Still,' she says, 'we were too busy to leave at all in the first term. But the militarisation worked. On the final day of term, we were lined up alphabetically outside the Flight Commander's Office in Whittle Hall office. The drill was – march in, salute and wait to be told whether we'd reached the standard for Term Two or were re-coursed for another Term One. I'd passed, and moved my kit up to a single room in College Hall Mess – just before Christmas and a week's leave.'

In Term Two, says the brochure, the focus is on Leadership Training, with Air Power Training and Force Development modules. There is time for sporting challenges between junior and senior terms, at soccer, volley ball and a physical challenge called 'Superstars' – Mark looks it up on Wikipedia and finds out it's an even more modern pentathlon.

Following a further Performance Review Board, the term ends just before Easter and the second week's leave before taking on the final term – 'the last step before becoming a Junior Officer'. The modules here include a five week carousel of Leadership Tasks, a Basic Air Warfare course and a week at a Force Development Training Centre.

And what about drill?

'We started ceremonial for graduation in Term One, with sword drill, but it became serious in the final two weeks of Term Three, when we became "Queen's Squadron". There was a final Performance Review just ten days before Graduation – and two were re-coursed.

'But I made it. See you tomorrow at the parade!'

***

And here Mark sits, at 10 o'clock on Thursday 26th May 2016, experiencing an RAF College Graduation Parade for the first time in fifty-four years.

The College, Orange and Saluting Base appear unchanged, as do the splendid College Band who have taken their place on the main steps. The College Warrant Officer, an RAF Regiment man, bang on time calls the Queen's Squadron onto parade. Under their Officer Commanding, they swing round the corner of the West Wing to a tune unfamiliar to Mark, *Eagle Squadron*.

Here's a change – no rifles, no tricky white belts, just swords and sword-belts for all. And the graduates are, save for the CWO, and their staff officers and NCOs at the rear, all alone. There are no supporting squads, just IOT Course 43, in all their splendour.

Initial Officer Training Course 43 marches on. (*RAF College*)

310

The SWO hands over command of the Parade to the OC, who gives the order, 'Present – Arms' and then, 'March on the Queen's Colour'. As the familiar tunes ring out – *Point of War* and *Lincolnshire Poacher* – Mark is glad that the Colour Party drills are still, after all these years, intact.

Promptly at 1028, the Reviewing Officer arrives. Mark was pleased to read that it's to be Air Vice-Marshal Andrew Turner, AOC 22 Group (and previously Officer Cadet Andy on IOT 89, 1985). He knows this man – he wrote the Foreword for a book Mark published in 2011 about RAF Air-Supply in Afghanistan. Escorting him is the current Commandant, Air Commodore Chris Luck (IOT 79, 1984).

The thought occurs that by now all Senior Officers in the RAF will be IOT Graduates – ex-Flight and Graduate Cadets are well into retirement.

As the Reviewing Officer takes post on the dais there's a General Salute – with a difference. The trumpets deliver the traditional fanfare, the Colour-Bearer does his stuff as four-score swords and the Colour are presented, before the entire show is stolen by the sudden, overwhelming roar of a Typhoon of No. 29 Squadron arriving over Number One Mess. Split seconds later, it screams away over the College roof.

The OC then invites the AVM to inspect the parade, which he does, accompanied by popular film scores – *Those Magnificent Men in their Flying Machines*, *Band of Brothers* and the heroic *Longest Day* of Maurice Jarre.

The departing Officer Cadets march past in slow and quick time, before advancing in Review Order for a further General Salute. Same marches, same manoeuvres – not much of the drill has changed, reckons Mark.

The Reviewing Officer presents the prizes. There's the Sword of Honour of course, together with eight others, most unknown to Mark. He notes the MacRobert Prize, awarded to the cadet who, in the opinion of his or her peers, has made the greatest contribution to the course – a welcome touch of democracy there. But his favourite is the RAF Club Prize, for the cadet who, throughout the course, has shown grit and unwavering perseverance, meeting every challenge with enthusiasm. Back in 81's day, Robin the potholer, sailor, mountaineer and gutsy pilot would have walked away with that one.

The remainder of the parade follows the lines of every graduation since the new College building opened in 1933. Air Vice-Marshal Turner makes an address which is short and to the point – not for nothing was he the RAF's Head of PR. The OC hands the parade back to the SWO and the Queen's Colour is marched smartly off, up the steps. *Auld Lang Syne* works its usual magic as the entire parade of Officer Cadets slow-marches in line astern up the steps.

Left: The Rotunda Gallery in 2016. (*RAF College*)

Below: College Hall Dining Room. (*RAF College*)

The College Hall Dining Room

As the Parade Commander disappears into the Atrium, and the hats soar up into the gallery, the cheers can be heard out on the Orange.

After the parade, there is, as usual, a Service of Dedication in the College Chapel, which the guests are invited to attend. Mark is reminded how openly the RAF declares its commitment to the Church of England. He knows nowhere else in his world where such religious devotion is more solemnly demonstrated. In the fighting Services, it must truly be a help to believe that your God is on your side.

***

At a convivial luncheon, Mark learns that in the evening there's to be a Graduation Ball, as there was in his day. His host says there'll be plenty of entertainment, with a James Bond theme. Just before midnight and in the Rotunda, names and commissioned ranks will be read from a scroll – dramatically delivered earlier by parachutists of the RAF Falcons – confirming the graduates' transformation to Officer in the Royal Air Force. She and her colleagues look forward to that as the most symbolic moment of the day.

After the post-prandial speeches and loyal toast, Mark finds himself admiring the Queen's portrait by the Founders' Gallery at the very moment when Air Vice-Marshal and Air Commodore, in great good humour and splendid in their blue and gold, erupt through the Dining Hall doors.

Seeing Mark, the AVM greets him like a long-lost friend and explains to the Commandant his role in the writing of the Afghanistan book. He then cheerfully adds, 'You should write a book about the RAF College – centenary coming up and all that.' The Commandant nods enthusiastically in agreement.

So Mark sets to – and the research begins.

Chapter 15

Graduates and a Prince on Parade

1966-1978

In 1966, the first of 81 Entry's ex-Flight Cadets returned to witness how changes were affecting the College then.

In December that year, following OCU at RAF Thorney Island and a first operational tour with Danny and Robin on the Hastings transports of 48 Squadron in the Far East Air Force, Flight Lieutenant Anthony took up the post of Flight Commander 'B' Squadron. He was responsible for the discipline and development of the fourth Junior Entry to experience the Holder Syllabus.

He recalls:

> I was aware that the Flight Cadets in the Senior Mess were still on the old three-year syllabus but we were too engrossed in what we were doing to take much notice.
>
> To me, the way of life of the lads in the Junior Mess was pretty much like my Junior Entry time in 1959 – bull, square-bashing, Strikers and GD studies, but no boxing or bullying. There were more Guest Nights – one a week. And another big difference – the South Brick Lines huts were centrally-heated.
>
> We Flight Commanders had a handover from the previous incumbent which I think lasted a week and then we had to get on with it. There was a much increased amount of leadership training. The leadership syllabus was in the process of being formalised along the lines of the work of John Adair, a senior lecturer at Sandhurst, but the manual, on 'Functional Leadership', wasn't to come out until three years later.

The first Technical Cadets had arrived at Cranwell in January 1966, comprising 104 officer students from the Technical College at Henlow together with officer students for newly-introduced courses. Instruction started in Trenchard Hall while construction teams were still putting the finishing touches to the building – the official opening was in May.

Cranwell was now on the way to providing facilities for 300 staff officers, 380 student officers, 506 Flight Cadets and nearly 1,700 airmen and civilians. There were now four messes, one for the Station Officers, another for the Senior Entries in the renamed College Hall, plus a new one in East Camp for Junior Officers together with the existing Junior Cadets' Mess in West Camp.

Such an establishment required a command structure to suit – reporting to the Commandant (now an Air Vice-Marshal) were Assistant Commandants (Air Commodores) for Cadets and Technical. The flying Wing remained separate, reporting direct to Flying Training Command.

Scheduling the variety of courses and entries demanded considerable ingenuity from the Progress and Plans Department, not the least by providing an imaginative system of transport to get everyone around the place, on time.

***

In October 1966, Group Captain E.B. Haslam MA was appointed Assistant Director of Studies, based in Whittle Hall. He writes that while ostensibly attached to the Department of Cadets and willingly identifying with their activities, he also had to oversee the relevant academic studies in Whittle Hall of some of the students from Trenchard Hall. It was a 'bewildering campus', comprising no fewer than twelve separate courses, ranging from Technical Officer (Graduate) Electrical together with Mechanical, through Advanced Weapons to Non-MOD Maintenance Engineering Course for Foreign Services.

Around the same time, Squadron Leader Bobby Robson arrived from a stint in Berlin to take command of 'C' Squadron in the Cadet Wing. He recalls, 'Cadets and Staff of Henlow had moved en-masse to Cranwell to occupy the College Mess alongside their GD colleagues, sharing the initial officer training aspects of the three-year course but enjoying the technical facilities of the newly-opened Trenchard Hall. It was a time of considerable strife, with the demands on both cadets and staff causing damaging tension.'

***

By then, the Air Force Board had decided that advanced pilot and navigator training would not after all take place at Cranwell but would be undertaken, following graduation, at the appropriate Flying or Navigation School. The Holder Syllabus was already undergoing change.

So, when Flight Lieutenant Mike (following his thrilling tour with the Argosies in Borneo and a Captaincy on the same aircraft at RAF Benson) arrived at Cranwell in March 1968 as a newly-qualified Jet Provost QFI, it was to teach basically the same course he'd completed on 81 Entry. He recalls:

> The Flying Wing was a world apart. I remember no formal procedures for co-ordinating reviews of students' flying progress with those in academic and officer studies. Flying chops came about with reference to flying progress only.
>
> They were usually caused not by the mechanics of flying, save for the tricky work on instruments under the hood, but rather by failure in the field of airmanship. Here, the JP's stability as a platform led to more time and attention being given to essential airmanship so the chop-rate was low.
>
> Wings were still awarded on graduation. It was then the AFTS Gnats that sorted the men from the boys.

Soon after Mike's arrival back at the College, a further change was announced. Despite intense lobbying, the attempt to persuade the Council for National Academic Awards (CNAA) to recognise Cranwell studies as degrees had only partially succeeded – just the engineering degree course brought over from Henlow was accepted. At the same time, budgetary restrictions imposed on all three Services by the Labour Government, under Defence Secretary Denis Healey, meant that the College had to find other ways of attracting the university graduates it needed.

The Air Force Board went for the solution it had forecast in 1964 – an all-graduate intake scheme was announced in December 1968.

The summer of 1968 had seen student revolutions worldwide. So-called 'baby-boomers', born after the Second World War and tripling the number of undergraduates in many countries, ran riot in protest at the Cold War as well as ageing governments with entrenched attitudes. The leader of the Free French in the war, and now President De Gaulle, became a prime target of abuse.

Cranwell sought to catch more of the more rational undergrads, by offering them an alternative to the uncertainties of the civilian marketplace. The basics for the scheme were in place – there were at the time 150 RAF Scholars at the UK's universities. The plan pleased Mr Healey – financially, an all-graduate recruiting scheme made sense.

The recruiting circular stated, 'Because of the increasingly complex nature of defence systems and techniques the Air Force Board has decided that a high proportion of direct entrants to commissioned ranks should be graduates. For this reason the RAF looks to the universities, polytechnics and other colleges for the young men and women who have the high personal and academic qualities required in an officer entering a full and progressive career with good opportunities of promotion to the highest ranks.'

The changeover took a few years – the first Graduate Entry was expected in September 1970. In February of that year, 97 Entry was due to pass out, leaving 98, 99 and 100 in residence. These last three Flight Cadet entries varied in format, as they bridged the gap to the Graduates. On arrival in September 1968, 99 Entry was 134 strong, the largest ever. Before starting academic training, every Flight Cadet had to decide whether to seek entrance to university after twelve months or to follow the standard Cranwell course. Those transferring (as Acting Pilot Officers) would, given success in University exams, return to Cranwell for professional training. No fewer than sixty decided to transfer. Those remaining (fifteen pilots, twenty-five engineers, seven suppliers, three navigators, one secretarial and one Regiment) were tasked with introducing the first two graduate entries to the life and traditions of the College. They responded with a will.

In 1971, the selection criteria for the College changed to those for an all-graduate entry. Successful candidates were offered 'Cadetships' at university with the rank of APO with all expenses met and membership of UAS provided – the latter for primary flying training and RAF-style social life. On graduation, they would report to Cranwell for officer and professional training, with varying seniority in ranks depending on their degree results.

To square things up with those who had achieved degrees while at Cranwell, the Air Ministry approved seniority awards to officers of the College Engineering Branch, as well as to the nineteen Flight Cadets from 81 to 90 Entries who had made the degree-level milestone.

The final entry of Flight Cadets, No.101 graduated on 16th March 1973, with the last of the full parades. The Reviewing Officer was 81 Entry's old friend, Sir Denis Spotswood, now Air Chief Marshal and Chief of the Air Staff.

With that parade, the College had seen 3,571 cadets graduate since February 1920.

81 Entry's Flight Lieutenant Chris returned to Cranwell as QFI from March 1969 to December 1971 (latterly as Flight Commander) and saw in the first of the all-graduate entries. But he saw little of all that organisational turmoil since, like Mike, he found that Flying Wing had scant contact with College life. What he did notice was that his graduate students were remarkably well behaved – on the ground and in the air.

'They were older than we were during our time at Cranwell. Maybe they'd worked off their high spirits at university.'

***

APO Gavin Mackay was a member of No. 1/70 Graduate Entry, whose course at the RAF College ran from September 1970 to August 1971. He was originally destined for the Royal Navy, having, in visits to Loch Ewe naval base with his father, been brought up among warships and sailors. With the aim of becoming a Fleet Air Arm pilot, he was on course for Dartmouth, but on seeing all his chums off to university, wondered whether he'd made the right choice.

Nevertheless, he went to Dartmouth, but after six months, hearing that all the new carriers were being cancelled, he resigned, and went up to Glasgow University for civil engineering studies. There, he joined the UAS and flew Chipmunks (totalling 250 hours) which inspired him to apply for a commission in the RAF.

He went to RAF Biggin Hill for a day of aptitude tests, before two days of officer selection. His timing was good – the RAF was looking to boost its graduate intake. He was awarded an RAF Cadetship, which gave him APO rank and pay.

Gavin recalls:

The armed forces had only recently decided that degrees were important, and the College was starting its transition from the Flight Cadet system to the Graduate Entry scheme, with all the attendant complications in revising and rearranging training courses. With one exception, all of my entry were to be pilots.

We arrived at Cranwell as Acting Pilot Officers, each proudly sporting the Preliminary Flying Badge (PFB) we'd gained at UAS, together with a very basic grounding in drill and Service Knowledge. We were all keen to get on with the flying, but it was apparent that there were some uncertainties about our status – for example, we were soon told to remove those PFBs!

We went straight into College Hall Mess, living alongside the remaining 'traditional' cadets, who were still on the Holder Syllabus. Graduate Entrants were known RAF-wide as 'Green Shielders' – implying that we gained our APO status and subsequent accelerated promotion by collecting sufficient numbers of the eponymous stamps. But I never encountered any antipathy at Cranwell. On the contrary, everyone – cadets, staff officers and SNCOs – were welcoming and supportive.

Sixteen weeks of officer training had been planned for 1/70 GE, but that was shortened to ten in order to fill slots available on the Jet Provost. For this flying stage of the course, they were joined by HRH Prince Charles.

Gavin remembers:

Prince Charles was also destined for the RN, but he came to Cranwell to get his RAF Wings. All College Hall Mess accommodation was being refurbished, and he shared what had been an SUO's flat in the West Wing.

I was one of four 'friends' detailed to look after him, but he also had one of two Close Protection Officers discreetly on hand at all times. One of them was a stocky, burly Glaswegian – a wrestling champion in the Met – who joined him, and us, in various escapades. They ranged from mess games – HRH had learnt those in his time on the UAS – to pub crawling the Trent in one of the College's rowing eights. We all got on well, very relaxed. It was fascinating to see so many god-like senior officers prostrating themselves before our course-mate.

The Prince's Squadron Leader Flying Instructor was 76 Entry's Dick Johns, who reports:

> There were two Mark 5 JPs custom-built for HRH's personal use, which were subjected to a much enhanced maintenance and spares-replacement programme. To become his instructor I had to obtain a special A1 Category.
>
> He had to show he was up to standard in all the syllabus exercises, except Pilot Navigation, for which he had a navigator sitting in the right-hand seat. Charles could then rightly log those trips as aircraft captain, while we could make sure that the Heir to the Realm, whose call-sign was 'Golden Eagle', didn't stray into forbidden areas or become embarrassingly or dangerously lost.

That navigator was a Flight Lieutenant, 81 Entry's Mitzi, back at Cranwell, on the staff. It can't have done him any harm – the very next year he was promoted Squadron Leader, his subsequent posting taking him into front-line Buccaneer bombers.

Gavin concludes:

> Prince Charles disappeared at weekends in his Aston Martin, and didn't stay on for our second stint of Officer Training – which, since we had all qualified for our Wings, turned out to be a very relaxed few weeks of adventure training and a detachment to Cyprus. He came back to join us for a bit of marching in preparation for the Passing Out Wings Parade. He was an excellent pilot, who fully earned his Wings.

Gavin and his colleagues each logged 120 hours of JP flying to Wings standard, all done in thirty-six weeks – Monday to Friday. There were no Saturday morning drill parades, no theses to write, no academic exams.

After the flying, there were eight further weeks of Officer Training before graduation in August 1971, by which time Gavin had been promoted to Flight Lieutenant. He was awarded the Sword, Kinkead and Dickson Prizes. 'I was heavily backed to win the aeros prize as well but forgot one barrel roll of my sequence!'

The Passing Out Parade was reviewed by Air Chief Marshal Spotswood, now CAS.

***

The pilots of 1/70 GE who were streamed fast-jet went on to Valley, where there was no conflict with Direct Entry chaps – by then, everyone who went to Valley had their Wings. But a fatal accident revealed a problem with the tailplanes of the Gnats, most of which were grounded – all serviceable ones were diverted to the Red Arrows. After a course of fifty-six hours (which should have been sixty) Flight Lieutenant Gavin Mackay's FHT was spent delivering a Gnat to RAF Fairford.

Meanwhile, No. 2/70 GE had arrived for three months' IOT in October 1970. The contingent comprised Supply and Secretarial trainees and included, for the first time at Cranwell, members of the Women's RAF. They all shared the same Passing Out Parade.

By December 1978, thirty-three Graduate Entries of Officer Cadets (four and then five per year) had been completed, but there were to be no more in the same pattern.

Chapter 16

The IOT Era

Dec 1978 to year 2000

By the time Squadron Leader Mike was again back at Cranwell in July 1977, tasked with setting up and commanding a third flying squadron, the Graduate Entry scheme appeared still to be in full swing. However, eighteen months later, in December 1978, the Cranwell College training syllabus was to consist of just eighteen weeks of IOT alone – three or four courses per year and no flying training. The Flying Wing at RAF Cranwell was to become totally divorced from the College 'boot camp' as an FTS.

In 1975, the Air Member for Personnel had set up a working party to examine Initial Officer Training in the RAF. By June 1976, it had concluded that for reasons of increasing efficiency and to minimize expense, there should be a 'Single Gate of Entry' for officers and that should be located at Cranwell. The Air Force Board concurred. At the same time, all basic flying training would be rationalized between RAF Linton-on-Ouse and RAF Cranwell and all navigator training at RAF Finningley. 'Very considerable' savings in manpower and running costs were foreseen.

By autumn 1978, the Department of Initial Officer Training (DIOT) had been established at Cranwell, making ready for the arrival of the first IOT course.

***

The new era began with IOT 34 in December 1978. The intake comprised University Cadet Graduates, Graduate and Non-Graduate Direct Entrants (all both male and female), together with airmen and airwomen. They had three months at the College before moving on for their specialist training. The Wings ceremony was no more. For the pilots among the graduates, primary flying training was to be undertaken at UAS and the North Airfield Chipmunk Flight was to be wound up.

Intakes and courses varied. IOT 37, arriving in May 1979, was made up of fifty-two Direct Entrants, and thirty-four former serving airmen and airwomen, of whom nine were WRAF cadets. That course had four months at the College.

From December 1979, all officer training for the RAF was being undertaken at Cranwell and by the end of 1980, the Single Gate had seen the commissioning of some 600 officers.

**

In 1982, Bobby Robson, now Group Captain, arrived for his second Cranwell tour, this time as Director of DIOT.

He writes:

> By then, the IOT course comprised a maximum of eighteen weeks and throughout, there were highly physical exercises, designed to weed out the wheat from the chaff. The aim was to deliver the 'right stuff' for further professional training in the cadets' chosen Branch. With three or four entries a year, there were Passing Out Parades at a rate of up to one per quarter.
>
> The result was that the elitism was being squeezed out. There were increasing numbers of ex-NCOs in the student numbers, as there were of females – many of whom managed to outperform their male colleagues.
>
> There were growing numbers of instances where cadets challenged the orders of those above them in the heirarchy. That was all very well and good but if everyone, everywhere is challenging orders then you're on shaky ground.
>
> There was little time to spend on etiquette and the finer points of 'gentlemanly conduct'.
>
> As always, Cranwell, together with Dartmouth and Sandhurst, was simply reflecting the culture in UK society at large, as well as the political and fiscal climate in the nation's affairs. The nation's way of life was making people uncomfortable with an 'officer class'.

There had indeed been major shifts in the political and fiscal climate in the 1970s, culminating in the 'Winter of Discontent' 1978/79, when, not helped by blizzards in the coldest winter since 1962/63, the Labour government of James Callaghan lost control of inflation, the unions and the refuse collectors. Margaret Thatcher, leader of the Conservative party since 1975, seized the moment and, after winning the election of 1979, she introduced laws to restrict unions' power and implemented fiscal deregulation in uncompromising style.

With continuing economic recession, her popularity waned. In early 1982, the Argentine Junta handed her a lifeline by invading the British Falkland Islands in the South Atlantic. War was never declared but by 2nd April 1982, the British had designated the South Atlantic a war zone. On 5th April, the British government dispatched a naval task force to engage the Argentine Navy and Air Force before making an amphibious assault on the islands. The conflict lasted seventy-four days and ended with the Argentine surrender on 14th June 1982. Margaret Thatcher was a war hero and with economic revival, triumphed in the 1985 election.

Navy and RAF air power had a high-profile and successful role in the 'Falklands War' – Harrier VTO fighters, together with Chinook, Wessex and Sea King rotaries proving crucial on convoy and assault duties. From a newly set-up RAF Base on Ascension Island, the Air Force provided an 8,000-mile air bridge from the UK together with a bombing force that prevented the Argentinians using the Port Stanley airfield. There was an increased flow of candidates for the Cranwell IOT pipeline.

In August 1982, 81 Entry's Anthony arrived back at Cranwell once again, to report to Bobby Robson.

He recalls:

> At that time there were two Wing Commander posts in DIOT. Bobby, who reported to the Air Commodore Assistant Commandant, decided that he only wanted one and that I was to absorb the duties of both. I would then assume the traditional post of Wing Commander Cadets which was recreated. Subsequently we also created the post of Squadron Leader Cadets to help ease my workload.
>
> A major element of the eighteen-week course focused on Leadership Training with two Leadership Camps away from the College, usually in an Army Training area. These

IOT Staff 1984. (*RAF College*)

were physically demanding and therefore earlier training focused on a build-up of physical fitness. The rest of the cadet syllabus covered such subjects as, inter alia, Service Writing, Academics including RAF History and War Studies as well as Regiment Training and the usual drill.

Our instructional and office accommodation was in Whittle Hall, where there were teams for War Studies, RAF Regiment Ground Studies and a French Liaison Officer.

There were around 140 on the DIOT staff at the time and each of my four Squadron Leader Flight Commanders had between ten and twelve Flight Lieutenants as Flight Commanders, each of whom was normally responsible for the training of ten to twelve Officer Cadets. The staff had been specially selected for the Flight and Squadron Commander posts and therefore were ripe for promotion, which often happened mid-tour, requiring a further Confidential Report to be written, often at weekends. That said, having such high quality and well-motivated staff had its benefits as they all generally set a fine example to their cadets.

The CWO and his eight Drill NCOs were superb. They were models of discipline combined with tact. The War Studies Team were great too – we had Navy, Army, and RAF instructors as well as Americans. War Studies seem to have been a constant in the College syllabus.

***

One of Anthony's early students was Officer Cadet Chris Luck, who joined IOT 79 on 10th June 1984, direct from school. There, he'd been an ATC cadet and gained a Flying Scholarship, as well as the necessary five O-levels (including the compulsory English and Maths) to apply for Cranwell and take the Aptitude and Leadership tests at Biggin Hill and Daedalus House.

He relates:

> I was allocated to the Junior Flight of 'B' Squadron – yellow gorgets and scarves – comprising two dozen souls. There was a mixture of direct-from-schoolers, ex-rankers, graduates and Commonwealth cadets.
>
> We were housed in Number Two Mess, a block to the east of the guardroom gate. There was no brutal haircut and hats were not compulsory. The craze at the time was for moustaches, with which the ex-rankers and the graduates were more advanced than those of us direct from school.
>
> Thanks to my ATC experiences – my final summer camp had been at Cranwell – my transition from sixth form to Cranwell Cadet was seamless. The regime was certainly strict but I took it for granted and did as I was told. I did get into trouble on one kit and quarters inspection, when the Flight Sergeant opened the window and checked with his white-gloved forefinger for dust on the barrack wall, that being the only way he could find something at fault. I was sentenced to a weekend's loss of privileges.
>
> The course was eighteen weeks in three terms, with short leave breaks between. There were leadership training camps in the second and third terms. For the second term, we moved to Number One Mess, below Cranwell Avenue and directly in sight of College Hall Officers' Mess (CHOM) to which we moved for Term 3. While to the south of Cranwell Avenue, we marched in squads to lessons and activities – in CHOM, life became easier, logistics-wise.

There were organized sports – but not too much, there just wasn't time to fit them in. I majored in equestrianism. There were however plenty of physical challenges throughout, including, in Term 1, humping pine logs around a cross-country course.

There were just the two formal occasions in CHOM – a Dining-in Night in practice for the Graduation Guest Night, which took place on October 11th, by which time there were less than a dozen survivors on my Flight, including two Jordanians and two ex-rankers. The 'chop' rate was high – there wasn't time to spend too many days in tender loving care for those falling behind.

I did just what was asked of me without a murmur. I was where I wanted to be, on track for becoming an RAF pilot. I took everything in my stride.

Following graduation, APO Luck moved on to flying training on the Jet Provost at Church Fenton, to be followed at DIOT the next spring by Officer Cadet Andrew Turner, another Flying Scholarship man, who continues the Single Gate story:

I joined IOT 89, which was 144 Officer Cadets strong. Of those 134 were university graduates and the rest of us were 'schoolies', of whom I was the sole public schoolboy. Five of the course were from overseas, and a few were female.

Two weeks into the first six-week boot camp – aimed at destroying our civvy and schoolboy and student character in preparation for building us up again as officers – I received my A-level results, three passes in science subjects.

In Term two, academics started – foundation courses in Air Power Studies and essential service knowledge. The leadership camp was in East Anglia.

In the third term, in College Hall, we had the services of batmen, just one per corridor. Academic studies moved up a gear and the Leadership Camp was on Salisbury Plain.

Drill began, with neither swords nor rifles, in preparation for the Graduation Parade.

When we graduated, we were 120-strong, an above-average pass rate, but notably, neither the Sword of Honour, nor the

Sash, were presented. Throughout the course, there was plenty of physical training but no regularly-organized sports. When the triangular events with Sandhurst and Dartmouth came around, teams were put together on a scratch basis.

Throughout the course, there were performance reviews almost weekly, and Restrictions were a regular event. There were no Under Officers appointed – the command structure was from Course, to Squadron, to Flight.

It was possible to keep a low profile below the radar, hold your breath and survive. That wasn't for me but nonetheless I survived, until a hiccup with service writing led to my being re-coursed for six extra weeks, along with nine others.

I graduated with IOT 90 and proceeded to Linton-on-Ouse and the JP.

***

Mike from 81 Entry arrived for his third flying tour at Cranwell in 1985, for three years in the post of CFI. 'We were even further removed from goings-on at the College but we were aware that by 1987 the College Hall had become a listed building – much to the annoyance of the Works and Bricks people who couldn't even change a window-frame – and there was a Passing Out Parade every six weeks.'

***

October 1989 saw the arrival at Cranwell of Officer Cadet Peter Squires B Eng (Hons). He took the full route of CCF (at Warwick School), Flying Scholarship and RAF Scholarship before going to Southampton University on a £1,200-a-year RAF Bursary to read Aeronautics and Astronautics.

He embraced the social and sporting life, and UAS Bulldog flying to such an extent that his tutor and UAS Commander both threatened to ground him unless he bucked his ideas up on the academics side. He listened, rebalanced and came through, gaining a 2.2 Honours Degree and reported to IOT 122, which was still running a three-term course of eighteen weeks in total:

There were approximately 120 of us, mixed men and women, the majority of whom had come from University, with an infusion of the 'old and bold' ex-rankers. We were organized into Flights and I confess to remembering little of it save the pine-poles, 'Knocker Run' around the North Airfield, the tented exercise camps, leaping from the top diving board and being exhausted come the weekends. It all passed in a busy blur.

My recollection, however, of the final two weeks before graduation is quite clear. At our practice Dining-in Night in No. 5s, we indulged in some novel after-dinner games – ironing-board surfing down the HQ stairs and foolishly as it transpired, jousting on bikes along the main corridor of College Hall.

I came a complete cropper, being caught in the chest by a wooden mop and catapulted into the wall, lying, bleeding on the corridor floor completely winded. I vaguely remember my Flight Commander shouting, 'Keep his bleeding head off the bloody carpet!' At hospital, broken ribs were diagnosed and there were only seven or eight days to graduation. The CWO put me into the middle of the parade so my limited arm movement wouldn't be so noticeable and fortunately I graduated on time.

For me, IOT at Cranwell probably knocked off a few immature edges but I saw it mostly as a stepping stone to my ultimate goal of flying fast jets. Having been awarded my Preliminary Flying Badge at UAS, I went straight to Basic Flying Training at RAF Church Fenton for course Number Two on the new Tucano.

***

Officer Cadet Ryan Roberts, whose father was in the RAF, was just nineteen when he came to Cranwell in 1991, in the Logistics Branch, for IOT 136. He arrived straight from A-levels and on the course had difficulties with application.

'I was recycled to 138 Reserve Squadron in 1992, where I came up against more forthright officers and NCOs. They were the making of me – I began to enjoy myself and engage with the training. I'd done pretty well by the time I graduated.'

***

This was the time when the Cold War had wound down but the Middle East had heated up with the Gulf Wars.

In 1982, with both Valiant and Victor already side-lined, the Vulcan was the last V-Bomber carrying the RAF's nuclear deterrent. By the end of the year, the Royal Navy's submarines had taken over the British deterrent and the V-Force was no more.

But in 1985, a reformer, Mikael Gorbachev came to power in the Soviet Union, preaching social 'glasnost' (openness) and 'perestroika' (economic rebuilding). By November 1989 the Berlin Wall, built in 1961 by East German construction workers, had come down and in December 1991, the USSR itself had collapsed. The crooks and the oligarchs moved in, and the Cold War became a fight to fill the pockets on both sides.

At the same time, tensions in the Middle East increased. The Iran-Iraq war (begun in September 1980, when Iraq invaded Iran) ended in August 1988 but left a state of tension in the Arabian Peninsula. By 1989, 81 Entry's Andy, the 'chap with a lucky face', had risen to the rank of Air Vice-Marshal as AOC No. 1 Group. In that role, he assumed the in-theatre leadership from 11 August to 30 September 1990 of British Forces Arabian Peninsula at the time of Operation Granby, the British contribution to Operation Desert Shield, the build-up of US-led Coalition forces in defence of Saudi Arabia.

The pot boiled over when Saddam Hussein ordered the invasion and occupation of neighbouring Kuwait, coveting its oil reserves, in early August 1990. He defied United Nations Security Council demands to withdraw from Kuwait and the Gulf. As a result, in mid-January 1991, the Gulf War began, with a massive US-led thirty-five nation air offensive known as Operation Desert Storm. By the end of February, the Iraqis were annihilated. The RAF had a high-profile role in the action, with some 6,000 personnel deployed.

A returnee to Cranwell in 1992 was David Cousins, as Air Vice-Marshal and Commandant. He recalls:

After my first tour on Lightnings, followed by the appointment as ADC to the CAS, I spent fifteen years introducing the Buccaneer, and then Tornado to the RAF, as Flight, Squadron and Station Commander, before two years at MoD saw me bouncing back and forth from Britain to Germany no fewer than three times. After that, being appointed Commandant of the RAF College was almost a rest cure.

The challenge there was in Command and Control. No fewer than six AOCs had a stake in Cranwell – IOT, College of Air Warfare, UAS, Flying, Cadets and Engineering. To say that this led to tensions is to say the least.

I dealt with the situation by letting five of those run their course while concentrating on saving the University Air Squadrons. I spent a lot of time on the road for them, on Annual Inspections, dinners and motivation. The latter was a problem in that they were due to be cut in one of the many post-war Defence Reviews. I was able to show that with UAS graduates the chop rate in subsequent flying-training was much below the average. They survived, much to the benefit of the RAF.

It was unusual to have a Cranwellian as Commandant – it helped in some quarters, especially in dealings with fellow Flight Cadets who'd made it to the Air Board and for finding good candidates for the job of Reviewing Officer every two months.

During David Cousins's time at the Lodge, the RAF College finally became the single point of entry for all RAF officers, no matter what their branch. Then, in his last year, 1994, came the implementation, following a full redesign, of a twenty-four week IOT course. The catchment was to include graduates, A-level students, serving airmen and airwomen – in all cases, just those with potential.

The course, now the only way to earn an RAF commission, was designed to be hard work. The structure was four weeks of transition from a civilian to a military lifestyle, followed by nine weeks of leadership training and another nine weeks in the academics phase. There were recovery leave periods of a week between each phase.

For his final years in the RAF, 1993 to 98, Air Chief Marshal Sir David Cousins was at RAF Innsworth, 'dual-hatted' as Air Member for Personnel and AOC-in-C Personnel and Training Command:

It was a time of huge defence cuts. The AOC-in-C 'fun' job, 800 aircraft and many bases, had to be relegated in order to drive continually down to Whitehall to argue the case with Ministers and Civil Servants on the future of the RAF.

Slimming the manning down from 93,000 to 54,000, in line with the 1997/98 Defence Review was an immensely tough job, involving many redundancies. There were knock-on effects on the Flying Training side. The reductions meant that Valley, expected to run at an impracticable one hundred per cent, was swamped. On my own initiative, and with help from a USAF colleague, we set up a flying-training programme run by the Royal Canadian Air Force.

***

From 1992-97, the CAS was ex-76 Entry Michael Graydon, now Air Chief Marshal Sir Michael. From that perspective, he has concluded:

Cranwell has always aimed to produce 'the right stuff' but in many respects its methods have been constantly in flux.

Post-war, the College tried to recapture the ethos of the pre-war regime – that which produced heroes such as the legendary Douglas Bader. But as the 1950s progressed, the authorities began groping their way towards a different kind of cadet – one still with the attributes of a career officer: flair, resourcefulness, loyalty, charisma and potential for making a fine pilot. And one who would stand out among the officers coming from the ranks, National Service and Short Term Commissions – some of the latter being graduates from University.

But, a degree was believed to be beneficial for future leaders, and this was also being reflected in the difficulty of recruiting into the College – many potential recruits looked for a University degree rather than a three-year course and no degree. Moreover, later on concerns emerged over graduates being recruited whose degrees were pretty irrelevant to the needs of the RAF – some of them were turning out to be poor officers. There was also the problem that graduates would arrive on the front line already in their mid-twenties, not the best age to start operational flying.

Thus, the College was seeking a way to involve degree studies but the External Degree experiment started with 81E did not last more than four further entries – it put so much pressure on Flight Cadets that their flying training standards were endangered. In any event, there were questions over the long-term purpose of External General Degrees, as well as AFRAeS Parts I and II, at this stage of training.

Throughout the 'sixties and 'seventies and onwards, the recruiters were still looking to recruit men – and from 1970, women – made of the 'right stuff' but the Graduate Entry experiment from 1971 had many flaws.

With IOT, the recruitment process looks for bright candidates from the ranks and from school, as well as from the right universities with relevant degrees – those with the right stuff as well as with the brainpower to study and achieve degree qualifications throughout their RAF career. This has the bonus of a mix of experience among the IOT recruits – people from the ranks bring their experience to bear in helping the others.

The old Cranwell was great but unsustainable. Time will tell, but it looks as if the RAF is close to getting it right today. More young people coming from school, mixing with experienced ex-rankers, getting to fly much earlier and picking up further education down the way. That will be especially important if the force is to be subject to further reductions, when everyone must continuously punch above their weight. As ever, the vagaries of defence cuts and subsequent expansions, still have a huge impact on the smooth flow of flying training.

**

Following Air Chief Marshal Graydon as CAS was another 76 Entry Air Chief Marshal, Sir Richard Johns, who held the post to the turn of the century.

He recalls:

The 1997/98 Defence Review sustained a decade of pressure on the defence budget.

Many graduate entrants enlisting in their early twenties were not giving sufficient length of service in return for the expensive investment in their flying training. We thus aimed to reduce the emphasis on graduate entrants while increasing the numbers of those joining direct from school – forty per cent was the target. If they decided to leave the Service in their mid–thirties, as were too many graduate entrants, the RAF would at least have gained three more years of productive service.

That said, we recognised that a degree remained an important aspiration and to that end arrangements were concluded with the Open University and Exeter University for officers to undertake a degree course if they so wished at a time of their choosing. The chosen subject would have to be one of value to the Service and RAF training would satisfy some of the requirements within agreed modules.

This was welcomed at the time but judgement of its success or otherwise should be left to those who followed on after my retirement in 2000.

***

Officer Cadet Andrew Ross undertook the IOT course in May 1998, as a graduate from Edinburgh University. With five A-levels to his name, he was in his fourth year of the Geology degree syllabus when his urge to fly became overpowering:

> I'd had no CCF or ATC experience but my grandfather had served in the RAF in the Second World War, flying Lancasters and Wellingtons – he got shot down over North Africa, imprisoned in Italy, escaped, made his way back and recommenced the war in a Lancaster. He was my inspiration – I wanted to fly.
>
> In my final year, I ran two approaches at once. I went after a trainee intake for British Airways and got to the last few before losing out. At the same time, I applied to the RAF and took the Aptitude and Officer Selection route at Adastral Hall.

The recently-opened Adastral Hall was a purpose-built facility with a hangar-sized hall chock-a-block with partitioned-off areas for officer-selection exercises, together with rooms full of computer screens for aircrew aptitude testing. The whole campus, commanded by a Wing Commander, went by the name of Officer and Aircrew Selection Centre (OASC) and was blessed with a candidates' accommodation block, as well as a separate mess, where the three-day selection process could run with no disturbances from the outside world. It was Cranwell's, and the RAF's pride and joy and was viewed enviously by military around the world.

Andrew found it absorbing:

> After a fitness test with the Physical Trainers, the first day was seven hours at a computer screen with all kinds of logic and

spatial exercises – the latter controlled by joystick in one hand, throttle in the other and rudder-bars at your feet. It was a kind of time out of time experience. It really tested your powers of endurance and concentration. At the end, the staff called us, exhausted, into one of two rooms – it turned out that one was for those who'd passed and the other for those who'd blown it. I passed – and was invited to stay for the night for the next day. Those who hadn't made it just disappeared. We assumed they'd just packed their bags and pushed off – sudden death stuff!

That night, still in our cocoon, the atmosphere was surreal. Small talk, not much more. Everybody nervous and chewing their nails for Day Two.

This was in those booths in the hangar for leadership and initiative testing. It was another intense experience. Small teams – climbing and swinging apparatus – impossible challenges – sweaty palms – and all the time, blokes with clipboards making notes, including some watching from a balcony high above. Noisy too – you could feel the determination to impress compressed into this echoing vault. A nerve-wracking, exhausting day.

Again, there was the weeding-out procedure. I made it through. That night, it was pretty quiet in the Candidates' Mess. People kind of kept their own counsel.

The third day was one of interviews, women and chaps who really knew how to get under your skin – terrifying and really made you think, mostly about yourself and what kind of person you really were.

Then, dog-tired, we all packed our bags and rejoined the real world – to wait for the letter telling us our fate.

A few weeks later, a letter dropped through Andrew's postbox saying he was accepted for IOT, to start 31 May 1998:

I was delighted. It was an incredible feeling.

I had a couple of months to get in shape – at twenty-two I was pretty fit. Nevertheless, Term One in Number One Mess was a tough transition – we were confined to barracks for the first four weeks. The instruction was good but in after-hours work the help from the thirty per cent of the course members who were ex-rankers, men and women, was invaluable.

I'd had no experience of drill but did fine nonetheless – the course was designed to cater for 'zero-experienced' intake.

Room inspections, by Flight Commanders and Flight Sergeants were an almost daily event. Defaulters consisted of so-called 'Sheet 3' offences, which resulted in parading at set times of day in the full appropriate uniform, for inspection, even if it was a weekend. Continual assessment was the key – there was a Performance Review at end of term.

Those not sent home moved their kit on the final day up to College Hall, ready for Term Two. The first week's leave came as a welcome break from what was an intense month.

Term Two focused heavily on Leadership, including a week of force development training in Wales. We also had masses of studies – Air Power etcetera, etcetera – hosted in Whittle Hall by the staff of OACTU, with help from King's College London. Sheet 3 disciplinary procedures continued, but with lesser impact – they were now designed not to affect our studies too much.

Again, at the end of term, there was a Performance Review – on 'Black Friday' – before a second week's leave.

Term Three concentrated on development from Officer Cadet to a Junior Officer. We had to write a full essay on a chosen current-affairs subject – this was assessed by King's College and if it was not up to standard, we had to start all over again on another.

We watched our step – Sheet 3 offences were still a possibility.

Two weeks before graduation there was a Dining-in Night rehearsal in Number Five Mess Dress. The following week, 'Champagne Tuesday' was when your graduation was confirmed, or otherwise – another nervous day. Some on my course found themselves pushed back a term, to deal with various points of weakness.

Things remained tense until you finally walked up those steps – which we did November twentieth, 1998.

There had been zero 'own request' drop-outs – a reflection of the efficiency of OASC selection procedures.

My only regret was that unfortunately, my university syllabus included no Maths or other subjects of use to the RAF. But I've never regretted abandoning a career in Geology!

After a short holding-post, Flying Officer Ross was back at Cranwell for ground school before being selected to go up to Church Fenton for elementary flying – where the training on the Firefly ('What a small aeroplane!') was delivered by sub-contractor Hunting Aviation. Despite his tyro status, Andrew went solo in just eleven hours.

He'd joined the RAF in the time following the Cold War and before the attack on New York's Twin Towers on 11 September 2001. In just a few years, he was flying a 70 Squadron Hercules to the 2001 relief of Kabul.

***

In the year 2000, Air Vice-Marshal Gavin Mackay (ex-1/70 GE) returned to the RAF College, as AOC and Commandant.

He recalls:

> I took over a busy organisation, with courses of Initial Officer Trainees starting every eight weeks. In 2000, more than 700 new officers, including Reservists and Foreign and Commonwealth trainees came through. That pace continued throughout my tenure.
>
> As well as the Officer Cadets and the College, the Commandant had responsibilities, via a dedicated HQ at Cranwell, for the sixteen UASs which had become an integral part of the RAF's Elementary Flying Training (EFT) system, together with the squadrons at Church Fenton and Wyton, for RAF trainees who hadn't flown at a UAS. We also had duty of care for Army and Navy pilot trainees at Barkston Heath. For Advanced Flying and other professional training purposes, the RAF Cranwell Station Commander reported directly to AOC Training, but he looked to my office for budgetary control, as well as discipline. On top of that, HQ Air Cadets reported to me, together, latterly, with Officer Selection and Recruitment.
>
> I found it a messy arrangement, with some areas of responsibility between myself and AOC Training far from clear. Also, although I loved my dealings with the UASs and the Air Cadets, in some ways I would have preferred to have more time to devote to the College and cadets. I sometimes envied my colleagues at Sandhurst and Dartmouth, who were focused on their own closely-defined campus. But we coped.

In my previous post, I'd spent eighteen months at Yeovilton and High Wycombe bringing the Joint Harrier Force into service, but before that, as Commandant CFS, also based at Cranwell, I'd qualified on most of the aircraft types based there. That was useful for, whenever possible, flying myself and my ADC in the Tutor to visit the University Air Squadrons.

Unlike the traditional Flight Cadets, we Graduate Entrants hadn't spent long enough of our formative years at the College to form a lifelong bond with it and our colleagues. But I still became very fond of the place and its people. I had a thoroughly enjoyable and rewarding time there as a trainee – and as Commandant.

Chapter 17

All Changed – Again

2017-2020

The date of the centenary of the RAF College has been set at 5th February 2020, the day in 1920 on which Entry No. 1 arrived. To complete the story, some brave assumptions will have to be made about what could be a turbulent few years.

But it soon becomes clear that the College staff are already working on that. In parallel with the RAF 100 initiative, celebrating the centenary of the RAF itself in 2018, plans are afoot to restructure the RAF College for its second century.

***

After several tours in the UK and overseas, Wing Commander Andrew Ross (IOT graduate 1983) returned to Cranwell in 2016 as Wing Commander I/C OASC in Adastral House.

He points out that the centre is already this year celebrating the twenty-fifth anniversary of the transfer of Aptitude and Selection from Biggin Hill in 1992:

> In all that time, finding the 'best potential' trainees has been the number one criterion – it still is, despite the changes being made in the RAF. For instance, the Aptitude Branches now include not only Pilot and Air Traffic but also ISTAR – that's Intelligence, Surveillance, Target Acquisition and Reconnaissance – the future of the RAF's combat air reconnaissance assets. There's also Battlefield Control, Flight Operations and Weaponised Platform – Drone – Operators.
>
> Nowadays, the aptitude tests are on a separate day, acting as a coarse filter. The candidates receive their results on the same day and those successful come back to join the Non-Aptitude

Branches – Engineers, Logistics and Personnel – for the two days of Officer Selection.

We work on the basis of Continual Assessment – that's a good preparation for Flying Training, where the same method applies. There's an Officer Reselection Board for those who can't make the grade in professional training.

Of the intake of candidates, thirty per cent are currently ex-rankers, but the biggest chunk come directly from school and university. They're the ones we want – catch 'em young for best results.

The model works well – results prove that with a ninety-eight per cent success rate at EFT – but we have to move with, or even ahead of the times. Young people these days look to have more than one career – OASC, and indeed the RAF, has to make sure their expectations can be met.

The Royal Air Force Recruiting and Selection staff have over thirty recruiting offices around the country, each with Outreach Programmes – they and the candidates keep us in tune with those expectations. We also keep close to the commercial world – many firms come to us, to see how it's done.

Continuous evaluation, that's the key. We at the OASC are continuing to work hard to eliminate unconscious bias from the selection process. The 'golden thread' for today and into the future is to select candidates with the 'best potential'.

***

Wing Commander Ryan Roberts (IOT Graduate 1992) arrived to command OACTU in the spring of 2017:

I arrived in post at the back end of a system of thirty-week courses – twenty weeks training with two weeks leave – some seventy men and women strong, which had been running for twelve years. The College is now in transition to twenty-four weeks training plus four weeks leave and the courses are 120-plus strong, in response to the surge in recruiting. There are now Graduation Parades every ten weeks.

The IOT course had been reset with IOT 200 in 2004, when King's College London was brought into partnership to strengthen the academics. There was a further analysis in 2005-6 which concluded that the syllabus throughout the 1990s was good in ethos and in leadership elements but there was room for much improvement in the fields of situation analysis and the management of people and times. The result was a partnership with the Portsmouth Business School.

That model has been very successful. Fundamentally IOT is now a course which gives the cadets the confidence to go out and lead – capably. The Officer Cadets graduate as junior officers ready for work, ready for leadership.

Four weeks ago, I went down to Dartmouth to confer with my opposite numbers in the Army and the Royal Navy. The conclusion from that meeting was that Cranwell covers everything needed before junior officers go on to their professional training and first tours. The IOT course is busy, but balanced between the military and the communication, management and confidence skills the cadets will need for their future. In short, it's a great success story.

OACTU badge. (*RAF College*)

The current rate of throughput for IOT is 600 Officer Cadets a year and that's straining the infrastructure, which has to run like clockwork to do its job. By 2020 that number is planned to reduce to 550, which is a sustainable level.

But now, more change is on the way. Project Mercury, a 22 Group initiative, is re-evaluating requirements from OACTU. The project will deliver its report in eighteen months' time – doubtless there will be changes.

There's a need to update teaching systems for the digital age, all the more so for students used to the Science, Technology, Engineering and Mathematics, STEM teaching methods prevalent in schools and university. Also, some of the effects of the compression have not quite been reset – peaks need straightening out.

For Project Portal roll-out, making Cranwell the gateway for all recruits to the RAF, a large amount of new building will be needed, especially for Halton's Phase One training to move here. The future of Whittle Hall, fundamentally sound but in need of some refurbishment, is assured.

Whatever happens, it's going to be an interesting few years.

It seems to me the Flight Cadet system of your day was set up to create an elite of officers, destined for the highest ranks but in effect, you graduated as inexperienced Pilot Officers with no leadership training whatsoever – except of the Public School Prefect type.

That's not to say that IOT Officer Cadets of today are not the elite of society – every year, just 600 out of about 30,000 applicants, two per cent, make it to an IOT course. But nowadays, every officer in the RAF goes through the IOT mill – RAF officers, NCOs and airmen and women are now all chips off the same block. They come from all levels and segments of society and are at various stages of maturity.

The whole affair is a true meritocracy.

***

The College Warrant Officer, Mister C.W. Shaw, gives a close-up, eyeball-to-eyeball view of IOT life, for cadets and staff both.

As well as his viewpoint on IOT, he gives a slant on Project Mercury:

It's an organized search for 'continuous improvement', and this time, it's asking the cadets for suggestions. They should know – they're going through the mill and should know what IOT's all about.

I have two reporting lines. The first is to the Commandant as the College Executive Warrant Officer, responsible for all discipline, protocols and ceremonial events on the entire campus. The second is to OC OACTU, responsible for behaviour, deportment and protocol for Officer Cadets.

In the latter, mine is a mentoring role, encouraging and directing cadets on their way to becoming basic officers, regardless of previous status or branch. The Flight Sergeants reporting to me are in effect Deputy Flight Commanders – they live day-by-day with the cadets as well as delivering weapons training and field skills. They, and all the staff, are role models for the trainees.

Right from the start, they are given the basics in what to expect. It is explained to them that the College is looking for

342

quality – if on IOT they don't display officer qualities then why should the RAF commission them? The rules of the game are made quite clear.

For the first two weeks, they are marched from place to place by the Flight Sergeants. If at the end of that period they pass a drill check, each Flight is marched by a nominated Duty Cadet for a week. That's a rite-of-passage for tyros – if they manage it, then they get a huge boost to their personal confidence, and that's what the IOT is all about. If they fail – and some last just one day in the role – then refresher training is required, including a further drill check.

The Officer Cadets' progress through IOT is against a background of militarisation – room inspections, drill and on the rifle range. But they also go on leadership development camps run by the Physical Education Branch. Alongside that, there's time for academics, and occasional pure reflection.

For me, the twice-yearly courses for Warrant Officers are special. For just two weeks, they leave the rank of Warrant Officer to become Officer Cadets just like everyone else on the course, no matter what their background – albeit they are not subjected to the whole syllabus, being properly militarised already. They concentrate on Air Power Studies. Then, they become brand-new officers, among many. It's a transition of mindset like few others.

The Padres come here for a quickie six-week course and they're something else again – all the time smiling and finding it difficult to take the whole thing seriously.

Double-barrelled and foreign names are a challenge, but they all have name-tags. 'Oi' works when all else fails, if shouted loud enough!

Big numbers are now coming through, in all Branches – the load on the staff's increasing. During the inter-term two-week breaks, there's a week of refresher training for all staff – proper leave has to wait for Christmas and summer.

But Cranwell's a special place to teach. It's a fantastic set-up – great environment. And always in our minds is the thought that somewhere out on that parade square is a potential Chief of the Air Staff.

***

Air Commodore Luck has been promoted Air Vice-Marshal and commands the Joint Services Command and Staff College (JSCSC) at Shrivenham. Posted in as the new Commandant is Air Commodore Peter Squires (IOT 122 in 1989) who explains that, by a combination of design and circumstance, he wears multiple hats:

> First, although I command just a third of the establishment at RAFC Cranwell, my position as Head of Establishment means I have legal accountability and duty of care for all Force Elements who work at the unit. As the Station Commander I am also responsible for discipline of all its personnel and have the task of binding the whole unit and the wider family unit together.
>
> Secondly, I am the Force Commander for everyone who goes through RAF Phase 1 training, from IOT at Cranwell for the officers as well as the airmen going through the Recruit Training Squadron at RAF Halton.
>
> Thirdly, as the Head of the University Air Squadrons, I oversee approximately 900 university cadets across fifteen UASs. Most have an Air Experience Flight (AEF) responsible for flying up to 25,000 Air Cadets each year.
>
> Fourthly, I am responsible for the RAF's National Youth Delivery that conducts outreach programmes for ten to fourteen-year-olds with the aim of sparking an interest in aerospace and STEM subjects.
>
> Fifthly, I oversee the RAF's embryonic Tedder Academy that is responsible for Command and Leadership training and education, from Airman to Air Marshal.

Leadership training on IOT is today based on the methodology enshrined in the mnemonic SMEAC, which outlines the procedures for a leader when briefing his team about a situation, a mission and how they are going to execute the mission. Situation, Mission, Execution, Any questions and Check understanding – it's ingrained in every IOT graduate's approach for the rest of his or her career.

The Air Commodore continues:

> Finally, I am the Air Officer Lincolnshire, which encapsulates Cranwell, Scampton, Digby, Coningsby and Waddington.

This entails hosting a regular meeting of base commanders to discuss myriad issues from local engagement to flight safety.

In the fifteen months I've been in post, it took six to get a sense of the span of command – both vertical and horizontal – and I continue to evolve my full understanding of the role.

At OACTU, I tend to leave the Officer Cadets in the hands of the Group Captain Training and his staff for the first two terms. Then, in the third term, I make the time to meet them all as their likelihood of passing increases and they have more capacity to absorb my advice about their future role as a junior officer. I entertain the prizewinners in the Lodge and I'm always massively impressed with both the diversity of backgrounds and the talent before me. Some keep a low profile, others make sure they stand out from the crowd. All show great determination – the success rate is high.

Of course, I'm always there for the five Graduation Parades per year. It's the pinnacle event that provides me an excellent opportunity to showcase the very best of Cranwell to family, friends and senior RAF officers.

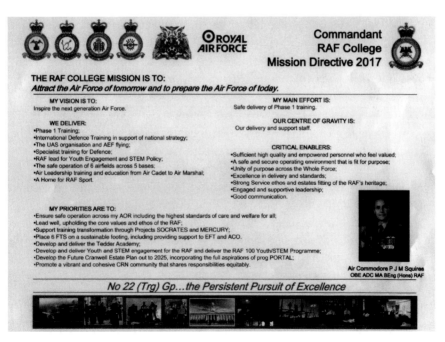

RAF College Mission 2017. (*RAF College*)

Looking to the future, the Air Force Board has made it clear that all Phase One Training Units are to be located at RAFC Cranwell as well as the leadership training and education for non-commissioned officers conducted by the Airmen's Command Squadron. The costing and design work is underway and plans are starting to cement.

The result will be a combination of new and refurbished buildings with a modern digital architecture to meet the needs of the Millennials. A new high-G training facility will be completed in 2018 ahead of the arrival from RAF Henlow of the RAF's Centre for Aviation Medicine due two years later.

All told, I am expecting up to 8,000 more students per annum to pass through Cranwell with several hundred more permanent staff – the additional support needs will be considerable. The result will be a super-base on the scale of RAF Brize Norton. Nonetheless, the position of Commandant will remain an Air Commodore post given that the majority of the new units are already under my command.

It will be a far cry from what was once the sleepy village of Cranwell, which had the good fortune to be chosen by the Royal Navy to become an airbase over a century ago.

***

The Air Officer Commanding, Air Vice-Marshal Andy Turner, puts his point of view:

> Since the change to IOT in 1971, the intake for the College has become far more egalitarian, reflecting the changes in society, and our national culture.
>
> In today's climate, IOT has to give far greater value from the investment than was the case in the Flight Cadet era. Because of that, throughput at Cranwell has increased out of sight – two entries of sixty or so per year in your time to a potential of 700 today. Of course, the two eras don't compare – three years for you, three terms of eight weeks today. And there's no professional training at the College today– that all follows afterwards at the Phase 2 'finishing schools'. But this new approach to IOT works – the Selection and Training procedures

today find candidates who are ready, able and willing to go through the rigours of training and in general they nearly all pass. This has preserved the baseline of what we think of as the 'Cranwell standard'.

The future? In my time as AOC 22 Group, we've overseen the setting-up of the Centennial Legacy project, a cultural reset of the Trenchard legacy in the pursuit of training and educational excellence. It includes more apprenticeships and a modernised approach to studies – available to all ranks, delivered when needed and not force-fed. It is offered periodically throughout service and is closely linked to civilian standards and qualifications. It offers degrees for all servicemen and women.

This centennial legacy includes more bursaries for RAF Scholars at the University Air Squadrons – increasing from thirty to 300. There will be an RAF Think Tank for Air Power and Leadership research, as well as a new Air Cadet College, where some 200 cadets a time will undergo a GCHQ 'Cyber Hygiene' qualification, protecting the next generation.

As a firm base for all that, we intend that Cranwell will become the single point-of-entry for all recruits to the RAF – where they'll get an egalitarian, 'all of one cloth' start. Turf-cutting for the Tedder Academy of Leadership is to start soon, for a planned opening September 2021.

That's not too long after the Centenary of the College and the launch of this book. All the best with that!

Postlude

It's now 2019, and the manuscript has to reach the publisher soon if the book is to be on the shelves at the end of the year. Time for Mark to consider his conclusions.

Were three years spent in public school conditions at the College in the 'sixties worth it? Was that Term Four a waste of time? Would a Direct Entry route after University have been the better bet? The answer depends on whom you ask.

Elitism? Public School? Andy of 81 Entry makes the point that four out of those five 81 Entry Air Rankers were from HMC schools. Perhaps exposure to their ethos was an advantage for the Flight Cadets of that time.

Direct Entry versus Cranwell and the new syllabus? Sid (who was incensed when he found out that their Wings didn't qualify the AFRAeS chaps for Fellowship in any case) was not alone in saying that his studies were useless, but he made Group Captain nonetheless. Peter (also a Group Captain) and Dave seemed to find them good value, and Aerodynamics gave Kraut the edge which won him a career as a test pilot. After a thrilling supply-dropping tour in Borneo and a year as a QFI, Mark, in the wake of Denis Healey's manpower cuts in the late 1960s, used his degree as a parachute into the nascent computer industry.

But the overall judgement of that much-derided academic experiment might come from the fact that of the five who made Air Rank, four were general 'A' Streamers. Concentration on flying and activities were certainly no bar to career success for them.

Between the World Wars and in the social changes of the 1960s, the RAF was perhaps slow to adapt to the times. But change, perforce, it did. As Dick Kingston says, 'The Flight Cadet system was wonderful, but – just like Singapore, Hong Kong and RAF Germany, with its tax free cars and tax free petrol – it had to go.'

And go it did, to be replaced by IOT. Since 1978, the flexibility of IOT has quite obviously suited British culture and fiscal policy, as well as the RAF's recruiting needs.

As Air Chief Marshal Sir David Cousins, ex-84 Entry Flight Cadet, puts it:

> I am constantly hearing that twenty-four weeks on course led and still leads to a poor quality product. I contend that it was, and is, quite the opposite. The quality of instruction, together with the motivation imparted to students was, and is, as high. Many of those cadets are now Station Commanders and Air Rank Officers.
>
> IOT works. It's part of the training continuum, keeping up with the times and progressing. It deals with the aspiration for university by delivering degrees during an RAF career. It develops social skills.
>
> University vice-chancellors have told me that Cranwell is getting, not the First Division graduates, but the best all-rounders with 2.1 and 2.2 degrees, men and women motivated to make an RAF career.
>
> Those who graduate from IOT have shown their ability to take on the toughest of challenges and overcome them. The Flying Training Schools teach the pilots to fly to Wings standard and Cosford instills the Engineers with the RAF ethos. The ISS course and the Junior Commanders' courses will teach them to write to a high standard and to think in a structured way.
>
> Another part of the continuum.

***

In October 2018, Mark is invited back to the Orange to watch the rehearsal for a truly unique event, the Joint Graduation Parade of the RAF College's IOT Course No. 55 (104-strong) and Commissioned Warrant Officers' Course No. 17 (seven strong), alongside RAF Halton's recruit Training Squadron No. 619 (ninety-one strong).

All non-commissioned ranks enter the RAF through the Recruit Training Squadron, on a ten-week course focusing on teamwork, discipline and the core values of the RAF. Similarly, all commissioned officer ranks graduate from Cranwell's OACTU after six months when leadership is top of the curriculum. The Warrant Officers, all seven of whom have held the rank for at least two years, spend two weeks in officer conversion and two more in Air Warfare studies.

The event, the last in a series celebrating the centenary year of the Royal Air Force, is a splendid spectacle. Two flights, from each of the west and east wings, led by the Cranwell cadets with swords – the Halton graduates following with rifles – march proudly to take their place in line of review along the full extent of the College Parade Ground. The Queen's Colours of the RAF College and RAF Halton are then marched on together, to take their place in the centre of the ranks.

On the actual parade in two days' time, as the Reviewing Officer, the CAS, Air Chief Marshal Sir Stephen Hillier, a Tornado man, arrives at the Saluting Base, a Spitfire from the Battle of Britain Memorial Flight together with the RAF's newest and shiniest, a F-35 Lightning II from 617 Squadron are scheduled to roar overhead.

After a general salute, the CAS will then inspect the serried ranks of graduates, over 200-strong and parading under the title of Queen's Squadron. This duty is today carried out by officers from the College staff but the College Band does its stirring stuff, and Mark has time to consider the immense changes in British and world affairs since his graduation in 1962.

He's seen punched-card machines grow through the IBM 360 and the BBC £75 Micro into the servers and hand-held devices of today, powered by Internet and Google. Over the same period, the aviation industry has expanded from the sound barrier to Mach 2, while the RAF has contracted from 148,000-strong to some 32,000 Regular and Reserve personnel today – the equivalent of a couple of Army divisions – albeit supported by nearly 5,000 Civil Servants and thousands of contractors.

At the same time the global instability created by the upheavals of the Balkans, 9/11, Al Qaeda and the Taliban have in the twenty-first century given the Air Force plenty of high-profile work. From the time of the conflicts in Afghanistan and Iraq, and throughout the struggles in the Middle East – not forgetting continual standby in the UK to provide 'Military Aid to the Civil Authority' – the tasks have always put pressure on available resources.

The RAF, writes the CAS in the advance programme, is currently running sixteen separate operations in twenty-three countries across five continents. 'These graduating officers and recruits will write the next chapter in our astonishing history.'

The band have given their *Pirates of the Caribbean* and *Test Drive*, but *Lawrence of Arabia* takes Mark's thoughts back to the 1960s, and memories of his colleagues on 81 Entry.

***

POSTLUDE

Five of them made Air Rank in the RAF. Air Commodore John, who flew Hunters in Borneo, was ADC to the Queen before forming the Air Warfare Centre, while AVM Robert was the RAF's first Tornado pilot before handling the tricky post of Air Secretary at the time of the defence cuts. AVM Nigel was one of the youngest of Vulcan captains before rising through the ranks of Bomber Command and the MoD while ACMs Sir CJ and Sir Andy put in four years of service together on the Air Force Board. Sir Andy served in the Falklands and the Gulf and was the RAF's last C-in-C RAF Germany, while Sir CJ became the first chief of the new NATO command, Allied Forces North-Western Europe.

Group Captains totalled nine. Air transporter Sid, with SHAPE and USAF postings under his belt, served latterly as Station Commander RAF Newton and soon after retirement re-mustered into the RAF Volunteer Reserve where he flew with No. 2 AEF into old age, while after a full fighter-boy career, Peter has gone on to keep bees and fly-fish. Mike, after a tour as the youngest Argosy captain, went on to forge a reputation as the most congenial of Air Attachés and Defence Advisors (Saudi Arabia, India and Algeria) while Hugh, after clipping the waves around the coasts of Borneo in his Shackleton, attended the French Staff College and prospered as Attaché in Algiers and Berlin before taking post on the Queen's Flight.

Chris, after Hunter, Harrier and Jaguar tours, spent eleven years at MoD working with the other nations on the Operational Capability for the Eurofighter, right up to the production go-ahead of what was to become the RAF's Typhoon. Jock made a full and successful career as an RAF policeman with Wings, while Anthony extended his busy service life by becoming Deputy Head at the MoD's Air Historical Branch. Vernon had a noteworthy career, from three tours on PR Canberras to CO Joint Air Reconnaissance Intelligence Centre and a CBE, while Welshman Frank, fully belying his early airborne trials at Barkston, took command of the Red Arrows in the 1977-78 season.

Mark spares a thought for the 81 Entry graduates no longer with us. Two perished on their first flying tours – Kiwi, whose RNZAF Canberra slipped one starry night into the South China Sea and Martin, whose breakaway underwing drop-tank took out an aileron in a Hunter ground-attack training sortie in Aden.

Others suffered untimely deaths. ACM CJ, within days of taking up his NATO post, died in July 1994 from what proved to be a brain haemorrhage. Wing Commander Mitzi, after a full operational and staff career also died in service while Terry, Ross, Tom, Vernon and Welshman Frank have sadly not lived to enjoy their old age.

Those who have flown for a lifetime include Kraut, who has enjoyed a long career as a test pilot and is still, just, training QFIs for light aircraft. 'Low-profile' Guy certainly made the most of his coveted Wings – on an eight-year tour as OC Flying at St Athan, he qualified as Unit Test Pilot to fly and test eight aircraft types, from Chipmunk to Tornado. Pete graduated with 82 Entry before clocking up six full transport tours, while Frank flew Victor K2's in the Falklands War and Nimrod R1's in the First Gulf War. Brawn confounded the London BA examiners by becoming a tutor at Staff College, and concluded 6,000 hours of tactical transport operations with two Squadron Commander tours on Hercules, before rounding off his career with the Sultan of Oman.

The rebellious Michael engineered an early transfer out of the V-Force to helicopters and did a brave first tour in Borneo before flying, on and off, for a full fifty years. Dave, the AFRAeS champion, left the V-Force when the Valiants were grounded in 1965 before also joining the rotaries in Borneo, going on to fly helis for a long living in the air, including UN service in the Balkans. Potholer Noel remained a proud 'truckie navigator' Flight Lieutenant, flying operationally until age fifty-five and running fifty marathons before becoming a mature MSc graduate in Computer Studies. His subterranean colleague Danny was another to prove his brainpower post-Cranwell, gaining an Open University BA while captaining a Transport Command Belfast.

Wing Commander Zak flew Vulcans and Canberras before switching to the Supply Branch, latterly becoming OC Supply Wing at Lyneham. While at Odiham, he found a new respect for the Station Warrant Officer, Jack Holt. Despite a brief return to piloting, Adrian's eye injury had him changing trade, to navigator. Blind Bill, after escaping the V-Force for Edinburgh UAS and PR9 Canberras in Malta, left at the thirty-eight-year point for the business world – George and Tony took a similar route.

David, another V-Force and Canberra man, left for the airlines at about the same age – joining Mac (who after appeal was awarded his BA London), Robin, Danny and Terry (all three having been tactical-support pilots with the RAF in Borneo) and Tim. He'd enjoyed an exchange tour on RAAF Hercules before, with a VIP Endorsement, taking the first VC10s to China and Prime Minister Heath to Japan.

Jim the Nav, having taken eight years to get onto the Vulcans of 617 Squadron (of dam-busting fame) went on to give the RAF full value for the investment in his training – joining BAe in 1979, he air-tested their Buccaneer and Phantom weapons systems up to 1987.

POSTLUDE

The Rhodesian and Zimbabwe Air Forces certainly profited from their funding of Air Commodore Phil's six years of training, as did the Jordanians from their bets on Mahmoud, who ran their Civil Aviation Authority and then their national airline, and Lieutenant General Sam, who became Chief of their Royal Air Force.

***

The Joint Graduation Parade progresses through the slow and quick marches past and, although this is just the rehearsal, when it's time for *Auld Land Syne* to send the two-hundred graduates slow-marching off through all three sets of College doors, there's certainly a lump in Mark's throat.

Halton and Cranwell, men and women, girls and boys, all graduating together – would Lord Trenchard ever have believed that?

***

From the vantage point of the Commandant's chair at the Joint Staff College, Air Vice-Marshal Christopher Luck has asserted:

> Current arrangements with the IOT programme at the College are the best for attracting a coherent mix of entrants – bright young men and women direct from school. For them and us, there's the benefit that they reach an operational squadron earlier.
>
> Alongside are the ex-rankers, who bring experience and inspiration for others in the ranks to follow. Then there are the graduates, with three years UAS experience and relevant degrees, and finally Commonwealth Air Forces students with much-needed multi-national contacts.
>
> A big factor in that attraction is the prospect of further education throughout their service career. I personally took that up with a will. No A-levels but a long list of educational qualifications now and the boss of JSCSC – I'm living proof that the system delivers what it promises.
>
> Out of the RAF College, Cranwell, now comes an officer cadre with an intellectual edge – an edge that is further developed at the JSCSC, in the interest of success on operations and leadership in government.

Mark buys into that judgement. For what it's worth, he personally holds the RAF College, and its staff, in the highest regard for maintaining the brand over ten decades.

Events have made it clear that it wasn't necessarily star quality at Cranwell that led to Flight Cadets' success in their RAF careers – it was what they did after passing out that counted most. Nowadays, the same applies, but everyone who graduates from the IOT course begins his or her career from the same starting line.

As the recipient of a three-year professional and technical education to go with his pilot's Wings, Mark has every cause for gratitude, to both the RAF and the Public Purse. In common with the majority of his interviewees, he counts himself fortunate to have been a Cranwell cadet.

ROYAL AIR FORCE COLLEGE

CRANWELL

Left: RAF College Coat of Arms, with supporters of 'Trenchard Eagles' granted 1971. (*RAF College*)

Below: Twenty-First Century Cranwell. (*RAF College*)

Author's Note

Following the prompt from the Air Officer Commanding in May 2016, the first step in producing this book was to trawl the 81 Entry veterans' network for willing sources. The response was magnificent. Along with contact details came a wealth of facts, figures and anecdotes as well as extracts from Flight Cadet diaries. The network widened to include ex-Flight Cadets from other 'fifties and 'sixties entries and the core narrative was secured.

To cover developments in cadet life over the decades, access to the records in the RAF College Library was essential and I am indebted to librarians Tim Pierce and Julia Harrison for their patient help. Archive copies of the College *Journal* from 1921 up to the final edition of 1971 proved a rich seam of facts and incident, as well as a source of illustrations.

For research into developments leading to the all-graduate-entry experiment of the 1970s, the National Archives at Kew came into play, as well as further meetings with ex-Officer Cadets of the era, many of whom had returned to the College on the staff, or had driven events from levels of responsibility up to and including the Air Board.

To cover the Initial Officer Training system from its inception in December 1978 to date, introductions from the College Commandant, Air Commodore Squires, himself an IOT graduate, helped the witness network expand further. He and his senior training staff gave priceless testimony from the standpoint of IOT cadets and bosses both.

It is thus a substantial team that has made the writing of this story possible. Every source quoted has given time, attention and approval to their contribution and heartfelt thanks go to all sixty of them, including five widows of late 81 Entry cadets.

Extra thanks are also due to the Commandant for his kind permission to publish RAF College-sourced pictures, to Air Chief Marshal Wilson for penning the Foreword and to Pen & Sword for their support. Keeping a watching brief throughout has been my wife Jenny whose editorial skills, as ever, have been invaluable in helping to ensure that the focus of *We Seek the Highest* has remained firmly on the point-of-view of the Cranwell cadets themselves.

Roger Mark Annett
Buckinghamshire, 2019

Bibliography

Entry No 1:   *Cranwell Cadet 1920,* ACM Sir George Mills, RAF College Journal, 1970.

Entry No.'X':   *Recollections of 'X' Entry 1930,* Anon, RAF College Journal Summer, 1962.

Entry No. 54:   *From Blue to Grey*, Fred Hoskins *inter alia* (1949-52), 2005.

Entry No. 54:   *There I Was – Memories of an Old Aviator*, Brian Meadley, Moyhill, 2012.

Entry No. 54:   *An Airman of the Queen my lads!* Richard Robson, Bright Pen, 2012.

Entry No. 60:   *Flight Cadet – the Royal Air Force College, Cranwell*, Rutherford M. Hancock, Pentland Press, 1993.

Entry No. 81:   *Looking Skywards*, C.B. Adcock, Woodfield Publishing, 2017.

Entry No. 81:   *Wings, Prizes and Awards*, Royal Air Force College, 30th July 1962.

Entry No. 81:   *Passing Out Parade*, Royal Air Force College, 31st July 1962.

Entry No. 81:   *Order of Service of Dedication, Royal Air Force College,* 31st July 1962.

IOT Course No. 43:   *Queen's Squadron Graduation Parade*, RAF College, 26th May 2016.

Joint Graduation Parade Programme:
Queen's Squadron IOT 55, CWO 17 and Recruit Trg Sqn 619, 4 Oct 18.

Fifty years of Cranwell, a history of the Royal Air Force College, 1920-1970, RAF College.

History of Officer Selection in the Royal Air Force, 1958-69, G.A. Roberts, MoD *ca*1970.

Per Ardua ad Astra, a Handbook of the Royal Air Force, Philip Congdon, Airlife, 1994.

RAF Cranwell – a pictorial history, Peter Green and Mike Hodgson, Midland Pubs, 1993.

Royal Air Force College, Cranwell Journals, 1921-1971.

The Flight Cadet Era, Gp Capt Christopher Finn, RAF Historical Society *Journal* 65, 2017.

The History of Royal Air Force Cranwell, E.B. Haslam, Crown Copyright, 1982.

The Royal Air Force – an Illustrated History, Michael Armitage, Cassell, 1993.

Wings – the RAF at War 1912-2012, Patrick Bishop, Atlantic books, 2012.

Wings – and other things, Hugh Lynch-Blosse, Square One Pubs, 1990.

First Impressions of Cranwell, Anon, RAF College Journal, 1963.

Papers from the archive of Wg Cdr Colin Cummings.

RAF Handling Squadron, Boscombe Down.

AP.4560C-PN Jet Provost T. Mk. 3 Pilot's Notes (October 1959 – Reprinted October 1960).

Squadron Leader Dick Kingston.

AP.4560C-PN Jet Provost T. Mk. 3 and T. Mk. 4 Flight Reference Cards (December 1964).

Notes for the Guidance of Flight Cadets, RAF College, Cranwell, 1961.

National Archives, Kew

Air 2/4321	Purchase of land 1020-21.
Air 2/10494	Provision of Batmen for pupil pilots.
Air 2/12060	Selection Policy 1953-58.
Air 8/2265	RAF College, Cranwell, Revision of Flying Syllabus, 1959-62.
Air 20/9084	CW/HEN Amalgamation 1954-55.
Air 20/9849	Ministry of Education Inspection of RAF College 1957-58.
Air 28/2212	Operational Record Books RAF Cranwell 1Apr79-31Jul79.
Air 29/3555	Operational Record Books RAF College, Cranwell 1961-65.
Air 29/3556	Operational Record Books, Appendices, RAF College CW 1Jun61-30Sep62.

***

Index

INDEX